Computers Don't BYTE!

Family & Kids Edition

Written by Linda Pereira, Tim Haag, and
Jessica H.G. Schroeter

Illustrated by Karon Walstad and Wendy Chang

Teacher Created Materials, Inc.
6421 Industry Way
Westminster, CA 92683
www.teachercreated.com
© 2001 Teacher Created Materials, Inc.
Made in U.S.A.

ISBN-0-7439-3457-1

Editors:

Evan D. Forbes and Lynn C. Gustafson

Important Information

Web sites frequently change addresses or become unavailable for myriad reasons. Teacher Created Materials attempts to offset this problem by posting changes of URLs on our Web site. Go to www.teachercreated.com. From the sidebar on the home page, click on URL Updates. Enter a number in the box to find the latest updates. For Part I: Best Web Sites, enter 2000; for Part II: Internet, enter 0621; and for Part III: Computers Don't Byte, enter 0813.

Table of Contents

Table of Contents (cont.)

Part III: Computers Don't Byte

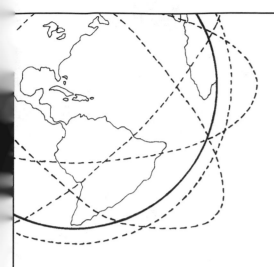

Part I

Best
Web Sites

Written by Jessica H. G. Schroeter, M.A., M.L.I.S.

Illustrations by Denice Adorno

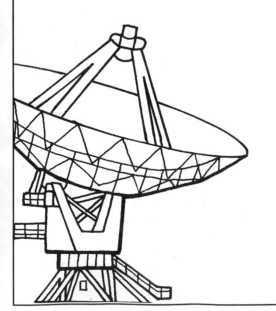

So Many Places To Go!

The World Wide Web (WWW) is a wonderful resource for children. It can be compared to a gigantic library containing information on almost every imaginable topic. But unlike a library with books arranged according to clearly defined categories, the ever-expanding number of sites appearing daily on the Internet can be overwhelming and seem to have no organization whatsoever. The Internet does not discriminate between sites created by professionals and non-professionals or by educators and advertisers. Locating Web sites that are educational and enjoyable for an appropriate age level can be extremely time consuming. Parents and teachers are also concerned about sending their children to computers unsupervised. So now that more and more people have access to the Internet from their homes and schools, they are asking themselves the question: "Now that I am connected to the Internet, what should I do with it?"

This book attempts to answer this question by offering a clear and concise collection of some of the most intriguing children's sites for available on the Web today. Highly recommended sites are arranged in a variety of interesting sections. For example, a useful category like "Find That Fact!" offers numerous research Web sites, and the chapter "Kiddie Korner" presents a sampling of sites for the very young Web surfer. You can visit the recommended sites in this book or use them as starting points for your own explorations. Don't fret about spending hours locating appropriate Web sites for kids. All the sites in this book have been reviewed and are safe, informative, and often very entertaining.

Best Web Sites launches you on the Information Superhighway for the 21st Century. Use this book as a guide, and as you flip through the pages, take the opportunity to discover some of the best sites on the Internet for kids. Visit zoos, museums, and travel the world, but most of all, have lots of fun on your explorations!

Important Information

Web sites frequently change addresses or become unavailable for myriad reasons. Teacher Created Materials attempts to offset this problem by posting changes of URLs on our Web site. Go to www.teachercreated.com. From the sidebar on the home page, click on URL Updates. Enter a number in the box to find the latest updates. For Part I: Best Web Sites, enter 2000; for Part II: Internet, enter 0621; and for Part III: Computers Don't Byte, enter 0813.

Who Can Use This Book?

Whether you are a teacher or parent searching for information for school projects or a child looking for fun activities on the computer, this book is for you! To get started, all you need is the following:

- A computer
- Access to the Internet with a modem or cable
- An Internet service provider (ISP)
- Basic experience using search engines
- A desire for advice about Web sites to visit.

If you fit this description, or even if you already have a lot of surfing experience, you will enjoy **Best Web Sites**. Use this book to find and explore new places in Cyberspace, but don't allow your explorations to end there. Once you have visited and enjoyed all the sites described in this book, follow the many recommended links provided within the Web sites listed in this book and become confident navigating the World Wide Web, where time, space, and location seem to disappear!

Managing Web Resources: Bookmarks

Millions of Web sites are available on the Internet, and it is impossible to remember the lengthy URLs (addresses) associated with all your favorite spots. Since you will undoubtedly want to revisit useful locations again and again, you will need to create a system of organization for your Internet explorations.

That is when bookmarks come into the picture. An electronic bookmark (also called the Favorites List) does the same thing a regular bookmark does: it marks your place. No matter what the feature is called, all current browsers make it possible to "bookmark" a location on the Web for future use. By selecting **Add Bookmark** from the Bookmark menu, the title of a Web page is added to the bottom of your bookmarks list, allowing you to return to the same Web page over and over again.

However, a long list of bookmarks can soon become unmanageable. Often a list grows so long that it seems you are scrolling on and on, making it difficult to find your favorite places on the Internet. Fortunately, browsers contain editing features that make it easy to keep track of the wonderful tools available on the Internet.

The following pages contain directions for using this bookmark feature with *Netscape Communicator* (previously called *Navigator*) and *Internet Explorer.*

Netscape Bookmark Feature

To Create a Bookmark

1. Open **Netscape**.

2. Go to the Web site you want to save.

3. Click on the **Bookmarks** menu on the Location toolbar.

4. Select **Add Bookmark**.

5. Click on the **Bookmarks** menu again to make sure the site has been saved.

After awhile, your list of bookmarks will increase. Add order to it by grouping the bookmarks into folders according to topics. For example, you may organize folders for games, animals, or online dictionaries depending on your interests.

To Organize your Bookmarks (Folders)

1. Find the **Bookmarks** or **Edit Bookmarks** command. In earlier versions of **Navigator** this is found under the **Navigator** icon. In later versions, it is found under the **Bookmarks** menu.

2. Go to the **File** menu and click on **New Folder**.

3. Type in the name of the new folder in the **Name** box.

4. Click **OK** when finished.

Managing Web Resources: Bookmarks *(cont.)*

To Put Bookmarks in a Folder

1. Highlight the bookmark you want to move.

2. Hold down the left mouse button and drag the item (the Web site name) over to the folder.

3. Drop the item into the folder by releasing the mouse button.

To Delete Bookmarks

1. Highlight a bookmark.

2. Press the Delete key.

To Edit Bookmarks

1. Highlight the bookmark.

2. Go to the **Edit** Menu.

3. Select **Get Info**.

4. Change the name or alter the URL at this window.

5. Click **OK**.

To further organize each folder, you can create folders within folders. For example, you may want to create in a science folder subcategories for weather, planets, ecology, and so forth.

To Create a Subfolder

1. Go to the **Bookmark** menu and select **Edit Bookmarks**.

2. Click on the Bookmark folder to which you want to add a subfolder.

3. Either click the arrow or double-click the folder to open it.

4. Go to the **File** menu and select **New Folder**.

5. Type a name in the **Name** box.

6. Click **OK** when finished.

7. Click and drag appropriate bookmarks into the new folder.

8. When you open the main folder, you will see your subfolder beneath it.

Managing Web Resources: Favorites

Internet Explorer Favorite Feature

To Create a Favorite

1. Open **Microsoft Internet Explorer**.

2. Go to the Web site you want to save.

3. Click on the **Favorites** menu on the location toolbar.

4. Select **Add Page to Favorites**.

5. Click on the **Favorites** menu to make sure the Web site has been saved.

To Organize Your Favorites (Folders)

1. Click on Favorites.

2. Select **Organize Favorites**, and a list of your favorites will appear.

3. Go to the **Favorites** menu and select **New Folder**.

4. A folder will appear. Type the title of the folder in the box.

5. Press **Return**.

To Put Favorites in a Folder

1. Highlight the favorites you want to move.

2. Hold down the left mouse button and drag the item (the Web site) over to the folder.

3. Drop the item into the folder by releasing the mouse button.

To Delete Favorites

1. Highlight the favorite.

2. Press the **Delete** key.

To Edit Favorites

1. Go to the **Favorites** menu and select **Organize Favorites**.

2. Highlight the favorites you want to edit.

3. Go to the **File** menu and select **Get Info**.

4. Change the name or alter the URL at this window.

5. Press **OK**.

To Create a Subfolder

1. Click on **Favorites.**

2. Select **Organize Favorites**, and a list of your favorites will appear.

3. Go to the **Favorites** menu and select **New Folder**.

4. A folder will appear. Type the title of the folder in the box.

5. Press **Return**.

6. Highlight the new folder.

7. Hold down the left mouse button and drag the new folder into the main folder.

Plug-Ins

Do you really need plug-ins? The answer to this question is definitely yes! Even if you are using a state-of-the-art browser, technology is still changing at an unprecedented rate. This means that *Netscape Communicator (Navigator is an earlier version)* and *Microsoft Internet Explorer* cannot handle all types of files found on the Internet.

This is why plug-ins are essential for optimal interactions with Web sites. You can think of plug-ins as helpers that aid in displaying files the browser cannot accommodate on its own. For example, audio files, video clips, and animations can't be viewed by your browser alone. Without plug-ins, you will not be able to experience the array of variety found on the Internet.

Fortunately for the World Wide Web user, it is easy to find and download these applications to your computer. Listed on this page are suggested plug-ins along with their Internet addresses. Again, it is highly recommended that you install them before you plunge into the multitude of sites in this book.

One word of caution: There may be costs associated with these downloads so be sure to read the information carefully at each Web site.

Name: Adobe Acrobat Reader

Function: Allows you to read electronic documents

URL: http://www.adobe.com/

Name: Macromedia Shockwave

Function: Allows you to view interactive content like games and animations

URL: http://www.macromedia.com

Name: Real Audio

Function: Allows you to listen to sound on the Internet (This application lets you listen to radio broadcasts over the Internet)

URL: http://www.realaudio.com

The plug-ins mentioned above are suggestions. Keep your eyes open for future developments and additions to this basic list!

Ancient & Medieval Times

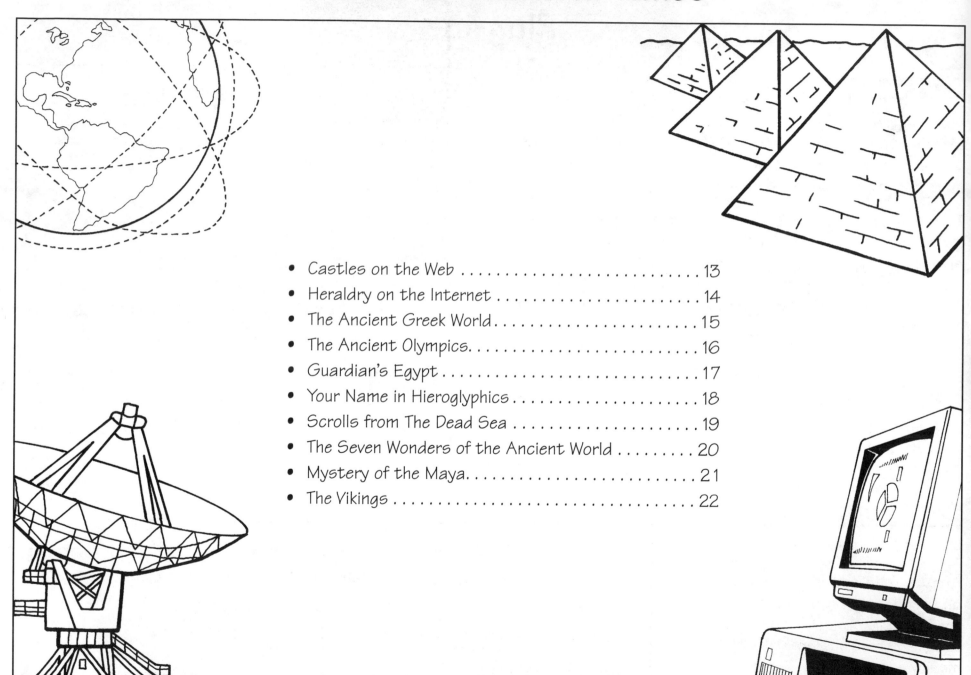

http://www.castlesontheweb.com/

Overview:

Do you like books about King Arthur and Sir Lancelot? If you do, enter the wondrous world of *Castles on the Web*. This comprehensive site organizes the many online resources about medieval castles. If you are interested in heraldry, chivalry, and castle adventures, this is the perfect site for you. Try these sections:

- Castle Tours
- Abbeys and Churches
- Myths and Legends
- Weapons and Supplies
- Castle Greetings

A special section called *Castles for Kids* offers sites with kids' interests in mind. Some places to visit:

- Journey Through the Middle Ages
- Life in the Middle Ages
- Castle Builder

Go back to the time of imposing castles, monarchy, feudalism, and knighthood as you discover the wealth of activities available at this site.

Try this:

Are you reading a Brian Jacques book and need a photograph for a HyperStudio project? Use this site to collect fabulous graphics of medieval imagery.

Highlights:

This site is clearly designed and well organized.

A glossary and links are included.

See also:

The Official Redwall Page

http://www.redwall.org/

Heraldry on the Internet

http://digiserve.com/heraldry/

Overview:

This informative site is designed to help you find heraldry on the Internet. Heraldry appeared during the Middle Ages when people wore armor to protect their faces. This made it impossible to recognize the person behind the armor. So to easily and quickly identify a person or group of people, different coats of arms with specific colors, crests, and symbols were used.

Look for a family name coat of arms used by someone who has the same surname (last name) as you. Search for coats of arms of cities and towns or use *Pimbley's Dictionary of Heraldry* to identify symbols found on coats of arms. The section on clip art contains hundreds of images and a few blank shields so that you can create your own personal coat of arms.

The site is divided into the following sections:

- What's Hot
- Reference
- Heraldry
- Coats of Arms
- Heraldry Articles

- -

Try this:

Click on *Surnames* in the Reference section. Search for your last name and see if there is a coat of arms listed for your family. To create your own, go to the *Clip Art* link under Heraldry.

Highlights:

Teachers would benefit greatly by incorporating this site into a Middle Ages unit.

You will find everything you always wanted to know about heraldry at this site.

See also:

Middle Age Art Exhibit

http://www.learner.org/exhibits/middle ages/

The Ancient Greek World

http://www.museum.upenn.edu/Greek_World/Intro.html

Overview:

Welcome to the online exhibit of The Ancient Greek World presented by the University of Pennsylvania Museum of Archaeology and Anthropology. This site offers artifacts from the museum's permanent collection that provide a backdrop for a vivid story of real life in Ancient Greece.

The site is divided into four thematic units:

- Land and Time—Visit Hellenistic, Classical, Archaic, and other time periods.
- Daily Life—Visit a Greek house and read about fashion.
- Economy—Check out Greek coins, pottery, and cosmetics.
- Religions and Death—Learn about Greek heroes or visit a cemetery.

Try this:

Look at artifacts in the *Geometric Period* (Land and Time). Create your own original work of art using the geometric style.

Highlights:

This is a good starting point for learning about Ancient Greece.

Photographs of artifacts are excellent.

See also:

Mythweb

http://www.mythweb.com/

This site is devoted to heroes, gods, and monsters of Greek mythology.

The Forum of Trajan in Rome: A Virtual Tour

http://www.artsednet.getty.edu/Arts EdNet/Browsing/Trajan/index.html

© Perseus Project

The Ancient Olympics

http://www.perseus.tufts.edu/Olympics/

Overview:

Discus, Chariot racing, Wrestling, and running were all part of the ancient Olympic Games. But which of these events remain part of today's Olympics, the world's largest pageant of athletic skill and international competition? You will find answers to these questions and others at this informative site about the Ancient Olympic Games.

Note: Shockwave plug-ins are required at this site.

- -

Try this:

Go to Athletes' Stories and read about Milo of Kroton, the famous six-time Olympics victor. According to ancient sources, how did Milo show off his strength?

Highlights:

A comprehensive overview of ancient games is provided.

Try the slide show of Olympia; it takes a few minutes to download, but it's worth it!

See also:

The Real Story of Ancient Olympic Games

http://www.upenn.edu/museum/ Olympics/olympicintro.html

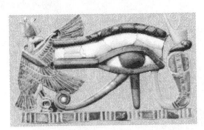

copyright © 1995-1999 Andrew Bayuk

http://guardians.net/egypt

Overview:

Welcome to Guardian's Egypt, a site where you can explore the mystery and splendor of Ancient Egypt! Find articles, pictures, essays, songs, games, and facts about everything Egyptian. Start by touring some of the sophisticated monuments at the *Great Pyramid* link. Once arriving there, take a virtual tour through its ancient chambers and tunnels. Then visit the *Mummies*, go on a *Cool Dig*, visit Egyptian Museums, and find information about Kings and Pharaohs.

An exciting part of this site is the *Guardian's Cyberjourney*. Enjoy photographs of tombs, temples, antiquities, and more at this fascinating section.

Try this:

Particularly worth visiting is the *Ancient Egypt Kid Connection*. Try *Make Your Own Mummy*, *The Pyramid Crossword Puzzle*, or *Design and Make an Ancient Egyptian Box*.

Visit the Little Horus Web site designed for children to explore Egypt in English or Arabic.

Highlights:

From pyramids to mummies, hieroglyphs to pharaohs, this site is packed with information, links, photographs, and interactive activities.

See also:

The Rosetta Stone Exhibit at the Cleveland Museum of Art

http://www.clemusart.com/archive/pharaoh/rosetta/

Mysteries of Egypt

http://www.civilization.ca/membrs/civiliz/egypt/egypt_e.html

Your Name in Hieroglyphics

http://www.iut.univ-paris8.fr/~rosmord/nomhiero.html

Overview:

Enter this site created by Serge Rosmorduc and have your name transformed into hieroglyphics, an ancient Egyptian language from 3,000 years ago! Don't be concerned when you see the title "Nom en Hieroglyphes" in French on your computer monitor! You have arrived at the correct destination and if you read on, you will notice that English is also used to explain how to use this site.

This site, while visually unimpressive, is actually widely accessed and lots of fun. To use this page, write your name phonetically in the space provided, and then click on *Send*. Wait about 10 seconds, and you will see your name in hieroglyphics.

- -

Try this:

Find out how to write a family member's name in hieroglyphics and then design a piece of jewelry with the new name as a gift.

Highlights:

This site loads quickly and is fun to use.

Teachers: Use this as a companion to a unit on Egypt.

See also:

Hieroglyphic Page from Seaworld

http://seaworld.org/Egypt/hiero.html

http://lcweb.loc.gov/exhibits/scrolls/

Overview:

View the ancient Dead Sea Scrolls on the Web and read about the people who hid these documents, the secrets the scrolls might reveal, and why, after their discovery in this century, the scrolls' custodians restricted access to the information contained in the scrolls. Young Bedouin shepherds searching for a goat in the Judean Desert discovered these scrolls in 1947. After entering a cave, they found jars filled with ancient scrolls. Thanks to their initial discovery, you can experience a taste of this old world at this site. Leap into the Qumran community 2,000 years ago and delve into the history of this interesting archaeological discovery. Interesting parts of the exhibit include images of artifacts from the Qumran community including the following:

- textiles
- combs
- pottery
- vases
- jugs
- wooden objects
- basketry

Try this:

Using papyrus and a pen, write your own scroll and ask a friend or family member to solve the mystery in your text. (Make sure your message opens secrets to the universe!)

Highlights:

This online, virtual museum gives you an opportunity to view a world-famous collection from the comfort of your home.

See also:

Ancient Sites.com

http://www.ancientsites.com/

$\mathfrak{The\ Seven\ Wonders}$
$\mathfrak{of\ the\ Ancient\ World}$

Seven Wonders of the Ancient World

http://ce.eng.usf.edu/pharos/wonders

Overview:

Few people can name all the Seven Wonders of the Ancient World. Poets and historians have written about these monuments with great admiration. Today, only one of the Seven Wonders still exists: The Great Pyramid of Giza. That is why these monuments from time immemorial are the subject of much mystery and speculation. Only recently, have archaeological discoveries revealed some of the mysteries surrounding these monuments for centuries.

Seven Wonders of the world:

- Pyramids of Egypt
- Hanging Gardens of Babylon
- Statue of Zeus (at Olympia, Greece)

- Temple of Artemis (at Ephesus, Greece)
- Mausoleum of Halicarnassus
- Colossus of Rhodes
- Pharos of Alexandria (ancient lighthouse)

Try this:

If you are studying Egypt in school, use this site to learn about the building of the Pyramids.

Highlights:

Go to the clickable map and check out the locations of the Seven Wonders.

There are an abundance of links in the Forgotten Wonders section.

See also:

Modern Wonders

http://ce.eng.usf.edu/pharos/wonders/modern/index.html

Mystery of the Maya

http://www.civilization.ca/membrs/civiliz/maya/mminteng.html

Overview:

Why did the Maya, at around 900 A.D., give up their kings and return to a simple lifestyle as farmers? Despite the fact that this unsolved mystery still lingers after one thousand years, there is much to learn and explore about the Mayan civilization. Their remarkable achievements include an advanced system of mathematics and calendrics (calendars), developed writing, and expert astronomers. Take a journey deep into the jungles of Mexico, Guatemala, and the Yucatan to learn about the legacy of the classic Mayan civilization.

- -

Try this:

Take a detour to other *Exhibits on the Plaza*, and explore a variety of excellent materials produced by the Canadian Museum of Civilization.

Highlights:

A Teacher's Guide offering questions, projects, and activities is included.

The slide show found in the Mayan Civilization section offers excellent photographs of architecture, sculpture, costumes, and other aspects of the Mayan world.

See also:

Rabbit in the Moon

http://www.halfmoon.org/

Find information on Mayan writing, Mayan calendar, Mayan architecture, and more.

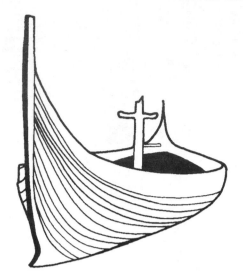

The Vikings

http://www.viking.no/e/eindex.htm

Overview:

Come to this site and find out everything about Vikings. Were Vikings really a group of seafaring men on ships seeking wealth and glory in foreign lands? Were they bloodthirsty pagans who attacked and robbed villages? No one is sure who the Vikings were or what the word "Viking" actually means. There are many theories ranging from being a people of Viken (from the Oslo fjord area in Scandinavia) to being a cove-searching people.

Take the opportunity to learn about Vikings at this site and click on the main menu to find:

- Everyday Life
- Viking Travels
- The Viking Heritage
- Viking Regions, Countries and Places
- Famous Vikings

- -

Try this:

Follow the route of Viking movements at the *Travels* link. Test yourself on geography and see if you can identify places on the map with their modern English names.

Highlights:

This site provides a general understanding about the Vikings.

Find out the basic things that the Vikings needed in life.

See also:

The World of the Vikings

http://www.pastforward.co.uk/vikings/index.html

Creatures & Crawlers

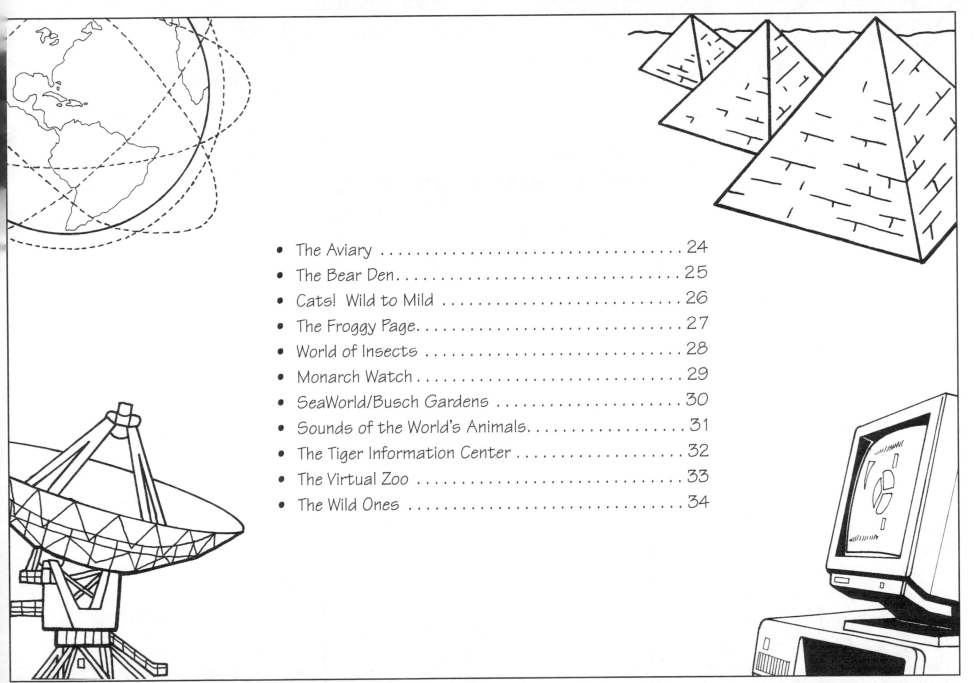

If you love birds . . . *Welcome Home!*

your avian info center

Your complete information resource for birds!

http://theaviary.com

Overview:

Welcome to this informative and richly illustrated site dedicated to everything you would want to know about birds. If you love birds, don't pass up this comprehensive information resource about one of nature's most graceful and beautiful creations.

Click *Birding, The Aviary,* and find tidbits on wild and domestic birds, birding events, bird migration, bird anatomy, bird flight, bird links, resources, supplies, free clip art, bird postcards, wildflowers, pet birds, mailing lists, newsgroups, and teacher and parent resources.

Try this:

Follow the link for *Types of Birds* and find information on over 100 different types of birds. Use this information as a starting point for a report.

Go to the *Post Office* and choose from over 100 free birding postcards to send to a friend or family member.

Highlights:

A massive amount of free clip art is available at this site. Use it for a *HyperStudio* slide show of our feathered friends.

See also:

Audubon Society's WatchList 4Kids

http://www.audubon.org/bird/watch/kids/index.html

Peterson Birds Online

http://www.petersononline.com/birds/month/

http://www.nature-net.com/bears/index.html

Overview:

Did you know that a bear cub is about the size of a squirrel when it is born? Or that bears stand on their hind legs to smell and see better? Find out interesting tidbits like these and more at this site featuring your furry pals, the bears! Here you will find everything you ever wanted to know about bears, including news updates, information, photographs, and other entertaining information.

A list of eight species of bears is provided.

- Brown and Grizzly Bears
- American Black Bears
- Polar Bears
- Giant Pandas

- Asiatic Black Bears
- Spectacled Bears
- Sloth Bears
- Sun Bears

Click on the name of any of these bears to find information on population, vital statistics, physical characteristics, diet, home range, reproduction, and hibernation.

- -

Try this:

Check out the *Cub Den*, a section of the Web site for younger readers that contains *Ten Facts About Bears*, *Amazing Facts About Bears*, and *Books for Young Readers*.

Highlights:

An excellent bibliography of bear books is provided.

This site is colorful, and informative and can be used for beginning or intermediate readers.

See also:

Koalas at Lone Pine Koala Sanctuary

http://www.koala.net/

Cats! Wild to Mild

http://www.lam.mus.ca.us/cats/

Overview:

Visit this "purrfect" site which features America's number one pet, the cat. From cat behavior, cat biology, cat history, and cat conservation to Cat Lotto (a game)and working with cats, this site is packed with enough information to satisfy any cat enthusiast!

If you are interested in finding information about a particular cat breed, click on *Egypt & Domestication*, and then *36 Flavors*. A list of domestic cat breeds with hyperlinks will provide you with the breed profile, attractive photographs, as well as related links.

Try this:

Are you up to a challenge? Then go to *Cat Facts* and play Smiley the Cat's flash-card game. To play, click on the picture of the cat and try to answer the question that appears. Click a second time, and the answer will appear.

Highlights:

A complete teacher's guide is available.

Produced by the Natural History Museum of Los Angeles, this site is very informative and graphically pleasing.

See also:

The Cat Fanciers' Association

http://www.cfainc.org/

http://frog.simplenet.com/froggy/

Overview:

Do you like frogs? If you do, visit this site! Everything having to do with frogs is here, including the following:

- Froggy Pictures
- Froggy Sounds
- Froggy Tales
- Songs of the Frog

- Scientific Amphibian
- Famous Frogs
- Net Frogs

Try this:

Click on *Scientific Amphibian* and take part in a virtual frog dissection. (This is not for the tender hearted!)

Highlights:

Froggy Sounds gives you a sample of the different sounds frogs make.

Many froggy graphics can be found at this site.

See also:

The Lily Pond

http://www.thelilypad.org/

The Interactive Frog Dissection

http://curry.edschool.Virginia.EDU/go/frog/

http://www.earthlife.net/insects

Overview:

Welcome to the Wonderful World of Insects, a site loaded with information about the world's most successful life form. From ladybirds to spiders, and from grasshoppers to earwigs, you are sure to locate loads of facts about any insect beneath your feet or over your head!

Use the jump menu, "A short index of the files of this site," to choose a topic and browse through hundreds of items, including general information about each insect, a selection of graphics, a bibliography, and links to other Web sites.

Kids: If this page is too confusing, follow the link to *The Bug Club*. This part of the site is dedicated to young people who "find insects and other creepy crawlies interesting and even fascinating"!

Try this:

Check out *Bug Pets* at *The Bug Club* and find out how to take care of these miniature pets. Follow links to the *Invertebrate Care* sheets to prepare for your future with a pet insect!

Highlights:

A glossary is provided.

Information on classification of the insect orders is excellent.

See also:

O. Orkin Insect Zoo

http://www.orkin.com/html/o.orkin.html

The Microbe Zoo

http://commtechlab.msu.edu/sites/ dlc-me/zoo/

THE UNIVERSITY OF KANSAS DEPARTMENT OF ENTOMOLOGY &
THE UNIVERSITY OF MINNESOTA DEPARTMENT OF ECOLOGY

MONARCH WATCH

DEDICATED TO EDUCATION CONSERVATION AND RESEARCH

http://www.MonarchWatch.org/

Overview:

How do monarch butterflies move across the continent; do they move in certain directions or take specific routes? How is their migration influenced by weather? To answer these and other questions, the Monarch Watch Outreach Program was created at the University of Kansas.

This site, designed as a companion to the program, offers great ideas, projects, and graphics about butterflies. *The Multimedia Gallery* gives monarch watchers a place where they can share their experiences online through artwork, essays, and photographs. At *Monarch Biology*, read about the monarch lifecycle from egg to larva to pupa to adult. Visit *Research Projects* and look at projects that are particularly interesting for students.

Try this:

Follow the tips in *Butterfly Gardening* and create a garden which will attract monarchs.

Highlights:

Teaching materials are available at this site.

Use this site for a school research project.

See also:

Children's Butterfly Site

http://www.mesc.usgs.gov/butterfly/Butterfly.html

http://www.seaworld.org/

Overview:

Come visit SeaWorld and find lots of interesting information about animals. Need quick facts about an aquatic animal? Visit *Animal Bytes*. Need to find answers to common questions about animal life? Click on *Ask Shamu*. Looking for up-to-date information about SeaWorld? Try *Animal News*.

Another great place to visit at this site is *Just for Fun!* You can try out activities on *Egypt*, go to *Key West*, or follow scientists in *Antarctica*.

A fabulous resource at SeaWorld is its animal database that includes the following:

- Baleen Whales
- Beluga Whales
- Birds of Prey
- Bottlenose Dolphins
- Endangered Species
- Flamingoes
- Gorillas
- Harbor Seals
- Killer Whales
- Manatees

Try this:

Click on *Aquariums as a Hobby*, located in the menu on the left side of the screen, and create your own aquarium at home.

Highlights:

A wealth of animal facts can be found here.

Teacher information and guides are offered to enhance classroom activities.

See also:

Monterey Bay Aquarium

http://www.mbayaq.org/

Zoom Whales

http://www.EnchantedLearning.com/subjects/whales/

Sounds of the World's Animals

http://www.georgetown.edu/cball/animals/animals.html

Overview:

What does a bird say? It's "pip" in Danish, "tweet-tweet" in English, and "chunchun" in Japanese. How about a rooster? It's "cocorico" in French, "ake-e-ake-ake" in Thai, and "chicchirichiii" in Italian!   At this site have fun learning how people all over the world—20 languages altogether—describe the sounds animals make.

- -

Try this:

Play a game with your friends. Choose an animal from the site and then take turns guessing what sound the animal makes in different languages.

Highlights:

This site has a simple menu. Choose sounds listed by the animal or by the language. Also included for young readers is *Spelling the Sounds of the World's Animals*.

See also:

Just Cows

http://www.arrakis.es/~eledu/justcows.htm

The Tiger Information Center

http://www.5tigers.org

Overview:

Visit the Tiger Information Center and find loads of valuable information, photographs, and fine interactive materials about tigers. Start at the *All About Tigers* section and find quick facts at *Tiger Basics*. Then follow the links to *Five Tiger Subspecies*, *Tigers in Zoos*, and *Tigers in the Media*.

Take a fast trip to the Cubs' n' Kids page and read about Tigers in Trouble or play some games.

An appealing part of this site is at Tiger Adventures where you can become involved in online simulation games that draw you into the world of tiger ecology. For example, try any of the following:

- Survive—You are a Bengal tiger and must survive in the wild.
- Tracking the Tiger Trade—Travel to India to capture tiger poachers.
- Tiger on the Loose—Help the police track an escaped tiger.
- Zoo Tiger—Design a zoo exhibit to house a runaway tiger.

Try this:

Join a conservation organization and see what you can do to help save tigers.

Use the *Tiger Basics* section as a starting point for a report on tigers.

Highlights:

Virtual experts offer tiger advice, and simulated newspapers report the results.

Teacher Resources will direct you to grade-level materials.

See also:

Learning All About Tigers

http://www.tigerlink.com/read@tigers.html

http://library.advanced.org/tq-admin/month.cgi

Overview:

Take a journey to the Virtual Zoo and visit Monkey Island, Cat's Corner, Amazing Aviary, Ocean Life, African Animals, Pandas, and more. This site offers you a lively excursion to the zoo. Start at the virtual map (an X marks "You are here") and click on your section of interest. The Amphibians, for example, include frogs, toads, salamanders, newts, and sirens. At African Animals visit antelopes, cheetahs, elephants, giraffes, hippopotami, hyenas, and zebras. Finally, stroll over to the Cat's Corner and watch frolicking jaguars, leopards, lions, and cheetahs.

Try this:

Only a Virtual Zoo could offer an area for extinct species! Check this one out for visits with the *Cynognathus*, Dinosaurs, Mammoth, and Saber-Tooth Cat.

Highlights:

Color photographs and sound clips are integrated into this wonderful zoo.

This site provides a good database of animals.

See also:

The Birmingham Zoo

http://www.birminghamzoo.com/

http://www.thewildones.org

Overview:

The Wild Ones offers an exciting opportunity for children, teachers, and conservation professionals in countries around the world to work together to preserve endangered species. Each section at this site is designed to improve survival prospects for endangered species. Click on *Scientists* and meet people who protect endangered animals, visit *Projects* and view students' work, or read the *Wild Times*, an online newsletter with animal updates.

You can gather information about endangered animals at *The Wild Ones Animal Index*. For each animal you will find information in the following categories: general animal description, habits, threats to survival and defending the animal against extinction. Some animals covered are the following:

- Sandhill Crane
- Scarlet Macaw
- Poison Arrow Frog
- American Alligator

- Green Iguana
- Sea Turtles
- Fruit Bats
- Jaguar

- Asian Elephant
- Red Ruffed Lemur

Try this:

Become a member of The Wild ones and share your observations, research, artwork, or creative writing in *the Wild Times*, a newsletter.

Highlights:

The Teacher Connection includes classroom, schoolyard, and field trip activities as well as pedagogical articles.

See also:

Rain Forest Action Network

http://www.ran.org/

Cards, Creativity, & Celebrations

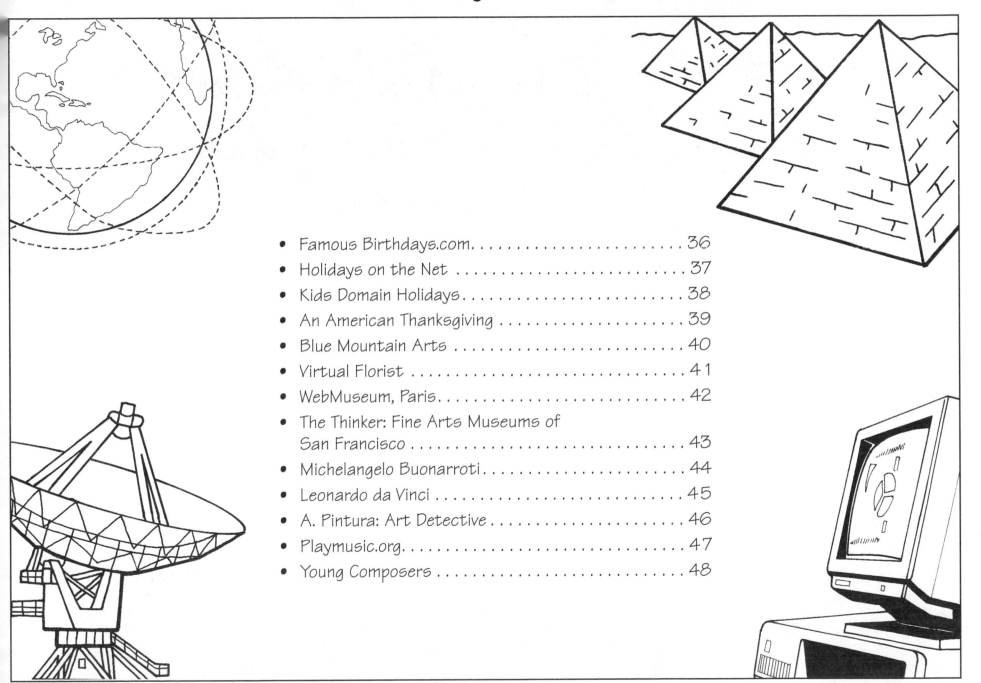

http://www.famousbirthdays.com

Overview:

Keeping up to date on birthdays is no longer a chore once you visit this site. At this quirky, yet entertaining birthday page, celebrate your birthday and famous people's birthdays by participating in several online birthday-related activities:

- Click on *Today's Birthdays* and find out who was born on this day.
- Find out who else was born on your birthday.
- Look at birthday listings of famous people by the month or year.
- Take a birthday quiz.
- Read birthday jokes.
- Check out birthdays of sports figures, writers, and Nobel and Pulitzer winners.
- Look up birthday listings by first or last names.

Before leaving this site, visit the *Other Favorite Birthday Sites*. Included are not only birthday-related sites but also movie databases, actor and actress links along with an autograph database, rock & roll sites, and more!

- -

Try this:

Use the *Free Birthday Coupons* as gifts for friends or family members.

Sports buffs, use this site to find information on your favorite athlete.

Highlights:

Use the search box to find a famous name at this Web site.

This site uses a simple, kid-friendly interface.

See also:

dMarie Time Capsule

http://dmarie.com/timecap/

Input your birthday information and receive a screen full of information about that day in history.

http://www.holidays.net

Overview:

Holidays on the Net is a terrific site for celebrating your favorite holiday. Enjoy a combination of animation, audio, video, and colorful graphics for each holiday. Try activities or craft projects, read stories, or learn about religious traditions.

You can choose a holiday from the menu, browse through the holiday listings and descriptions, or check the days and dates of holidays. This site includes a range of holidays from Jewish Passover and High Holy Days to Christian Easter and Muslim Ramadan. Of course, Mother's Day and Father's Day are included in the collection, along with Thanksgiving, Martin Luther King Jr. Day, and Independence Day.

Try this:

Register with the *Holiday Calendar* and receive holiday e-mail reminders.

Send a friend or family member a holiday greeting card!

Highlights:

This is a colorful and kid-friendly site.

Teachers: Find out how you can use this site in your classroom.

See also:

Holidays and Celebrations by NOBLE (North of Boston Library Exchange)

http://www.noblenet.org/year.htm

http://www.kidsdomain.com/holiday/index.html

Overview:

Holidays are more enjoyable than ever with these great activities and projects at Kids Domain. There are lots of creative ideas at this site, and for every holiday there is a diverse menu. Celebrate *Valentine's Day* with some great clip art and then deliver e-cards to your family and friends. *Father's Day* includes great gift-making ideas, and Easter offers a virtual *Adopt a Lil Chick* option. Browse through this site before every holiday and get ready to celebrate!

- -

Try this:

Go to *Fall Icons* and download the pictures. Add them to your school newspaper or to a writing project.

Visit *Earth Day* and follow directions for making coffee ground fossils.

Highlights:

Each holiday is updated one to two months before the actual holiday occurs.

Excellent gift-making ideas are included along with creative gift-wrapping instructions.

Links are provided to other holiday sites.

See also:

Holidays at Billy Bear's Playground

http://www.billybear4kids.com/holidays/fun.htm

An American THANKSGIVING

http://www.night.net/thanksgiving/

Overview:

Go to this site about Thanksgiving, the American holiday in November which reminds us to give thanks for all that we have, and find information on its history and traditions. This site recounts the first Thanksgiving at Plymouth when the Pilgrims and Native Americans shared their winter feast together. It also includes original Thanksgiving documents such as these:

- Mayflower Compact of 1620
- Peace Treaty with Massasoit, 1621
- First Thanksgiving Proclamation, 1676
- George Washington's 1789 Thanksgiving Proclamation
- Abraham Lincoln's 1863 Thanksgiving Proclamation

For a little entertainment, click on *Thanksgiving Fun* and find special certificates to download and color, stories, songs, poetry, games, and more!

Try this:

Want to help with the cooking this year? Try some of the recipes at *Thanksgiving Feast* and surprise your family with some great-tasting dishes!

Highlights:

This site provides a balance of serious historical information as well as playful interactive fun.

See also:

Caleb Johnson's Mayflower Web Pages

http://members.aol.com/calebj/mayflower.html

Blue Mountain Arts

http://www2.bluemountain.com/

Overview:

Brighten someone's day with a personalized card from this site... for free!

The process is simple. Once arriving at this site, follow these steps:

1. Browse through the ever-expanding categories of cards:
   - Holidays
   - Events & Milestones
   - Family
   - Comfort & Encouragement
   - Earth, Animals & Plants
   - Arts & Literature
   - Religions & Nations

2. Select your card.

3. Fill out the To: and From: information in the form.

4. Type a personal message in the box.

5. Preview your card.

6. Send it.

Now a special someone is having a happier day!

(Holidays are included for every celebration you can think of, including: Pet Day, Groundhog Day, Chinese New Year, Purim, and Mardi Gras.)

- -

Try this:

Instead of mailing invitations for your birthday party via "snail-mail," gather your friends' e-mail addresses and use this site for creating and sending electronic invitations.

Highlights:

The musical accompaniment gives a special touch to each card.

Animations, colors, and designs are very creative.

See also:

Free Electronic Postcard

http://www.electronicpostcards.com/

http://www.virtualflorist.com

Overview:

There is no better way to show someone you care than to send a lovely bouquet of flowers. For Mother's Day, birthdays, or special occasions, visit this site and e-mail a friend or family member some virtual flowers for free!

To send your bouquet follow these steps:

1. Click on *Send a FREE Virtual Flower Bouquet*.

2. Choose an image from the display and click on the one you'd like to send.

3. Type a message and fill in the subject line and the e-mail address of the recipient.

4. Check what you've written by clicking on the *Preview Your Virtual Bouquet* button.

5. If you are pleased with your card, click the *Send the Free Virtual Bouquet* button.

Warning: Do not click on Send Real Flowers because those cost money!

- -

Try this:

Don't wait for a special occasion to send flowers. Surprise a friend by sending virtual flowers on any day of the year!

Highlights:

This site is simple, kid-friendly, and always brings a smile to those who receive its images!

See also:

Free Web Cards

http://www.freewebcards.com/

WebMuseum, Paris

http://metalab.unc.edu/wm/

Overview:

Enter the WebMuseum, a veritable treasure chest of art and culture, and explore this fabulous collection of works of art. Begin your visit in the Special Exhibitions. Here you will find two links, one for Cézanne and the other for medieval art. Choose either one. Next, click on *Famous Paintings*, found in the General Exhibition Area, to view some of the great masterpieces of all times listed by artist or by theme. Scroll through a few of the themes, which include the following:

- the Gothic period
- Baroque
- Cubism
- Italian Renaissance
- Impressionism
- Pop Art

Visit the Artist Index and select Western masters from Giotto to Pollock or non-Western artists mainly from Japan. No matter which route you explore, this site is clearly presented, accurate, and a great resource for your art-hopping pleasure!

Try this:

Select *Seurat* from the *Artist Index* and then click on *The Circus*. Look at this painting carefully and see if you can tell how he painted this piece (he used small dots of contrasting colors). Create your own painting of a circus using this dot method!

Highlights:

Each artist page provides short biographies and images.

For better viewing, enlarge any work of art by clicking on its graphic image.

See also:

Museums of Paris

http://www.paris.org/Musees/

Directory of Artists at Yahoo

http://dir.yahoo.com/Arts/Artists/Masters/

http://www.thinker.org/

Overview:

The Fine Arts Museums of San Francisco presents a spectacular art imagebase as a growing, searchable catalog of their painting, drawing, etching, sculpture, porcelain, silver, glass, furniture, and textiles collections. At this site you will find 50% of the collection from the De Young and Legion of Honor museums online, which adds up to thousands and thousands of artistic images!

Try this:

Click on *Exhibitions* and then *Picasso and the War Years*. Then take the opportunity to view the *Slide Preview* of this exhibit to explore Picasso's artistic responses to the events from the Spanish Civil War through the Nazi occupation of France.

Highlights:

Teachers' resources and publications are available that further enable classroom preparation for museum visitations.

See also:

Art for Kids

http://artforkids.tqn.com/kids/artfork ids/

Fine art history, art projects, and more.

MICHELANGELO BUONARROTI
1475   1564

ENTER

http://www.michelangelo.com/buonarroti.html

Overview:

Meet Michelangelo, one of the greatest painters and sculptors of all time. This site provides an introduction to this famous Florentine artist, leading you from his early life through his final days. Here is your opportunity to visit Italy through Michelangelo's well-known works of art.

Read about:

- The David
- The Sistine Chapel
- The Laurentian Library
- The Last Judgement
- St. Peter's Basilica

This site is full of interesting historical tidbits such as Michelangelo's early life in Florence studying sculpture at the Medici Gardens and then, later, his difficult relationship with Pope Julius II as he painted the ceiling of the Sistine Chapel.

Try this:

Follow the hyperlinks from this page and take a fabulous tour of Michelangelo's work. Outstanding graphics are included at this site for your viewing enjoyment.

Highlights:

Check out the digitized five-minute video showing how IBM scientists and an eminent Renaissance art historian collaborated to reconstruct Michelangelo's Florentine Pieta.

See also:

The Uffizi Gallery in Florence

http://www.mega.it/eng/egui/monu/ufu.htm

Leonardo da Vinci

http://www.mos.org/leonardo/

Overview:

Experience the creations of this famous Italian Renaissance painter and inventor, Leonardo da Vinci. Although he is best known for his paintings, Leonardo conducted dozens of experiments and created futuristic inventions.

Take the opportunity to visit four different sections at this site:

1. Inventor's Workshop
2. Leonardo's Perspective
3. Leonardo: Right to Left
4. What, Where, When?

Try this:

Visit the *Leonardo Right to Left* page, and then try to write your signature in cursive from right to left. This is quite challenging!

Highlights:

After exploring *The Inventor's Toolbox*, try going to *Gadget Anatomy* and see if you can correctly choose which machine parts match the gadgets displayed.

Many aspects of da Vinci's genius are presented at this site.

See Also:

da Vinci's Inventions

http://www.lib.stevens-tech.edu/collections/davinci/inventions/index.html

http://www.eduweb.com/pintura/

Overview:

Grandpa died and left an old dusty painting to Miss Fiona Featherduster. Miss Featherduster wants to know if it is valuable, so she seeks the advice of Art Detective A. Pintura. To answer her question, join this mysterious twosome and discover who painted Grandpa's painting. Could it be Raphael, Titian, Millet, Van Gogh, Gauguin, or Picasso? Take the opportunity at this site to use your keen sense of awareness while viewing exquisite paintings from some of the world's most famous artists.

- -

Try this:

Check out the newest project, *ArtEdventures with Carmine Chameleon,* by clicking on this link.

Highlights:

Designed by Educational Web Adventures, this interactive site offers an online journey through the art world.

See also:

Inside Art

http://www.eduweb.com/insideart/index.html

Explore a painting from the inside out.

Reprinted by permission of Playmusic.org. ©1999 American Symphony Orchestra League

http://www.playmusic.org/

Overview:

If you are looking for entertaining and imaginative ways to develop your interest in classical music, visit *Playmusic.org*, the site where you can explore the many dimensions of an orchestra and even gain a sense of what it's like to be part of one. Begin at the *Main Stage* to discover each different section of the orchestra. Click on *brass, percussion, woodwinds,* or *strings* and listen to orchestral passages featuring, for example, how the flute sounds playing part of the Nutcracker Suite by Tchaikovsky. Then visit the *Backstage* where you'll find sections about composers and musicians, as well as links to other music sites. There are lots of opportunities to listen to music at this site, and kids can gain a good understanding of how orchestras work.

Try this:

Try some of the clever games included for each orchestral section. For example, help Dr. Strad put his violin back together at *Strings*, or match the sound with the correct instrument at *Name That Woodwind.*

Highlights:

This is a fully interactive site offering a wide variety of listening experiences.

See also:

Children's Music Web

http://www.childrensmusic.org

Check out *Pipsqueaks* for sing-along songs or *Musicians List* for information on musicians.

http://www.youngcomposers.com/

Overview:

This is a great site for aspiring musicians. Kids send musical compositions to this site, and when you click on *New Releases* or *Earlier Works*, you will find a list of their pieces available for your listening pleasure! Also available is a selection of pieces by famous composers.

Music is listed by category:

- Baroque/Classical
- Choral/Religious
- Jazz
- Modern

- New Age
- Rock/Blues
- Romantic/Impressionist
- World Music

Note: You need Javascript and frames for this site.

Try this:

Click on *Play Music Match* and see if you can name that tune! Listen to music by famous composers and see if you can identify the composer who wrote each piece.

Highlights:

This site offers numerous musical works from which to choose.

See Also:

ClassicalNet: A Guide to Composer Data & Works Lists

http://www.classical.net/music/composer/

Mysteries, Tales, & Magazines

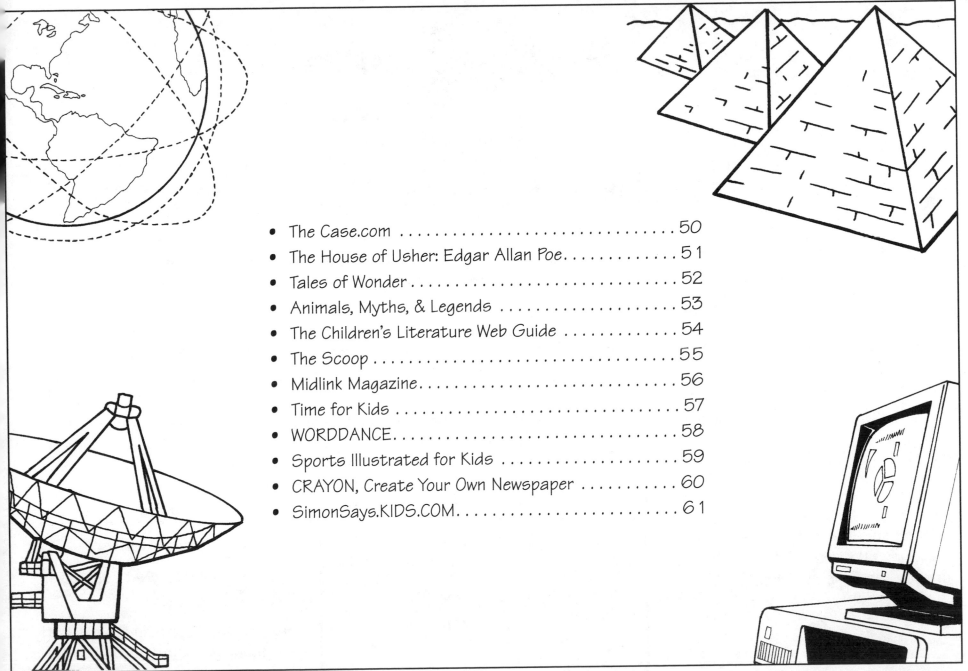

http://www.TheCase.com/kids

Overview:

Everyone loves a good mystery! For entertainment and engaging stories, go to The Case.com. At this site you can create your own mysteries, read scary stories, and try out magic tricks.

Special sections feature the following:

- Solve-it—Try a solve-it-yourself mini-mystery.
- Chiller—A chilling tale will scare you.
- Quick-solve—Can you figure it out?
- Magic Trick—Amaze your friends.

- Nancy Drew.com—Visit everyone's favorite teen sleuth.
- Writing Contest—Write a mystery about the mysterious photo of the week.
- Vote-n-Solve—Play an interactive mystery game.

At this site, you have the opportunity to submit solutions to mini-mysteries and to create original stories.

Try this:

Write a mini-mystery and enter the Mysterious Writing Contest (make sure you read the guidelines).

Highlights:

Lesson plans and ideas are included for using mysteries in the classroom.

For mystery buffs this is not be missed!

See also:

History of the Mystery Quiz

http://www.MysteryNet.com/learn/sites

Take this quiz and find out exactly how much you know about mysteries!

http://www.comnet.ca/~forrest/

Overview:

This eerie site featuring Edgar Allan Poe greets you with the "Adams Family Waltz" by Marc Shaiman from the 1991 movie. Once entering Poe's world, take a journey into the works and life of this macabre author and poet. Visit his homes and burial site under *Favorite Haunts*, read Poe's poems, or find information on his life and interests.

- -

Try this:

"The Raven," Poe's most famous poem, is often recognized by the lines in its first stanza. Click on this poem and make an attempt at memorizing this verse. Recite it for your friends before Halloween for a little fun!

Highlights:

This is a creepy and creative portrayal of Edgar Allan Poe.

See also:

The Edgar Allan Poe Society of Baltimore

http://www.eapoe.org/

http://members.xoom.com/darsie/tales/index.html

Overview:

Richard Darsie has compiled fairy tales, folk tales, and mythology from around the world at this site. If you are studying one country, you can print these stories to use in your classroom. Stories are available from the following countries:

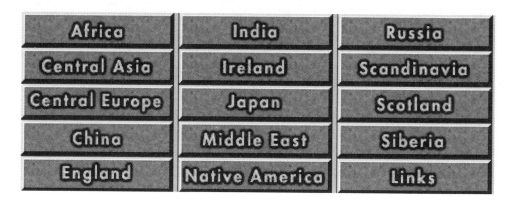

Africa	India	Russia
Central Asia	Ireland	Scandinavia
Central Europe	Japan	Scotland
China	Middle East	Siberia
England	Native America	Links

Try this:

Read "The Comrades" from the *Native American* section. Put on a play of this story and pretend that you are a set designer. Make sketches of trees, bushes, water, buildings, wildlife and the time of day or night for the different sets.

Highlights:

This is a great multi-cultural collection of stories. Tricksters from India and Africa provide humor and entertainment.

See also:

Aesop's Fables
http://www.cruzio.com/~seaweb/corbin/aesop.html

Author Online! Aaron Shepard's Home Page
http://www.aaronshep.com

Animals, Myths, & Legends

http://www.planetozkids.com

Overview:

Come visit Oban the Knowledge Keeper and his fellow storytellers who take you through the world of myths and legends. Discover Oban's collection of games, activities, and folklore and explore different cultures from around the world. This site presents common themes found in stories from various cultures of the world and invites you to learn about the myths and legends of your country and other cultures.

Try this:

Select Channel 1, and click on Animals Myths, and Legends. At this screen, go to the Playroom and try Oban's Brain Torture crossword puzzle. Then, do a word search or travel to another playroom in the Internet universe!

Highlights:

Find a legend or myth about an animal from your country, write it in your own words in an e-mail, and send it to Oban. He'll put some of the legends he receives on his page!

See also:

Myths and Fables

http://www.afroam.org/children/myths/myths.html

The Children's Literature Web Guide

http://www.acs.ucalgary.ca/~dkbrown

Overview:

The Children's Literature Web Guide (CLWG), developed by David Brown of the University of Calgary, gathers together and categorizes resources related to books for children and young adults. This excellent and highly-rated site organizes the best of the Web, compiles book award lists from print sources (Newbery/Caldecott Awards), publishes submissions from kids, offers book reviews, stories, author information, teaching ideas, and a host of other features.

- -

Try this:

Go to *What We're Reading* and find out what the author of this Web site likes to read.

Check out the current Newbery winners. Do you agree with the winning selections?

Highlights:

This is a great site for teachers, librarians, parents, avid readers, and kids!

The list of *Best Books* provides an invaluable resource.

See also:

Candlelight Stories

http://www.CandlelightStories.com/

Children s Book News

http://www.friend.ly.net/scoop

Overview:

Welcome to The Scoop, an electronic publication, where you'll find reviews of children's books, plenty of activities, information about books, interviews with authors, and more.

Browse through award-winning books, biographies, and favorite links and then check out the *Activity Center* including:

- Arts & Crafts—Build a birdbath.
- Contests—Try the World Almanac for Kids Contest.
- Cooking for Kids—Bake yummy taste treats.
- Jokes & Riddles—Share rib-ticklers and knee-slappers.

- Science Projects—Be a science professor.
- Sewing Project—Design great crafts.
- The Scoop Coloring Book—Enter the coloring contest.

Try this:

Use the book reviews as a guide next time you want to choose a book to read from the library.

Highlights:

The Scoop Resource Page offers high-quality literature links on the Web.

Read the current issue of The Scoop or search for older issues in the archives.

See also:

Berit's Best Sites for Children

http://www.beritsbest.com/

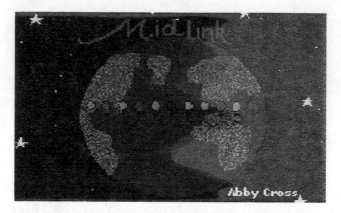

Midlink Magazine©

The Digital Magazine for Kids By Kids

http://longwood.cs.ucf.edu/~MidLink/

Overview:

Midlink Magazine, established in 1994, is an award winning electronic magazine for kids and by kids in the middle grades. It includes exemplary Web sites for teachers and students, as well as exciting and interactive projects with student-created content. The site encourages students to publish their own work and is a fine example of an effective classroom design on the Net.

Explore this site by reading new articles, and then meander over to the archives and browse through older editions of Midlink. Don't forget to check out *Cool Schools* to find some of the most interesting wired schools.

- -

Try this:

Tell your older brother or sister about *Secondary Roads*, the section of Midlink Magazine for students in the upper grades.

Go to *Best Web Sites Honor Roll* and surf through A+ sites. The section entitled *Just for Fun* is quite enticing!

Highlights:

Resources for teachers include information on Acceptable Use Policies, Best Web Sites, Search Tools, Copyright Guidelines, and much more!

See also:

The Vocal Point

http://bvsd.k12.co.us/schools/cent/ Newspaper/Newspaper.html

http://www.timeforkids.com/TFK/index.html

Overview:

Enjoy the kids' version of *Time Magazine* in its online form. This site focuses on kids in the news as well as other news stories that would be of interest to kids. This colorful and graphic news source will hold your interest while providing comprehensive articles in the following categories:

- Who's News
- In the News
- Cartoon
- Top 5
- Kids Talk Back
- Search TFK/Archive
- Multimedia

Check out *Multimedia* and read about fascinating topics like the *Robotlab* (you can try building your own robot), the exploration of Mars, or *Diamond History Fast Facts!*

Try this:

Send e-mail to Time for Kids and express your opinion about a news issue covered in this magazine.

Highlights:

The searchable archive provides access to previous articles according to subject or date.

The magazine is available according to grade level: Click on Grades 2-3 or Grades 4-6.

See also:

Kids Magazine

http://www.thetemple.com/ KidzMagazine/

Letters   Field Trip   World Word   Haiku Corner   Grab Bag

http://www.worddance.com/

Overview:

Visit the home of *Word Dance* magazine online, and become inspired with the variety of creative opportunities provided at this site. Kids in kindergarten through eighth grade can read samples of student-created stories, articles, and poetry, and view artwork as well. The site is divided into sections which include the following:

- Letters
- Field Trip
- World Word
- Haiku Corner
- Grab Bag
- Art Gallery
- Kids Links
- Word Games

For some additional fun, try *Word Scramble, MadLib, Checkers, Tic-Tac-Toe,* or *Paint,* all of which can be found in the Word Games section!

- -

Try this:

Try your hand at publishing by filling out a submission form with your own piece of writing, poetry, or art and send it to this magazine.

Highlights:

This site provides a "real world" application for language arts topics.

It is an excellent interactive site for classroom teachers.

See also:

For Young Writers

http://www.inkspot.com/young/

©Sports Illustrated for Kids

http://www.sikids.com/index.html

Overview:

Visit this colorful site with articles on famous sport greats from the NBA, NCAA, and NHL. Get quick sport updates at *Shorter Reporter* and then check out league standings, games, and the *Trivia Challenge*.

An exciting part of this site is called *Fantasy Sport* where you can play strange types of sports like these:

- Speed-O-Fantasy Racing—Rev up a NASCAR team.
- March-O-Fantasy Basketball—March into madness.
- Hoop-O-Matic Basketball—Guaranteed not to lock you out!
- Puck-O-Matic Fantasy Hockey—You shoot, you score!

As you would expect, this site offers great sports games online like *Indy Frenzy*, *Michael Jordan Trivia Jam*, *Deion v. Deion*, and more!

Try this:

Go to the magazine page and follow the clues at *Mystery Athlete* to figure out who he/she is!

Read the question sent in by a *Sports Illustrated* kid. Read it, think it over, and if you have advice to share, click on the link provided and send it in.

Highlights:

Check out the day's scores, stats, and standings at the *Stat Center*.

Good articles are included from the printed magazine version.

See also:

The Locker Room Sports for Kids!

http://members.aol.com/msdaizy/sports/locker.html

Create Your Own Newspaper
Your Personalized Internet News Service

http://crayon.net/

http://crayon.net

Overview:

If you are interested in news and current events, you'll want to try CRAYON, an acronym for CReate Your Own Newspaper. CRAYON automates the process of constructing a personalized, Web-based newspaper for free! To use this site, simply click on *Create Your Free Newspaper*, enter your e-mail address, and choose a password. Choose a title, motto, and layout for the paper. From there you fill out a form checking news categories you are interested in. Some of the sections follow:

- U.S. News
- Regional and Local News
- World News
- Politics

- Editorial and Opinions
- Weather Conditions and Forecasts
- Business Report
- Information and Technology Report

- Health and Fitness Roundup
- Funny Page
- Tabloid Page
- Cool Web Sites

When you are finished, select the *Create this newspaper now* button! Your newspaper will be given its own URL. Bookmark this page and go read your custom-designed paper every day!

Try this:

Try modifying your paper by changing the news categories or layout. Observe your reaction to these changes and reflect on why you prefer certain types of news.

Design a separate paper for a friend.

Highlights:

Depending on your selections, the newspaper will include a current weather map for your city along with comics you enjoy.

Nearly a thousand news sources are provided.

See also:

KidNews

http://www.kidnews.com/

http://www.simonsays.com/kids

Overview:

Visit SimonSays KIDS.COM, a site designed with kids' reading interests in mind. Here you'll find information about many well-known books and authors, and you can also browse through new books that pique your interest. A favorite section of this site is at *Find a Book*. Simply type as much information as you know about a book in the search box (a title, author, subject, or series), click on *Find It!*, and a review of the book will appear on a new screen.

Try this:

Go to *Cool Stuff*, and try some of the games at this section.

Use this site to find reviews of books you'd like to read.

Highlights:

Check *New Releases* from time to time to learn about recently published books.

Teachers: Check out the *Teachers Lounge* for classroom guides.

See also:

Education Place

http://www.eduplace.com

Go to the Kids Clubhouse for some reading fun!

Find That Fact!

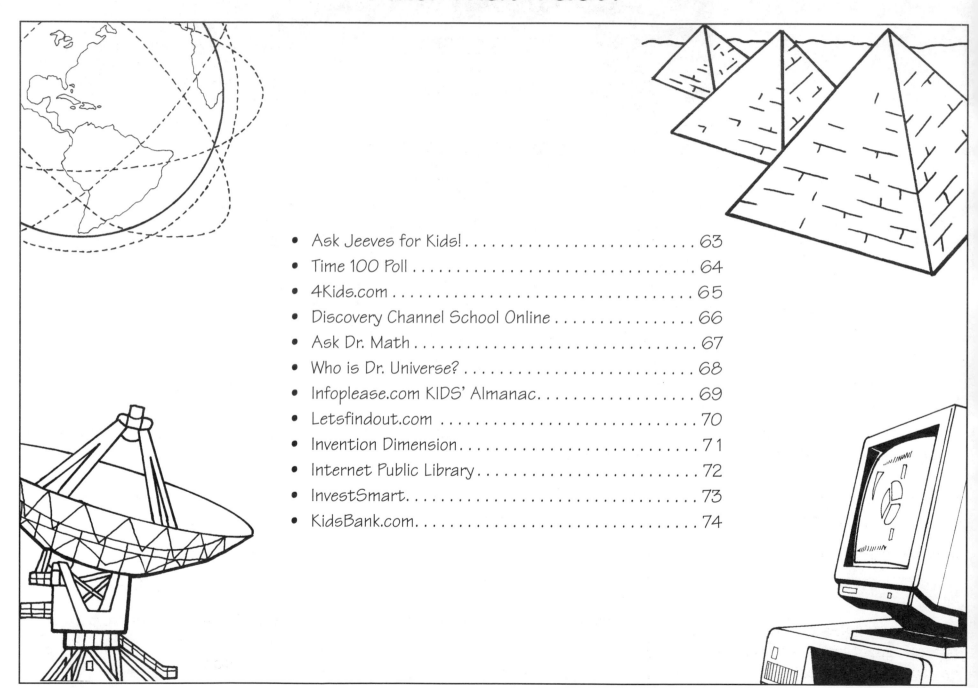

http://www.ajkids.com

Overview:

Welcome to Ask Jeeves for Kids, a highly-used tool among Web surfers! Why is Ask Jeeves so popular? Jeeves uses a unique search tool that lets kids ask questions on almost any subject while providing fast, easy, and safe ways to find answers.

To use Ask Jeeves:

1. Enter a question in plain English into the search box.
2. Jeeves will search his database and return lists of any related questions.
3. Select the question(s) that best matches your original inquiry.
4. Click on the Ask button and the answer to the question will lead to a Web page that has been reviewed by Jeeves' staff of researchers.

With thousands of question templates and millions of kid-safe researched links, it is difficult to imagine your questions won't be answered. But just in case Jeeves comes up empty handed, e-mail your question to him, and researchers will try to find an answer!

Try this:

Improve your vocabulary by clicking the *Today's Word* link on a regular basis!

Visit *Student Resources* and browse through questions that other kids have previously asked!

Highlights:

Teachers: You can ask Jeeves questions like, "Where can I find information on aquariums?" or, "Where can I find a quiz on tigers?"

See also:

Alta Vista

http://www.altavista.com

This is a search engine that allows adults to find information using a whole sentence.

Time 100 Poll

http://www.pathfinder.com/time/time100

Overview:

This site takes a look at people who have had the greatest impact on the twentieth century as selected by *Time Magazine*. This is a superb research site and is arranged in five categories:

- Leaders and Revolutionaries
- Artists and Entertainers
- Builders and Titans
- Scientists and Thinkers
- Heroes and Inspirations

Browse through these sections and find excellent biographical material.

- -

Try this:

Submit your choice for the most influential person/people of the century and vote in the *Time 100 Poll* or *Person of the Century Poll*.

Check out the *TIME Warp* link and find out how the world has changed during this century.

Highlights:

Each category features profiles of 20 people, including audio and video clips, archival material, quizzes, time lines, and related Web sites.

See also:

Biography.com

http://www.biography.com

4Kids.Com

http://www.4kids.com/4kidshome.html

Overview:

Climb up in the 4Kids treehouse and spend your day playing, studying, researching, or reading. Click on the *toy box*, *bookshelf*, *globe*, *bulletin board*, or *fish bowl* and be transported to reading material, science facts, dictionaries, and games. Or go to the bottom of the page and follow the subject links:

- Entertainment
- Playroom
- Projects
- Science
- Social Studies
- Study Resources

All in all, you will find a little bit of everything at this site, all arranged to provide hours of enjoyment!

Try this:

' Having a boring day? Click on *Entertainment* and find a wealth of cartoon sites.

Highlights:

View some kids' home pages or class projects that have been listed on the *4Kids Projects* page.

This site provides a variety of resources designed with the elementary student in mind.

See also:

Merriam-Webster Online

http://www.m-w.com

http://school.discovery.com/

Overview:

Explore natural phenomena, go back in time, or delve into a variety of exciting themes at the *Discovery Channel School Online*. The following is just a small sample of the many enticing themes that this site offers.

For example:

- Day in History—This presents historical tidbits for every day of the year.
- Theme Week—Click on a featured theme such as World Empires, Planet of Life, Systems & Structures, and a wealth of others.
- Features—Check out a science story, sneak previews, games, and more.
- Earth Alert—Natural phenomena and disasters are featured here.
- Discussions—Find out what leading experts and peers think about a particular subject.

Try this:

Click on Features and read the most current feature story in the news.

No time to visit the zoo? Click on *Animal Cam* to see live, real-time animals in action!

Highlights:

Can't find what you need? Search Discoveryschool.com's resources by grade level, subject, and resource type.

Lessons plans for teachers include vocabulary, study questions, related Web sites, hands-on activities, and more.

See also:

The Why Files

http://whyfiles.news.wisc.edu/

Ask Dr. Math

http://forum.swarthmore.edu/dr.math/

Overview:

Here is one of the best, most complete, and highly rated math sites on the Internet. Dr. Math is a rewarding place to go when you have questions about a math problem. Simply submit questions to Dr. Math by filling out his Web form or by sending e-mail for help, and you will receive an answer to your questions via e-mail.

Dr. Math also provides an archive searchable by grade level and subject matter for elementary throughout college levels.

Try this:

Looking for an intriguing math problem? Dr. Math offers a problem of the week for the courageous student.

Highlights:

FAQ (Frequently Asked Questions) offers a comprehensive list of topics.

Excellent link to other Math Sites are provided.

See also:

Math Forum

http://forum.swarthmore.edu/

It is a great math source for students and teachers.

http://www.wsu.edu/DrUniverse/

If you have lots of questions, this is the site for you. You can ask Dr. Universe almost anything. She'll answer your question herself or go to Washington State University's research team for advice. She goes to libraries, field sites, or virtually anywhere to find answers to kids' questions.

Here are some questions kids have asked:

- Why do cats hate water?
- What is a black hole?
- Why do we dream?

- Were dinosaurs just too picky?
- Why am I so tired after lunch?
- What's the point of leap year?

Your questions never end, and neither do the answers at Ask Dr. Universe.

Try this:

Submit a question to Dr. Universe. Do your own research at the library and then compare your answer with Dr. Universe's response.

Highlights:

This is an award-winning site that is perfect for kids who want to know everything.

See also:

B. J. Pinchbeck's Homework Helper

http://www.bjpinchbeck.com/

http://kids.infoplease.com/

Overview:

This reference site designed for kids is a great resource for any report or project. Do you want to know about the tallest mountain in the world? Do you need to know which country has the fewest number of household appliances? You will find the answers to these and all kinds of questions in the online *Infoplease* almanac, encyclopedia, and dictionary.

This site is loaded with numerous topics such as:

- People
- Sports
- Fun Facts
- World
- U.S.

- Science
- Homework Center
- Word of the Day
- Today in History—for famous events
- Today's Birthday—for people's birthdays every day of the year

---

Try this:

Give yourself a quiz on paper money. Whose picture is on a $100 bill? $500? $1,000? Check your answers in the homework center. Did you get them right?

Highlights:

You can search this site by keyword or by subject category.

This site has a clear, well-designed interface.

See also:

A Web of Online Dictionaries

http://www.facstaff.bucknell.edu/rbeard/diction.html

http://www.letsfindout.com/

Overview:

Another great site from Knowledge Adventure, *Letsfindout.com*, is an online encyclopedia which gives you the capability to access information on a variety of subjects online. Find facts at your fingertips by using the subject search that categorizes materials according to the subject, or use the search box and enter the item(s) you wish to find!

- -

Try this:

Click on the *Browse All* link and choose a subject you know nothing about. Take the opportunity to learn more about a new hobby, sport, or famous person.

Highlights:

The handy keyword search option has the following capabilities:

- Searching is case insensitive (you can use lowercase letters).
- AND can be used to combine words.
- A single space can be used to separate multiple keywords.

See also:

Encyclopedia.com

http://www.encyclopedia.com/home.html

"Courtesy of the Invention Dimension, Lemelson-MIT Program"

http://web.mit.edu/invent/

Overview:

Did you ever wonder who invented plastic? crayons? frozen foods? This site, created at the Massachusetts Institute of Technology (MIT), provides answers to these and other questions. The best part of this site for kids is the *Inventor of the Week* Archives. Search for inventors or inventions listed in alphabetical order.

Try this:

Do a report on an invention for your science class. Use this site for your research.

Highlights:

A thorough and well-researched database can be found here.

See also:

Inventors and Inventions at Discovery Online

http://school.discovery.com/lessonplans/programs/inventorsandinventions1/

National Inventors Hall of Fame

http://www.invent.org/book/index.html

Internet Public Library

http://www.ipl.org

Overview:

The Internet Public Library, a project of the School of Information at the University of Michigan, is the first public library of the Internet.   The librarians who manage the site are committed to providing valuable and worthwhile sites to the public while also creating a useful place on the Internet.

The reference center lists resources under the following headings:

- Arts & Humanities
- Business & Economics
- Entertainment & Leisure
- Health & Medical Sciences
- Law, Government, & Political Science
- Sciences & Technology
- Social Sciences
- Associations

Check this out!

Click on the special section for youth and go to the *Reading Zone, Dewey, Science Net, Sports, Reference, Our World, USA, Art, Fun Stuff, Math Whiz* or *Health*. J. J. the Librarian at the Youth Division will help you explore these sections!

- -

Try this:

Is it time to design a project for the annual science fair at your school? Visit *Dr. Internet* and explore the *Science Fair Project Resource Guide.*

Highlights:

A special teen division caters to the research needs of high school students.

This site is an excellent source for school projects.

See also:

Pitsco's Ask an Expert

http://www.askanexpert.com

InvestSmart

http://library.thinkquest.org/10326/

Overview:

Enter InvestSmart and learn about trading stocks. This site provides an interactive stock market simulation; each player is given $100,000 virtual dollars to invest in over 5,000 companies. Buy stock on the New York Stock Exchange (NYSE), NASDAQ, or the American Stock Exchange (AMEX). You can research companies and decide which stocks to buy or sell.

Also included at this site are the following topics:

- Investment Basics—Become a millionaire by investing only $100 a month.
- Investment Lessons—Find explanations of stocks, bonds, mutual funds, and taxes.
- Real-life Examples—View portfolios of teenagers.

Try this:

Use different logon names to sign up for this game more than once and trade different stocks in each account to test out a variety of investment strategies.

Highlights:

Throw that newspaper away and keep track of your profits with the real stock and mutual fund quotes delayed by only 20 minutes.

See also:

Kids' Money

http://www.kidsmoney.org/

The New York Stock Exchange (NYSE)

http://www.nyse.com/

http://www.kidsbank.com/

Overview:

Do you spend your allowance on candy and video games? Try using money in a different way and let some new friends at Bank.com—Dollar Bill, Interest Ray, Mr. Money, and others—help you learn about saving and then discover why a bank is the best place to do it.

Look for the professor who lurks around this site, and with a click he will offer more information about a particular subject area. Ask Mr. Money offers a bulletin board where you can read questions submitted by other kids. If your question has not been answered, send it to the professor and come back the next day for an answer. Checks, the dog, will show you how to write checks, and Mr. Electronic Funds Transfer (ETF) allows you to discover how money can be moved around the world!

- -

Try this:

Click on *Calculators* and find out how much money you will need to save to become a millionaire.

Highlights:

This is a great site for the beginning saver.

See also:

Universal Currency Converter

http://www.xe.net/ucc/

Going on a trip to France? Find out what dollars are worth in francs!

Games & Whimsical Fancies

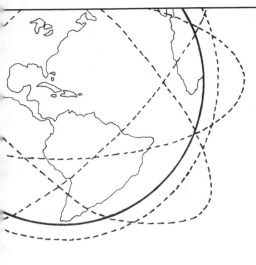

©Bonus Network Co

http://www.bonus.com

Overview:

Bonus.com is a colorful "SuperSite" offering hundreds of quality activities for kids. At first peek, it will seem as if this site offers only games, but with a second look, you will notice a site loaded with other kid-friendly experiences! Enjoy the following sections at this site including:

- Play—Brain Games, Weekly Arcade, Sports Action, and more
- Color—Lots of great coloring pages, including Cool Art, Animal Show-Offs, and Favorite Pets
- Imagine—Adventures, Storytelling, So Strange, Fashion, and other imaginative activities
- Explore—Use this section as a homework helper and find information on dinosaurs, Earth, natural disasters, the body, heroes, and more!

Note: Bonus.com is presented in a protected environment called NetScooter® and is available in another window on your computer screen.

Try this:

Register with Bonus.com (with parental permission, of course!) to compete in contests and earn medals.

Go to *Illusions* and then *Spirals*. Make the spirals rotate by pressing the "+" key on the computer. Then look at the rotating spiral and notice how it affects your vision!

Highlights:

Educators and parents: Curriculum content is available to supplement standard lessons in a non-standard, Bonus.com entertaining style!

A range of difficulty allows kids of many ages to participate at this site.

See also:

The Electric Origami Shop

http://www.ibm.com/stretch/EOS/

CyberJacques

http://www.best.com/~joshuas/

Overview:

Meet CyberJacques, the captain of the "grizzliest, silliest site on the high seas of the Internet"! Join CyberJacques and check out his collection of games, many of which are based around pirate themes. Then lower your anchor for awhile and select a game from the list below:

Try these:

- Tangram Game
- Tile Puzzle
- Memory Matching Game

- Connect the Dots
- Plank Jumper
- What's Inside?

- Secret World II
- Hangman
- Simon Says

Note: All games require Shockwave.

Try this:

Get a stopwatch. Select a game and challenge a friend to play it in a predetermined amount of time.

Play the *Memory Matching Game*. (Make sure your images are autoloading before you start.)

Highlights:

Games are kid-friendly and provide hours of fun.

See also:

Hangman
http://www.allmixedup.com/cgi-bin/hangman/hangman

Every wrong letter brings the stick man closer to the gallows. Nice little site.

http://www.funbrain.com

Overview:

Welcome to *FunBrain*, a collection of games for kids of all ages. This site organizes games in three ways. The first is according to age level: 6 and under, 7-10, 11-14, and 15 and up. The second is according to subject, and finally, you can browse through a pulldown menu that allows you to check out all the possibilities, including the games listed below:

- Math Baseball
- Power Football
- Shape Surveyor
- Line Jumper
- Change Maker

- Spellaroo
- Grammar Gorillas
- Piano Player
- Who Is That?
- Sign the Alphabet

Try this:

Try *Brainbowl*, a weekly current-event quiz that you can receive through e-mail or play over the Web.

Highlights:

Games include clear instructions.

Kids can choose the level of difficulty they wish to play.

See also:

Flashcards for Kids

http://www.edu4kids.com/math/

Game Kids

http://www.gamekids.com/

Overview:

Game Kids is a gathering place for kids of all ages to learn and exchange noncomputer games and activities. Each month, games, rhymes, activities, and recipes will be selected from around the world for you to download, print out, and enjoy. You are invited to submit your favorite games, stories, poetry, artwork, photographs, and recipes.

Try this:

Tired of kickball and soccer? Use this site to find other great physical education games that are kid-tested and approved.

Browse through Nail Party Games for some new inspiration!

Highlights:

Write a description of your favorite game and submit it to Game Kids.

Lots of creative ideas can be found here.

See also:

Game Kids Teens

http://www.gamekids.com/teenp1.html

http://www.headbone.com

Overview:

Enter the *Headbone Zone*, a spot where you can play captivating computer games on the Web. At this site you'll find lots of challenging scavenger hunts, puzzles, brainteasers, a game chat room, a chance to win prizes, and more!

This site features:

- hbz Voter—Check out Headbone democracy in action.
- Smirk City—Enter a town filled with laughter.
- Pojo's Digital Destiny Machine—Try this wacky gizmo.
- Hey Velma, How Come?—Check out weekly questions and answers with Velma the pig.

At Games and Prizes try:

- Rags to Riches
- FleetKids
- Hack.Back
- Mars or Bust
- Elroy PI
- Headbone Derby

There's only one rule at this site: "Be smart and use your headbone!"

Note: Most games require *Shockwave*.

- -

Try this:

If you don't have much online time, go to *Quick Games* for some fast fun.

Play *Rags to Riches* and take your shot at fortune and fame!

Highlights:

Headbone offers positive and kid-safe activities.

See also:

Imagiware's Game Zone

http://imagiware.com/games.html

http://www.humongous.com/

Overview:

At *Humongous Entertainment* play games, read comics, download Computer Goodies, and print Coloring Pages with loveable characters. Meet Pajama Sam, Freddi Fish, Junior Sports, SPY Fox, Putt-Putt, and Fatty Bear and join their irresistible world!

Each character has his own section of this fun-filled site. Simply click on one of their pictures from the menu and then roam through activities featuring that character.

Try this:

At Pajama Sam's page, click on Wacky Weather Game so you can check out Pajama Sam's Wacky World Wide Weather Report. To play, pick a newspaper title and headline. Then type words in the boxes and be prepared for lots of giggles!

Highlights:

This fun-packed, colorful site has a kid-friendly interface.

Lots of games, downloadable demos, and entertainment can be found here.

See also:

The Family Games Web Center

http://www.familygames.com/

Games at CyberKids

http://www.cyberkids.com/fg/index.html

Overview:

This is a favorite site for kids who love games, puzzles, and mazes!

Play a variety of interactive games such as the selections below:

- Alien Assembly
- Concentration using Egyptian Hieroglyphics
- Hippie Hockey
- Lockdown

- Music Match
- Pinball
- Why Do Birds Marry?

Note: Most games require Shockwave.

- -

Try This:

Play *Alien Assembly* and create your own alien by choosing alien body parts with the *New* button.

Highlights:

Games and puzzles are very creative and have interesting graphics.

Have hours of fun at this site!

See also:

Learn2 Play Checkers

http://209.24.233.206/05/0501/0501.html

Illusion Works

http://www.illusionworks.com

Overview:

Visit this innovative site about illusions to understand why our brains fool us into seeing things that aren't the way they actually exist. Illusion Works offers a comprehensive collection of mind-boggling optical and sensory illusions along with detailed explanations about why they are interpreted differently by different people.

Spend many hours at Illusion Works checking out interactive demonstrations, illusion artwork, interactive puzzles, 3-D graphics, perception links, and more. Tour some of the amazing parts of this site listed below:

- Ambiguous Images
- Motion Ambiguity
- Camouflage Illusions
- Stereograms
- Tesseract
- Adelson Brightness Illusions
- Shadow Illusions
- Cross-Modal Interaction

Don't be alarmed if you see double after leaving this site. Your vision will eventually return to normal.

- -

Try this:

Click on *Interactive Demonstration* to enter the Hall of Illusions. Next select *Impossible Figures and Objects*. Take a tour of these spatially inconsistent and paradoxical shapes and gain insights as to how the brain interprets 3-D verses 2-D images. Be patient as this incredible site loads on your computer.

Highlights:

This site features examples of some of the world's leading illusion artists, including M. C. Escher, Shigeo Fukuda, Scott Kim, Sandro Del Prete, and others.

Note: At the writing of this book, the introductory level was still under construction.

See also:

Grand Illusions

http://www.grand-illusions.com/

Exploratorium Online Exhibits

http://www.exploratorium.edu/exhibits/

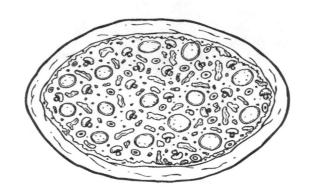

Internet Pizza Server

http://www.ecst.csuchico.edu/~pizza/pizzaweb.html

Overview:

Stop at this site and order a piping hot virtual pizza! Select the size and then choose from a menu of toppings, including the following:

- Meats
- Veggies
- Breakfast
- Sporting Goods

- Junk Food
- Hardware
- Misc

You can almost smell the yummy hammers and pop tarts. Let your imagination go wild at this site and try not to let your virtual appetite get out of hand.

Try this:

Do a report on pizzas and use this site to print pictures of pizzas for your project.

Highlights:

This site is simply delicious!

See also:

The Popcorn Institute
http://www.neology.com/portfolio/popcorn.cfm
Welcome to the World of Willy Wonka
http://www.wonka.com/Home/wonka_home.html

http://puzzlemaker.school.discovery.com/

Overview:

This site, sponsored by Ferguson Consulting, Inc., gives you the opportunity to create your own puzzles and games. A wide variety of choices is available at this site. For example, click on any of these:

- Mazed Things—Escape from hand-drawn mazes.
- Computer-Generated Mazes—Choose the shape and size of the maze.
- Word Search—Type in your own word list.
- Criss-Cross Puzzle—Enter your own words.
- Letter Tiles—Enter a phrase to be unscrambled.
- Number Blocks—Test your skills in arithmetic and/or algebra.

Try this:

Create a cryptogram for social studies. Test it on your classmates and see if they come up with the correct answer!

Design a computer-generated maze for your school newspaper.

Highlights:

This site can be translated into five languages!

When a new puzzle is submitted to the Puzzlemaker site, your creations are ready within about 20 seconds.

See also:

BrainBashers

http://www.brainbashers.com/

A collection of logic, language and math puzzles can be found here.

Thunk.com

http://www.thunk.com

Overview:

You've probably heard about spies using secret codes to conceal their messages from the enemy. At Thunk.com you too can use cryptology (the scrambling and unscrambling of secret messages) to make your own secret messages to send to friends or to keep personal diaries private! Thunk.com is very simple to use:

1. Type or paste a message into the text box.
2. Click the Scramble button.
3. Copy the secret message into e-mail or a word processing document.

To unscramble a message:

1. Type or paste a scrambled message into the text box.
2. Click the UnScramble button.
3. Copy the unscrambled message into your e-mail or word processing document.

Helpful HINT: Use CTRL and C keys to copy and use CTRL and V keys to paste.

Translate this message:

Ef zrccna qfj lfd dbn cqvb bvcn, lfd jvyy unovevcnyl qrin yfcb fo bntanc ode! (thunk.com)

Try this:

Go to the *Funnies* section and use the scrambled jokes to practice copying and pasting messages into the unscrambler. While you're at it, laugh at some corny jokes other kids have submitted to Thunk.com.

Highlights:

This site is entertaining and lots of fun!

See also:

CIA for Kids

http://www.odci.gov/cia/ciakids

Government Goodies

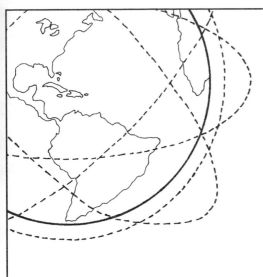

50States.com: States and Capitals

http://www.50states.com

Overview:

Here is the site you've been waiting for! Imagine this: Your social studies teacher has just assigned a report on a state, but all the books you need have been taken out of the library! Stay calm and visit this site. Use the image map and click the link of the state's name to find detailed information for every state in the U.S. Some of the facts at your fingertips are:

- Capital City
- State Bird
- College & Universities
- Constitution Information

- Economy Profile
- State Flag
- State Flower
- Governor

- Maps
- Congressional Representatives
- State Symbols
- Weather

- -

Try this:

Going on a summer vacation? Use this site to gather facts and travel information for your family.

Highlights:

Looking specifically for state songs? Try the *Song* link to avoid other facts.

This site is a gift to every elementary school student.

See also:

Stately Knowledge

http://www.ipl.org/youth/stateknow/

Try the State Capitals and State Flags game for some fun.

Bureau of Engraving and Printing

http://www.moneyfactory.com

Overview:

Have you ever seen a $10,000 bill? Visit The Bureau of Engraving and Printing to see this rare bill and pictures of other paper money online. Go to *The Currency* link and find out whose pictures are on large and small denominations of currency. Then check out *Money Facts & Trivia* where you can find out about the symbolism on money, and view all current currency.

Try this:

Follow the link to the Kids' page and play *Find the New Fifty, Face Flips, and Count the Cash!*

Highlights:

Lesson links are available for teachers at the Kids' Page.

This is an excellent source for pictures of cash!

See also:

The United States Mint

http://www.usmint.gov

Find coins at this site.

http://lcweb.loc.gov/

Overview:

Welcome to the Library of Congress, one of the most impressive libraries in the world. This Web site, a companion to the resources of the library, offers an amazing number of experiences for the Internet visitor. Some of the possibilities include: *Using the Library* (this includes an online catalog of the collections), *THOMAS* (Congressional Information), the *American Memory* page (America's history in words and pictures), *The Library Today*, *Exhibitions* (including the American Treasures of the Library of Congress) and much more.

Kids will enjoy checking out some of the online exhibits from the collections, all of which are very large Web sites. Take a tour of some of these amazing exhibitions:

- Frank Lloyd Wright
- The Gettysburg Address
- The African-American Mosaic

- 1492: An Ongoing Voyage
- Scrolls from the Dead Sea
- Rome Reborn

- Women Come to the Front: Journalists
- Temple of Liberty: Building the Capitol for a New Nation

- -

Try this:

Click on *Historical Documents* and browse through the Constitution, the Federalist Papers, or the Declaration of Independence.

Highlights:

This site is packed with photographs, famous documents, stories, books, and government records.

The site map clarifies the overwhelming amount of material to be found here.

See also:

The American Memory Page

http://memory.loc.gov/ammem/amhome.html

National Archives Online Exhibit Hall

http://www.nara.gov/exhall

Overview:

Studying the Declaration of Independence? Come to this site to see this and other original documents of American history online! The National Archives Online Exhibit Hall is the place to find unique primary source materials (original historic documents) for your school projects. Delve into a *Portrait of Black Chicago* and check out prize-winning photographs from the 1970s. Read about a behind-the-scenes meeting between Elvis Presley and President Nixon, or view famous documents like the Constitution, and the Bill of Rights.

A fascinating part of this site is called *Power of Persuasion—Posters from World War II*. At this section you can take a look at images of posters, some of which have become very well known:

- Man the Guns!
- It's a Woman's War Too!
- This is Nazi Brutality
- He's Watching You
- Stamp 'em Out!

Try this:

Print out your favorite poster on a color printer and write a poem to describe the image.

Try reading The Constitution from the original document. Can you read the words?

Highlights:

Take this delightful experience into the archives of the United States and view documents that have made history!

See also:

National Archives and Records Administration

http://www.nara.gov

This is the home page of this site.

U.S. Postal Service Kids' Page

http://www.usps.gov/kids/welcome.htm

Overview:

We all live in the age of telephone and e-mail. It seems natural to pick up the phone to dial a friend or to type a quick note on the computer to send via the Internet. But imagine a time without the telephone and computers. Whether it was a love note or an official government document, letters were the only way to correspond.

Here is a site where you can get to know more about the U.S. Postal Service. Try a game where you can deliver mail in silly ways, play concentration by delivering envelopes into mailboxes, and then answer some questions about the postal system at *Return to Sender.*

Try this:

Ever wonder how subjects for stamps are chosen? Go to *Criteria for Stamp Subject Selection* at *Stamp Information* and find out.

Can't locate a zipcode? It's at your fingertips at *ZIP Code Lookup.*

Highlights:

A wealth of games, puzzles, stamp collecting information, and more can be found here.

See also:

National Postal Museum

http://educate.si.edu/resources/programs/museums/postal.html

Presidents of the United States

http://www.ipl.org/ref/POTUS/

Overview:

Visit this site sponsored by the Internet Public Library that is entirely devoted to Presidents of the United States. Here you will find background information, election results, cabinet members, notable events, and points of interest for every president.

Simply select a president from the list provided, click, and be transported to a world of information. A picture is included for each president, along with information on first ladies and other family members.

Try this:	Highlights:	See also:
Do a multimedia report for President's Day and use this site as part of your report.	This site provides accurate and detailed information about presidents along with links to other sources on the Internet. Alphabetical indexes are provided for names, subjects, and topics in POTUS.	The American Presidency http://www.interlink-cafe.com/uspresidents/ Presidents of the United States http://www.whitehouse.gov/WH/glimpse/presidents/html/presidents.html

Smithsonian Institution

http://www.si.edu

Overview:

It doesn't matter if you can't make it to Washington, D.C. because the whole city is literally at your fingertips at this site. Share the wealth of the Smithsonian Institution, an amazing array of collections, offering a variety of museums and online exhibits. The Smithsonian collects art, artifacts, documents, and treasures, many of which are available online. This is with no doubt one of the highlights of the World Wide Web!

Choose your favorite museum from this partial list, and then sit back, relax, and enjoy the visit. Go to:

- The Cooper-Hewitt Museum
- The Hirshhorn Museum and Sculpture Gardens
- National Air and Space Museum
- Museum of American History
- Museum of Indian History
- National Portrait Gallery
- National Zoo
- National Postal Museum

Added to these museums are at least fifty online exhibits of which a few are listed below.

- Mysterious Manatees
- Ocean Planet
- Spiders
- Women and Flight
- The Jazz Age in Paris
- A Salute to American Musicals
- African American Sacred Music Traditions

For teachers only: This is a great source for education and curriculum materials.

- -

Try this:

Click on any topic from A-Z and find answers to frequently asked questions along with links to other Smithsonian resources.

Highlights:

This site contains more stuff than you could possibly imagine!

Check out *Kids' Castle* and find out about science, animals, sports, astronomy, the arts, and more.

See also:

The Carnegie Museums of Pittsburgh

http://www.clpgh.org/Carnegie.html

Voices of Youth

http://www.unicef.org/voy/

Overview:

Voices of Youth is an attractive and practical site for kids sponsored by UNICEF as part of its fiftieth anniversary celebration. At this site, you can take part in an electronic discussion about the future of children. Discuss ways in which the world can become a place where the rights of every child are protected.

Go to the *Meeting Place* and discuss your views about the following current global issues:

- Children and Work
- The Girl Child
- Children's Rights

- Children and War
- Cities and Children

Try this:

At the Meeting Place, explore the lives of children and their work through stories and photographs. *Take the Child Labor Interactive Quiz and give your opinion about the results.*

Highlights:

This site can be accessed in French, Spanish, and English.

It is packed with valuable information and is designed in a clear, logical sequence.

See also:

Free the Children

http://www.freethechildren.org/

http://www.whitehouse.gov/WH/kids/html/home.html

Overview:

Explore the residence of the President and the first family and read news about what's happening at the White House. Check out the History of the White House or read about kids and pets that have lived in the White House!

- -

Try this:

Take a virtual tour of the White House. You can do this by clicking the *White House History and Tour* link at the main page of the site at:

http://www.whitehouse.gov/index.html

Highlights:

Send an e-mail message to the President and try to convince him to support or not support some current legislation.

See also:

The House of Representatives

http://www.house.gov

History Helpers

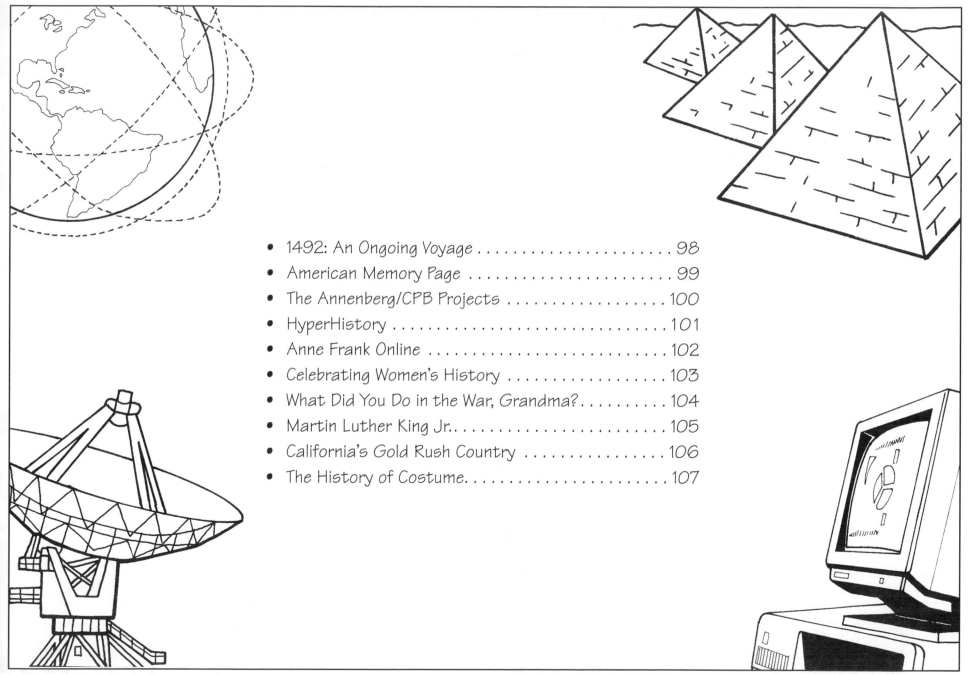

1492: An Ongoing Voyage

http://lcweb.loc.gov/exhibits/1492/intro.html

Overview:

Experience life in 1492, a date which brings to mind one of the most famous explorers in America—Christopher Columbus. This site delves into Columbus' explorations and adventures and the way in which his journeys brought two very diverse worlds, the Mediterranean area and the Americas in contact with each other.

This site addresses many questions, for example, "Who lived in the Americas before 1492?" and "Who followed in the wake of Columbus?"

Take your own journey through this online exhibit and travel through its six sections.

- What Came to Be Called "America"
- The Mediterranean World
- Christopher Columbus: Man and Myth
- Inventing America
- Europe Claims America
- Epilogue

This Web site requires a lot of reading on your part, but it's worth every second!

Try this:

Read about *Christopher Columbus: Man and Myth*, and follow the link to his coat of arms. Then, create your own coat of arms using images from the Heraldry Web site. (See p. 12)

Highlights:

This online exhibit includes images of 22 objects from the original exhibit, including maps and artifacts.

Teachers: This is an excellent addition to an explorers unit.

See also:

First People on SchoolNet: Nations Menu
http://www.schoolnet.ca/autochtone/nations_menu-e.html

Click on *nations* to locate information on specific tribes.

http://memory.loc.gov

Overview:

History comes alive at the American Memory Page! Sponsored by the Library of Congress, this very large site offers over 43 collections of oral histories, maps, papers, videos, and photography. Browse through *California Folk Music* and listen to old-time music. In the Prints and Photographs Division, view *Civil War Photographs*, look through *Baseball Highlights*, check out *Votes for Women*, and learn about the early days of motion pictures (movies), and so much more. This is only a small sample of the over one million items included at this site.

Note: You need the *Real Audio* plug-in, and the capability to play QuickTime, AVI, MPEG and WAV files to fully take advantage of this site.

Try this:

Create a slide show program with images from this site, using *HyperStudio, Kid Pix Studio,* or *ClarisWorks.*

Click on *Today in History* to get a glimpse of notable events from any day of the year.

Highlights:

This is an excellent starting point for researching American history.

A teacher's section is included.

See also:

The History Channel

http://www.historychannel.com

The Annenberg/CPB Project
Exhibits Collection
Interactive Learning Exhibits inspired by Video Series in the
Annenberg, CPB Multimedia Collection

http://www.learner.org/exhibits/

Overview:

Inspired by the Annenberg/CPB video collection, this online companion project offers high-quality multimedia exhibits on the World Wide Web. Educators develop the content for the exhibits along with a team of experts who specialize in Web design and technical applications. This site offers over 35 subject areas that can be used by students, teachers, organizations, and parents. Each month a new exhibit is added to the collection featuring science, art, writing, literature, psychology, geology, and many more.

Some highlights of the collection:

- Cinema—What goes into the making of your favorite movies?
- Collapse— Why do civilizations come to an end?
- Renaissance—Learn about the inspiration of this classical age.
- Middle Ages—Find out what life was really like during this period.
- Russia—What is Russia like now?

Try this:

Go to *Amusement Park Physics* to design your own rollercoaster and see if it passes the safety inspection.

At the *Personality* exhibit, take a personality test to find out how you are perceived by others!!

Highlights:

Each exhibit is packed full of valuable information and is an entire Web site in itself.

Teachers will find valuable classroom information at this site.

See also:

The History Place

http://www.historyplace.com/

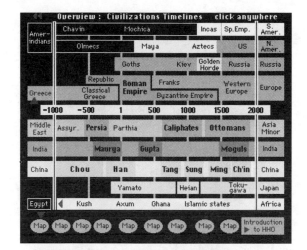

http://www.hyperhistory.com/online_n2/History_n2/a.html

Overview:

Based on a world history chart, HyperHistory covers 3,000 years of people, events, maps, and time periods. Imagine the chart from your history class coming alive, and with a click, all sorts of people and events from the past appear! For example, click on *Events* followed by a click on *1901-1910*. HyperHistory brings up a colorized chart (civilizations are color-coded) with a vast array of entries, including the *Boxer Revolt in China, Henry Ford Founds the Ford Motor Company, J. Barrie Writes Peter Pan, L. Lumiere Develops Color Photography, Congo Becomes a Colony of Belgium,* and many more. There is an incredible amount of information packed in this site that covers 3,000 years!

Try this:

Looking for a map of the Mongol Empire in a hurry? Click the Map button, and you will find it.

Highlights:

There is a huge number of files at this site, but individual pages are able to load quickly.

Updates and additions are continually being made to this page.

See also:

Any Day in History

http://www.scopesys.com/anyday/

Anne Frank Online

http://www.annefrank.com

Overview:

Learn about Anne Frank, a German-Jewish teenager who was forced to go into hiding during the Holocaust. Anne and her family, along with four others, spent 25 months during World War II living in an annex of rooms in Amsterdam. During this period, Anne wrote what was to become one of the most widely-read personal accounts of the Holocaust. This site offers a glimpse into Anne's story through several sections:

- A photoscrapbook of Anne's life and family
- Excerpts from her diary
- A tour of the Annex,
- A brief history of the Holocaust

Try this:

Find locations for the exhibit Anne Frank in the World: 1929-1945, and try to attend the exhibit when it tours your area of the country.

Highlights:

Excellent original archival materials are used at this site.

A section on education is available for teachers.

See also:

A Student's Forum of Art and Poetry About the Holocaust

http://remember.org/imagine/index.html

Celebrating Women's History

http://www.gale.com/freresrc/womenhst/index.htm

Overview:

Come to this site and celebrate the 150th anniversary of the Women's Rights movement. Read about courageous women whose unceasing work to achieve equality for the female half of the American population is still not fully recognized.

Go to the activities section to find a wealth of projects that will add to your understanding of women's history:

- Women's Rulers
- Champions of Women's Health
- Women and War
- Women Volunteers

- Anita Hill: Speaking Out
- Kate Chopin and *The Awakening*
- Mother Teresa
- Communicating Strength

You can go to the time line for key events in women's history, take a quiz on women's history, read excerpts from "Women's Rights on Trial," and find many references on this topic under *Featured Titles*.

- -

Try this:

March has arrived, and you are celebrating Women's History Month in school. Use this site to write a report on a famous woman.

Use the time line information to get ideas and then write a time line about your life!

Highlights:

One of the best parts of this site is the *Biography* section that tells the stories of more than 60 women.

See also:

Biography.com

http://www.biography.com/

Biography Maker

http://www.bham.wednet.edu/bio/biomak2.htm

This site will guide you through writing a biography.

What Did You Do in the War, Grandma?

http://www.stg.brown.edu/projects/WWII_Women/

Overview:

Learn about your grandparents' (and great-grandparents') generation, the years before and during World War II. Young students in the Honors English Program at South Kingstown High School interviewed Rhode Island women from this unique era and then created this site packed with memories and personal interviews. These are examples of some of the interviews:

- Coming to Terms with the Holocaust and Prejudice at Home
- A Pacifist in a Time of War
- A School Teacher Minds the Home Front

- Raising Six Children Alone
- War Sparks a More Active Role for Women

Twenty-six interviews are included as well as a World War II time line, links to oral history resources, articles, bibliography, an audio presentation, and reference pages.

Try this:

Make up a list of questions and interview your grandmother or another senior citizen; find out what she did during WWII.

Highlights:

This is an excellent example of a school Web site.

Teachers can integrate this site into a World War II history unit.

See also:

A People at War: Women Who Served

http://www.nara.gov/exhall/people/women.html

Martin Luther King Jr.

http://www.seattletimes.com/mlk/index.html

Overview:

Get to know Martin Luther King Jr. at this comprehensive site which covers the Civil Rights Movement and the role Dr. King played in the struggle for equal rights. Some of the highlights from this site are listed below:

- a time line of the Civil Rights Movement
- a time line of Dr. King's life
- sound clips taken from Dr. King's speeches

- an interactive quiz on Martin Luther King
- discussions about civil rights among students
- ways to celebrate King's birthday

Try this:

Click on *The Movement* and then *Images of History*. Follow the arrows at this section and take a photographic tour through the national civil rights movement in the Seattle area.

Highlights:

This is a very good site from *The Seattle Times* which takes an in-depth look at the impact of Martin Luther King.

See also:

African-American History

http://www.gale.com/freresrc/blkhstry/index.htm

©Leslie A. Kelly

Courtesy Show Me
The Gold® Logo

http://www.goldrush1849.com

Overview:

Strike it rich historically at this comprehensive site which covers the Gold Rush through stories and photographs. Take the virtual tour that begins when James Wilson Marshall discovers gold at Sutter's Mill in 1848. Read *The Way West* which describes the migration of the hundreds of thousands of gold seekers who flocked to California to get rich (the Forty-Niners) and tells about the addition of California as the United States of America's thirty-first state.

- -

Try this:

Do you need a writing project for school? Visit this site and then write a story through the eyes of a forty-niner. For example, include the trials of the journey westward as well as the obsession with becoming rich in California.

Highlights:

A map, extensive photographs, and information illustrate this site.

Related links and books are provided.

See also:

Gold Fever Exhibition at the Oakland Museum

http://www.museumca.org/
goldrush.
html

THE HISTORY OF COSTUME
By Braun & Schneider   c 1861 1880

http://www.siue.edu/COSTUMES/history.html

Overview:

Imagine this:

You have written a play set in sixteenth century Italy for your English class. The sets, characters, and lines are in place, but you are encountering one serious problem: what did the people wear during that time period?

Your problems are answered at this site which provides pictures of over 500 costumes from antiquity to the end of the nineteenth century. Originally published as individual plates in a German magazine, the plates were later collected and put in book form. While serving the needs of a modern-day student, the Victorian drawing style may seem a bit cumbersome and outdated. Still, this online book is an excellent source for costume designers and for anyone who is interested in fashion.

- -

Try this:

After browsing through the costumes from various time periods, become your own fashion designer and keep a sketchbook with new ideas.

Highlights:

Use the text index as your guide to view the time periods and costumes on this site.

This would be an excellent addition for period-related literature units.

See also:

The Costume Page

http://members.aol.com/nebula5/tcpmake2.html#schools

Favorite Picks

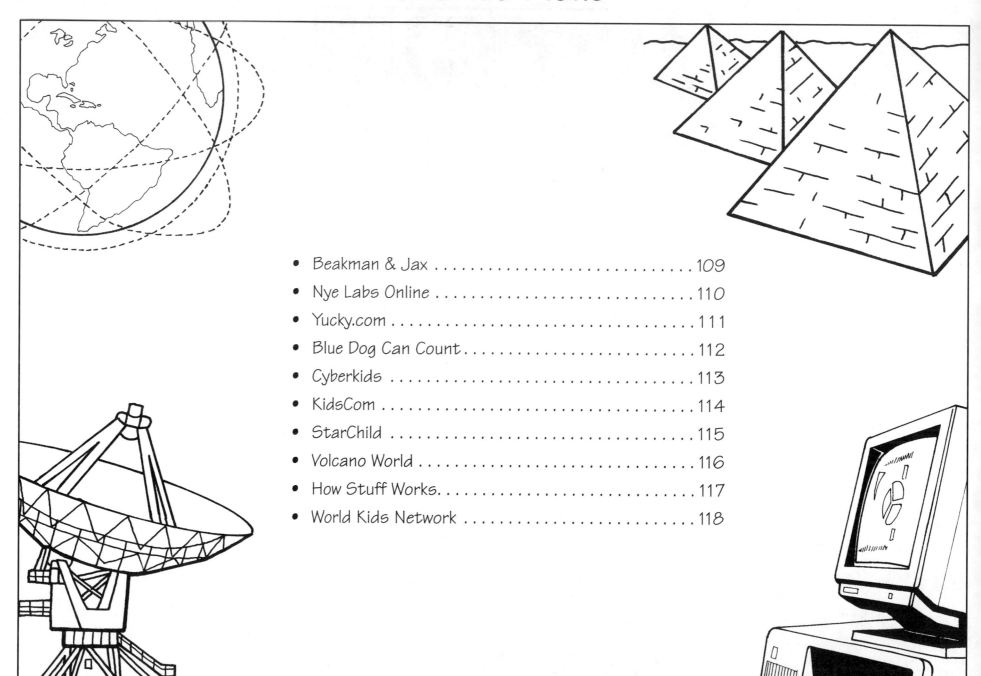

Beakman & Jax

http://www.beakman.com/

Overview:

Visit *You Can* on the Web and stay and play with Beakman and Jax. Click the *Answers to Your Questions* link and find answers to questions like *"How does soap work?"* or *"How does a lever make your stronger?"* Then find out what is coming up in future editions of the TV show or go on a world tour and visit museums with the sets and experiments from Beakman's World.

Try this:

Visit the *Other Tremendous Places to Go* section and find out why feet smell, how mucus protects us, or where Beakman & Jax like to go on the Web.

Highlights:

There is an abundance of funny questions.

If they don't have an answer to your question, simply send an e-mail and check the site in a few days.

See Also:

AskERIC

http://ericir.syr.edu/

Nye Labs Online

http://nyelabs.kcts.org/

Overview:

Did you know that lobsters make noises by rubbing their antennae together or that a computer can add 120,000 numbers in the time it takes a hummingbird to flap its wings? Ask questions from Bill of the TV show at Nye Labs Online and have fun while learning lots of fascinating facts about science! At this site you can check out the *Demo of the Day* and get instructions on how to do experiments that were done in an episode. Click on *Goodies* to hear songs or view photographs and video clips from the show. Go to the *U-Nye-Verse* to find facts about Bill Nye himself, and e-mail Bill Nye your question.

Try this:

Watch an episode of Bill's and then go to the Web site and read the follow-up activity in *Demo of the Day*. Then send an e-mail message with comments about the activity to Bill Nye.

Highlights:

Nye's entertaining approach to science provides hours of science fun!

See also:

Whelmers

http://www.mcrel.org/whelmers/

Find even more outstanding science activities.

http://www.yucky.com/

Overview:

Welcome to the yuckiest, most disgusting, and easily the funniest site on the Internet. First, click on the *Gross/Cool Body* button and find out why you burp, sweat, vomit, have bad breath, zits, pus, and more! Then go to the *Bug World* button and find out everything you always wanted to know about roaches!

- -

Try this:

Go to *Club Yucky* and try out *Yucky Science* or *Edible Science.*

Try creating a *Yucky E-card* and read the poems "Ode to a Worm" and "Worm Hate!"

Highlights:

Kids will be roaring with laughter at this site!

Lots of special effects are included, but they are too gross to be mentioned here. Try them for yourself!

See Also:

The Virtual Body

http://www.medtropolis.com/vbody/

Blue Dog Can Count

http://www.forbesfield.com/bdf.html

Overview:

This simple site is one of the most popular on the Internet. George Rodrigue's Blue Dog performs the arithmetic after numbers are entered in the blank squares. Then, the question is answered by a barking dog! You have the choice of addition, subtraction, multiplication, or division problems.

Try this:

Younger kids can go to this site to practice their math facts.

Test Blue Dog to his limit. If you add 100 + 100, will he bark 200 times?

Highlights:

This is a great beginning site for the younger user. The funny dog and his barking stimulate interest in the World Wide Web.

See also:

George Rodrigue

http://www.bluedogart.com/

Read George Rodrigue's biography and check out some of his other popular paintings.

Cyberkids

http://www.cyberkids.com

Overview:

The goal of this creative site is to create a community of young people from all over the world who share their thoughts and ideas. Take the opportunity to enter contests, tackle puzzles and brain teasers, show off your creativity, read reviews, try magic tricks, find keypals, listen to original musical compositions by kids, and join the Cyberkids Club. (To join the club, you need parental permission if you are under 12.)

Note: *Java* and *Shockwave* required.

Try this:

Register and join the Cyberkids Club (free). You can participate in member activities such as posting messages, chatting, entering contests, submitting drawings, downloading free software, and more!

Highlights:

The Cyberkids Launchpad provides interesting spots on the Web to explore. Immerse yourself in art, computers, music, science, nature, museums, entertainment, and all kinds of other activities.

See also:

KidsNews

http://www.kidnews.com/

Kids' writing from practically everywhere is at this site!

KidsCom

http://www.kidscom.com

Overview:

Enter this virtual playground for kids of all ages! Make new friends, find a keypal, travel to other countries, participate in a chat with kids all over the globe (chats are monitored for safety 24 hours a day), play easy or challenging games, and more.

At *Kids Talk About*, you have the opportunity to speak out on a new question every week, write a story with characters provided by KidsCom, or tell the Web community about your favorite pet.

Note: *Java* and *Shockwave* required.

Try this:

Young kids, go to *Mousers*, the section of the site designed for little KidsCom kids!

Offer your opinions to presidents and prime ministers by visiting the *Voice to the World* link.

Highlights:

Parents and teachers can visit their own special section at *ParentsTalk*. Share messages with parents from around the world or check out some activities at Family Fun.

See also:

Kids' Space

http://www.kids-space.org/

StarChild

http://starchild.gsfc.nasa.gov/docs/StarChild/StarChild.html

Overview:

Welcome to StarChild, a learning center for young astronomers put together by a special team at NASA. This site covers everything you'd want to know about the universe and includes many high quality photographic images. Click on The Sun, The Moon, The Planets, The Asteroid Belt, or Comets, and see what you can find.

The *Space Stuff* section is very interesting also and offers information on Astronauts, *Space Travel*, the *Hubble Space Telescope*, *Space Wardrobe*, *Space Probes*, and *Who's Who in Space*.

Try this:

Gather information at StarChild for a Science report. Include digital images from this site for your presentation.

Highlights:

An excellent glossary is useful for fact finding.

Printable versions of pages allow for higher quality printouts.

See also:

The Nine Planets

http://www.seds.org/nineplanets/nineplanets/nineplanets.html

Volcano World

http://volcano.und.nodak.edu/

Overview:

Volcano World provides fascinating information about volcanoes, one of the most dramatic phenomena in nature. At *Volcano World* you can experience the excitement of this unique natural wonder through many activities, numerous volcano images, volcano observatories, and even volcano video clips! Enrich your volcanic knowledge with interactive experiments, volcano indices, and by keeping involved with currently erupting volcanoes of the world.

Try this:

Go through the *Kid's Door* and check out *Volcano Art*, take the *Kid Quiz*, go on *Virtual Field Trips* at *Volcano Adventures* and e-mail questions to the Volcanologist.

Highlights:

Volcano World enriches learning experiences by delivering high quality images and other data.

See also:

Stromboli Online
http://www.ezinfo.ethz.ch/volcano/strombolihomee.html

Find even more volcano photos, eruptions, maps, drawings, and video clips.

How Stuff Works

http://www.howstuffworks.com

Overview:

Welcome to How Stuff Works, a wonderful place to explore the way things work in your everyday world. Join Marshall Brain, the creator of this site, as he helps you understand just about everything. For example, he answers the following questions:

- How does a VCR work?
- Why does a thermos keep the hot stuff hot and the cold stuff cold?
- How is a 500,000-pound jet able to get off the ground?
- How do Web servers deliver Web pages from anywhere in the world to your computer?
- What makes digital clocks and wristwatches tick?

Mr. Brain has an uncanny ability to communicate complex ideas clearly and has a passion to explain how just about anything works! To prove it, the traffic at this site has peaked to approximately 10,000 users a day!

Try this:

Send your e-mail address to How Stuff Works and receive information about new articles added to the Web site.

Highlights:

If you are searching for something in particular, a full text search facility is available.

This site is designed for both young and old kids!

See also:

The Last Word

http://www.last-word.com/

World Kids Network

http://www.worldkids.net/welcome.htm

Overview:

World Kids Network is a large site dedicated to the advancement of children's education. "Be anyone, do anything, or find out almost anything" is the motto of the site. You can join clubs, play games, do homework, visit museums, or even be a volunteer for the World Kids Network (WKN).

The WKN is a place where kids can explore the world with wonder in a safe and enjoyable environment with tons of new things to experience!

Try an excursion to one of the places below:

- The Marsupial Museum
- Internet Safety
- Channel of Wormholes

- Winnie the Pooh and Friends
- G.I.R.L. (Girls Internationally Writing Letters)
- Keypals Club International

- Atomniverse
- Rainbow Road
- Cast of Characters

Note: *Java* is required at this site.

Try this:

Take a guided tour of *Cosmotown* and visit the *Plastic Pink Flamingo* and the *Wiggly Family*. Then check out the *Cosmotown Mall*. How does this mall compare with the mall in your city?

Highlights:

Since this site has been put together by volunteers, you can offer your suggestions and make original contributions to this inspirational world.

See also:

Wacky Web Tales

http://www.eduplace.com/tales/

Touring the World

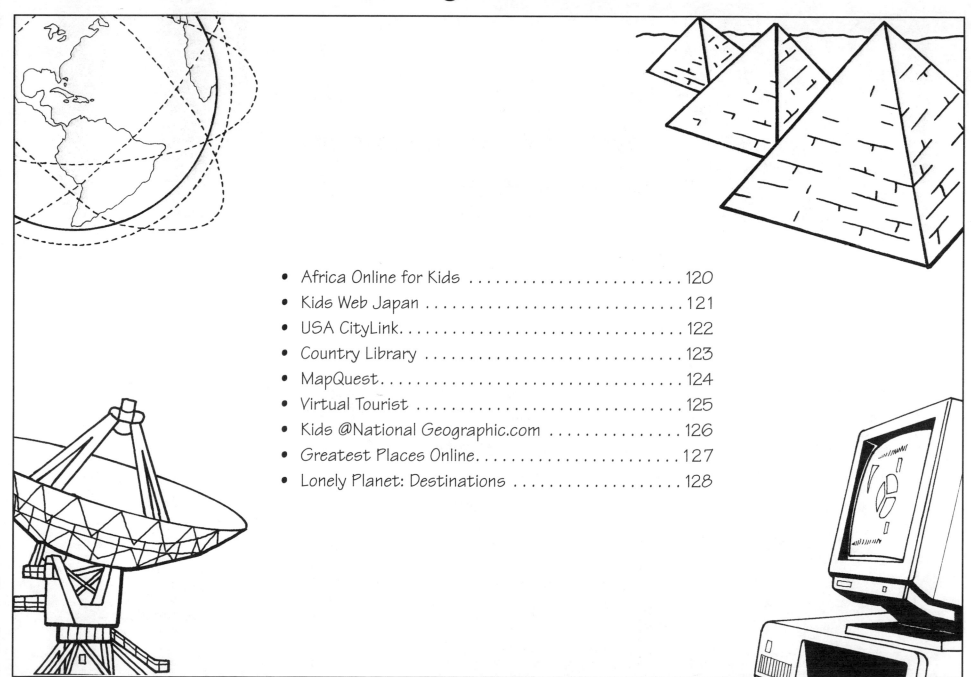

Africa Online for Kids

http://www.africaonline.com/AfricaOnline/coverkids.html

Overview:

Travel to Cote d'Ivoire, Ghana, Kenya, Zimbabwe and a host of other exciting countries in the second largest continent in the world, Africa.

Start at the *Kids Only Zone* and surf through many lands. Then take the online quiz about climate, cities, and names of countries.

A stimulating section to check out is the *Language Page*. Learn about the languages kids speak in Africa—over 1000! Have you heard of some of these languages?

- Arabic
- Berber
- Sudanic
- Setswana
- Teke
- Ubangi
- Cushitic
- Kikuyu
- Malinke
- Kiwahili
- English
- Fula

Give yourself a test and try to match these languages to the countries where they are spoken!

- -

Try this:

Go to *Games & Activities* and try an Africa Word Search, Crossword, or Decode a Message.

Check out the *Sasa Link* (a word in Swahili meaning "Now") and read poems and stories submitted to the site.

Highlights:

Refer to this site for your next report on Africa for social studies.

Lots of information is available here including travel, sports, and news.

See also:

Kids Zone Africa

http://www.afroam.org/children/

Kids Web Japan

http://www.jinjapan.org/kidsweb/

Overview:

Find out what kids are doing in Japan at this informative and colorful site. Read regularly updated news stories, find out what type of "once upon a time stories" Japanese kids grow up listening to, take part in Japan's rich tradition of Ikebana (flower arranging) and Origami (paper folding), assemble a jigsaw puzzle of the map of Japan, or try some recipes that are popular with school kids in Japan.

Note: *Shockwave* plug-ins are required at this site.

Try this:

Check out *What's Cool in Japan* for kids. Have you heard of any of these fads?

Need information for a report? Click on these sections: *History, Regions of Japan, Politics and the Constitution, Daily Life,* and any other link that is interesting!

Highlights:

Have a question? Go to KidsWeb Plaza and submit your question about Japan.

This excellent site is filled with factual and entertaining information.

See also:

Joseph Wu's Origami Page

http://www.origami.vancouver.bc.ca/

This is a wonderful paper-folding resource.

USA CityLink

http://www.usacitylink.com/

Overview:

The USA CityLink project is a comprehensive city and state listing on the Web. At first glance, the site seems quite simple, but it is one of the most visited sites on the Internet today. It provides users with a starting point when accessing information about cities and states. To use this site, simply follow these steps:

1. Select a state.
2. Browse through the cities available in the state.
3. Choose your city.
4. Gather facts about that city.

- -

Try this:

Doing a state or city report? Start your project at this site and go on a virtual tour.

Play a treasure hunt game. Develop a list of items to gather about various cities, and navigate through the city sites to find these secret treasures.

Highlights:

Comprehensive information is provided in an easy-to-follow format.

See also:

Flag Bazaar

http://www.niceeasy.com.au/flags/worldmap.html

Click on a section of the world to find your flag.

Country Library

http://www.tradeport.org/ts/countries/

Overview:

Visit this comprehensive reference site dedicated to providing worldwide facts. This page is your one-stop, perfect spot for locating all the data you need for class assignments. When you arrive at this site, you will realize that this description is no exaggeration; Country Library offers loads of information on any country of the world and will point you to a variety of helpful resources. Click on a region of the map or on a particular country. You will find:

- Country Overview
- Background Notes
- Demographics
- Trade Information

This site provides high level-material that is suitable for older kids in middle school and above.

- -

Try this:

Use the Country Search capability and enter keywords to locate the country information you are looking for.

Highlights:

This is a one-stop source for country reports.

Find *Background Notes* from your desk at home without having to wait in long lines at the library!

See also:

Mr. Dowling's Electronic Passport

http://www.mrdowling.com/

MapQuest

http://www.mapquest.com

Overview:

MapQuest is an interactive mapping service that includes two parts. *Find a map* allows you to find a map of any place in the world. Simply select a U.S. or International city, click *GO*, and quickly get a map. *Driving Directions* provides city-to-city maps or personalized maps for the United States, parts of Canada, and Mexico. For a personalized map just type in your starting and destination address, click on *Calculate Directions*, and your map will appear. The directions are clear and simple to follow. To print your map, don't forget to select the print version option.

Before going on your journey, make a stop at this site. Be prepared!

Try this:

Use the *Find a Map* section to do research on the geography of any part of the world.

Before your next vacation, collect all the maps you need from this site!

Highlights:

This service is free, fast, and easily accessible.

Use this site with students to plan a route to travel. Extend this activity by asking students to estimate traveling time and distance per hour.

See also:

How Far is it?

http://www.indo.com/distance/

The US Census calculates the distance between two places.

Virtual Tourist

http://www.virtualtourist.com

Overview:

Are you planning a trip, or do you simply like to travel? At this site the world is at your fingertips! The Virtual Tourist provides an electronic map of the world with a hyperlink at each section. Simply click on the part of the world you would like to visit and find general information and thousands of pictures of places all over the world. Other useful links at the *Tool* section include a currency converter and time zone information.

- -

Try this:

Collect media on any country and design a pamphlet advertising that country.

Play an online geography scavenger hunt.

Highlights:

Information provided is excellent for a country report.

E-mail tourist information offices in different countries for more access to country facts!

See also:

CIA Home Page for Kids

http://www.cia.gov/cia/ciakids/index.html

Kids @National Geographic.com

http://www.nationalgeographic.com/kids/index.html

Overview:

Join National Geographic's site for kids and check out some of the activities provided. Go to the *Cartoon Factory*, visit the *World of Tarantulas*, read *World Online Magazine*, or even go to the *Pen Pal Network*.

Looking for in-depth explorations? Browse through the lengthy site index at the top of the page, and search the archives. A great section for kids is at *Information Central* that provides information on many topics, for example:

- Animals—bats, manatees, gorillas, tigers and more
- Biographies—famous scientists
- Environmental Concerns—acid rain and the rain forest
- Geography—continent facts
- History—the real *Titanic*!
- Phenomena—unexplained subjects of interest

Try this:

Find *Geography Education* in the index and click on *Map Machine*. Explore continent maps, look at flags, and collect world facts at this interesting part of the site.

Highlights:

The site index provides an accessible menu at every page.

Nice photographs and world information are available at this site.

Teacher information is provided.

See also:

National Geographic.com

http://www.nationalgeographic.com/

| Amazon | Greenland | Iguazu | Madagascar | Namib | Okavango | Tibet |

Greatest Places Online

http://www.sci.mus.mn.us/greatestplaces/

Overview:

Explore the Greatest Places Online site sponsored by the Science Museum of Minnesota and visit the Amazon, Greenland, Madagascar, Namibia, Okavango, and Tibet. Created as a companion to the *Greatest Places* film, this site features colorful tours through these remote areas, interesting activities from the various countries, a travel journal of Namibia, and a chance to get to know the animals from the Amazon to Tibet.

- -

Try this:

Go to the *Making Stickers* section. Follow the recipe for mixing your own sticker glue and then print out a Greatest Place sticker and use the glue for placing it on your bedroom wall.

Highlights:

Hands-on activities give you the opportunity to try engaging projects and games that kids do in some of these great places.

Global systems information is provided and could be used as part of a geography unit by teachers.

See also:

Let's Go Around the World

http://www.ccph.com/

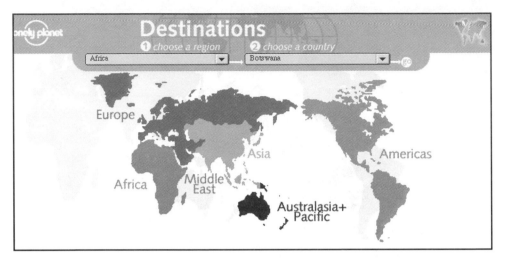

©LonelyPlanet

Lonely Planet: Destinations

http://www.lonelyplanet.com/dest

Do you dream about traveling around the globe from country to country? At this site, your fantasy becomes reality. Start at *Destinations* and use the scroll-down menu to choose a region and then a country. You will instantly be transported to your ideal travel spot and will find photographs, history, attractions, maps, a slide show, facts at a glance, events, and a variety of relevant country topics.

There are neat things to do at this site. For example, click on *Optic Nerve*, and find photographs of almost any country. Go to *Postcards* and read mail which fellow travelers have sent to the site!

Try this:

Use this site to design a travel guide for your favorite country. Include maps, photographs, and historical information.

Highlights:

Easy and quick navigation through this site makes travelling a breeze!

Other travel links are included at *subWWWay!*

See also:

World Safari

http://www.supersurf.com

From Neutrons to Numbers

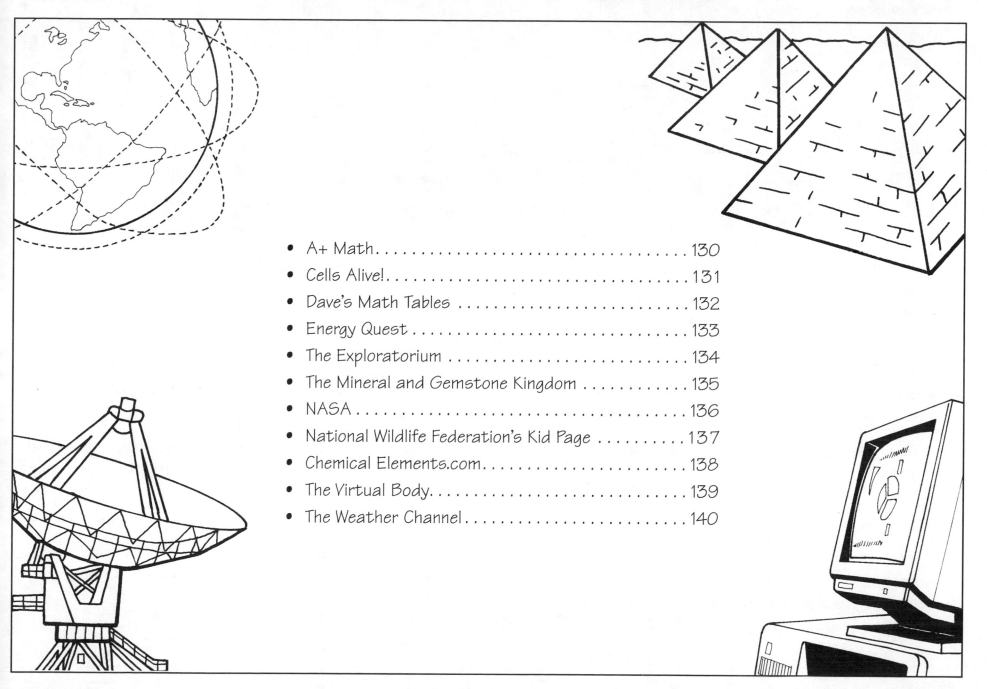

Flashcards

Homework Helper

A+ Math
www.aplusmath.com

Game Room

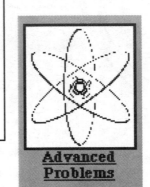

Advanced Problems

http://www.aplusmath.com

Overview:

Go to this site when you are working on your math skills and want a little extra help. Simple and colorful graphics make learning math lots of fun, especially when you play games like *Matho*, a combination of *Bingo* and math, *Hidden Pictures* and *Concentration*, or use a wide variety of flash cards.

A valuable feature is the interactive *Homework Helper* that allows you to input a problem and your answer. Then it will figure out if your solution is correct without giving you the answer! Try problems in addition, subtraction, multiplication, division, or division with remainders.

Try this:

Challenge yourself and work on problems in the advanced section.

Highlights:

This is a useful site for elementary and middle school students working on their basic skills.

Flash cards are generated quickly and are provided for many topics.

See also:

MEGA Mathematics

http://www.c3.lanl.gov/mega-math/welcome.html

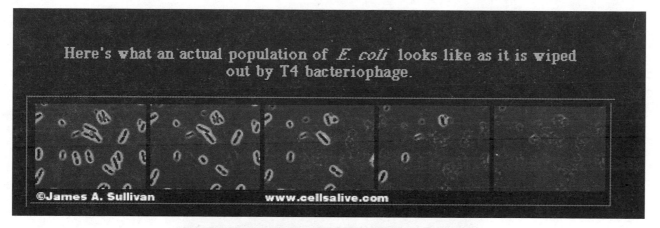

Here's what an actual population of *E. coli* looks like as it is wiped out by T4 bacteriophage.

©James A. Sullivan   www.cellsalive.com

http://www.cellsalive.com/

Overview:

Visit this awesome site that brings biology to life! It is packed full of graphics showing different types of cells in motion. Start with *Penicillin* and watch the video clip of its battle with bacteria. Next, check out *Making Antibodies, Parasites* (especially gross-looking things!), and *Dividing Bacteria*. Finally, click on *Pumping Myocytes* and get close to a beating heart.

Try this:

Have you ever gotten a splinter in your finger? To watch a splinter in action, go to *OUCH!* and see how immune cells work in your body.

Highlights:

Kids love this site because of its video clips and animations used to illustrate each subject.

See also:

The MAD Scientist Network

http://www.madsci.org

cup = 8 fluid ounces = (1/2) pint = (1/4) quart = (1/16) gallon
mile = 63360 inches = 5280 feet = 1760 yards
yard = 36 inches = 3 feet = (1/1760) mile
foot = 12 inches = (1/3) yard = (1/5280) mile
pint = 16 fluid ounces = (1/2) quart = (1/8) gallon
inch = 2.54 centimeters = (1/12) foot = (1/36) yard
liter = 1000 centimeters³ = **1 decimeter³** = (1/1000) meter³

Roman Numerals

I=1	V=5	X=10	L=50	C=100	D=500	M=1 000
	$\bar{V}$=5 000	$\bar{X}$=10 000	$\bar{L}$=50 000	$\bar{C}$ = 100 000	$\bar{D}$=500 000	$\bar{M}$=1 000 000

mile = 1760 yards = 5280 feet
yard = 3 feet = 36 inches
foot = 12 inches
inch = 2.54 centimeters

Dave's Math Tables

http://www.sisWeb.com/math/tables.htm

Overview:

Kids, this site will be a valuable resource for you when you are trying to solve a particular problem and can't find the correct formula. At first glance, it may seem as though this site is for older students. But if you look at the tables under the General Math heading, you will find useful materials for your math needs. Some tables you can find are listed below:

- Addition Table
- Number Notation Table
- Roman Numeral Table
- Number Base Systems

- Multiplication Table
- Fraction to Decimal Conversion Table
- Conversion to the Metric system
- Volume Relationship

Try this:

Have a math question? Post your question on this site's Math Message Board for math talk, questions, and answers. There are sections for elementary math through calculus.

Highlights:

Much of this material is suitable for printing.

Conversion utilities are also included at this site.

See also:

The Math Forum

http://forum.swarthmore.edu/

http://energy.ca.gov/education/

Overview:

Learn about energy conservation and environmental issues at this comprehensive site filled with information for both the novice and the seasoned science buff. Created by the California Energy Commission, this site will lure kids into entertaining games, activities, and projects, all packed with science facts.

A few of the site's features include:

- The Energy Story—Go from fossil fuels and solar energy to ocean thermal energy conversion and biomass energy.
- Science Projects—Create a lemon-powered battery or find out how much energy is in a single peanut.
- WATT's That?—Join an entertaining energy game show.
- Percy's Puzzles—Play games, and solve puzzles and riddles.
- Poor Richard's Energy Almanac—Find important energy facts.

Try this:

Get involved in the *Energy Patrol* and find out ways to monitor electricity in your classroom.

Click on *Kid's Tips* and find out what you can do in your daily life to conserve energy.

Highlights:

Energy Quest provides students and teachers with lessons, ideas, and inspiration.

All activities and projects are available in varying degrees of difficulty.

See also:

EnviroLink

http://www.envirolink.org/

The Atoms Family

http://www.miamisci.org/af/sln/index.html

About Us — Online Store ———— Programs — Visit the Museum

www.**exploratorium**.edu

the museum of science, art,
and human perception

http://www.exploratorium.edu/

Overview:

This incredibly large and impressive site was originally developed as a guide for The Exploratorium Museum in San Francisco. It has branched out to include digital representations of experiments that are performed in the actual museum. Online exhibits include brainteasers featuring *Changing Illusions*, *Disappearing Act*, *Depth Spinner*, and others.

Don't forget to drop by the Learning Studio and browse through the following sections:

- Cool Sites at the Exploratorium
- Online Exhibits
- Science Explorer
- Science Snackbook Series

- Cow's Eye Dissection
- Light Walk
- Past Exhibits
- Webcasts

FADING DOT
IF YOU STARE AT THIS DOT FOR A FEW MOMENTS IT DISAPPEARS.

Some of these experiments are quite amazing! This site is not to be missed!

Try this:

Go to *Online Exhibits* and click on *Shimmer*. Your eye movements cause this design to shimmer. Click on *Fading Dot*—if you stare at this dot for a few moments, it disappears.

Highlights:

Check out *Changing Illusions* and tease your brain.

The *Science Snack* section has ideas for creating your own miniature versions of some of the most popular exhibits at the Exploratorium.

See also:

Franklin Museum of Science

http://sln.fi.edu

THE MINERAL AND GEMSTONE KINGDOM

http://www.minerals.net

Overview:

At this sparkling gem of a site, dig into the world of minerals and gemstones. Find comprehensive information at Minerals A–Z and search for a mineral alphabetically or according to a variety of groupings.

Once locating your ruby, diamond, sapphire, or other gem, be transported to a page of information with everything you'd possibly want to know about a stone. Find the following information:

- Color
- Hardness
- Luster
- Chemical Composition

- Uses
- Varieties
- False Names
- Similar Gemstones

The pictures included of Gems and Minerals are absolutely fabulous. Many of the shots can be enlarged, providing a clear view of each stone.

Try this:

Click on *Gallery* and spend some time viewing the beautiful photographs available in the online Image Gallery.

Highlights:

All materials are arranged with an easy-to-use interface.

Content is for both amateurs and experts.

See also:

The Mineral Gallery

http://mineral.galleries.com

NASA

http://www.nasa.gov

Overview:

Enter the National Aeronautics and Space Administration (NASA) home page and be prepared to browse through another mega-site. Even visitors who want to remain earthbound will be impressed with its wealth of resources. Look through video and audio clips to gain a fuller understanding of NASA's advancements in aerospace. Enjoy reviews of space missions, visits to various space centers, the question and answer section, daily NASA news updates, and a variety of NASA projects.

This site may feel like an endless black hole of space facts, but it is best to take your time, be patient, and return for future space missions.

Try this:

Use the Search Tool to find NASA Astronaut Biographies and then write a report on an astronaut.

Go to the Multimedia Gallery and browse through NASA's still images at the *Photo Gallery*.

Highlights:

To get a handle on this large site, use one of the two search options. First, there is the NASA Subject Index, which is organized WWW information by subject. Second, you can search the NASA web by entering keywords in the search box.

Check out these related NASA sites!

SpaceLink

http://spacelink.nasa.gov

SeaWiFs Project—including the Jason Project

http://seawifs.gsfc.nasa.gov

The NASA K–12 Internet Initiative Page

http://quest.arc.nasa.gov

National Wildlife Federation's Kid Page

http://www.nwf.org/nwf/kids/

Overview:

Learn about nature with the National Wildlife Federation. Go on a *Cool Tour* by following animal tracks through *Water*, *Wetlands*, *Endangered Species*, or *Our Public Lands*. Then check out articles in English and Spanish from *Ranger Rick*, the environmental magazine for children. Click on *Games* and then check out the list below:

- Mad Libs
- Mix'em
- Match'em
- Quiz Yourself
- Rick's Riddle Picks
- Did you know?

A favorite game is Match'em where you identify animal tracks by clicking on the pictures of animal paws. Do you know what pig prints look like? pigeon feet? Ever seen turtle prints? Good luck!

Try this:

Did you ever think about helping the Earth but didn't know where to start? Click on *You Can Help the Earth* and learn about how to become an Earthsaver or about how to start an Earthsavers group.

Highlights:

Check out Ranger Rick's *Homework Help* and find information about Wildlife, the Environment, Math, Science, a Big Library and a PANIC BUTTON!

See also:

National Wildlife Federation

http://www.nwf.org/

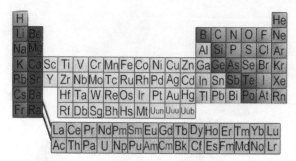

Chemical Elements.com

http://www.chemicalelements.com/

Overview:

Studying chemistry this year? Then you must check out this exceptional site. Yinon Bentor created this site as an eighth grade science project several years ago. Since then, this page has evolved to become an excellent source of information as well as a fine example of a truly interactive Periodic Table.

Using this chart is simple. Simply click on any element, and a page of basic information will pop up with almost everything you'd want to know about any element:

- Name
- Symbol
- Atomic Number
- Atomic Mass

- Melting Point
- Boiling Point
- Number of Protons/Electrons

- Number of Neutrons
- Classification
- Crystal Structure

Try this:

Click on *Help* and find explanations for words like symbol, mass, atomic number, melting point, and more.

Try viewing the Periodic Table in different ways. To do this, use the links found under the "Show Table With" menu heading.

Highlights:

Working on atomic structure as part of a homework assignment? Go to this site for help and look at in-depth diagrams showing electron distribution, energy levels, protons, and neutrons.

See also:

Web Elements

http://www.webelements.com/

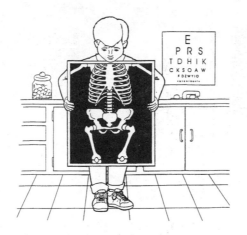

The Virtual Body

http://www.medtropolis.com/vbody

Overview:

Come to The Virtual Body, an absolutely amazing site! Experience an interactive and animated tour of the brain, digestive system, heart, and skeleton. Roll your mouse over a graphic of the human heart, and the name of the anatomical part along with a description of its function appears! Watch the heart pump blood as you adjust the heart rate slider to control blood flow. Then listen to a narrated tour. This is quite fascinating!

Don't forget to check out the *Human Brain, Human Skeleton* and *Digestive System* sections, which provide equally exciting graphics and information.

Note: *Shockwave* plug-ins required at this site.

Try this:

At the *Human Skeleton* section, drag bones from a pile and build your own skeleton.

Check out the Brain Book and find out what foods give neurons (brain cells) the most nourishment.

Highlights:

Teachers: Use a projection device in your classroom and display this site as an exciting addition to an anatomy unit.

See also:

Human Anatomy Online

http://www.innerbody.com/

The Weather Channel

http://www.weather.com

Overview:

Weather affects everyone. It offers daily variety and combines elements of prediction, anticipation, and surprise. The influences of weather are everywhere and make a difference in your day-to-day school activities. At the Weather Channel, take the opportunity to become more involved with weather. Telecommunications provide the opportunity to track events, manipulate data, and gather and compare real life-information.

Some handy features of this site follow:

- A pull-down menu allows you to find weather information on over 1,700 cities/countries.
- Weather maps have current conditions, US Doppler radar, and a U.S. Satellite Picture.
- A weather glossary is handy.
- A Storm Encyclopedia provides preparation for a storm.
- Disaster safety tips are available.
- You have the option of customizing your own weather home page.

Try this:

Locate the city where you live at Weather.com and find a five-day weather forecast. Print the forecast and then compare the daily predictions with the actual weather.

Highlights:

The *Teacher's Lounge*, found on the Education page, provides extraordinary resources for teaching and learning about weather phenomena.

See also:

Intellicast

http://www.intellicast.com

EarthWatch Weather on Demand

http://www.earthwatch.com/

Kiddie Korner

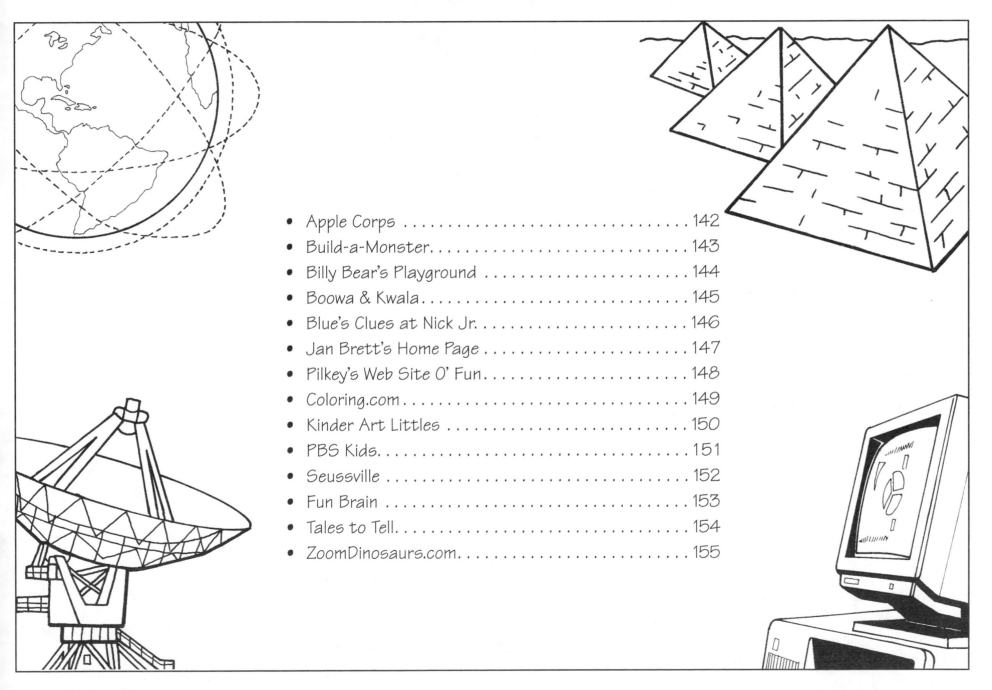

http://apple-corps.westnet.com/apple_corps.2.html

Overview:

Create faces on fruit and vegetables at this irresistible site based on the popular Mr. Potato Head by Hasbro. At Apple Corps, however, you are not limited to potatoes only. This site provides the opportunity to design faces on a variety of fruits or vegetables.

Directions:

1. Select the fruit or vegetable you wish to design by clicking on *Change Vegetable*.
2. Click on a button next to a facial feature.
3. To place your piece on the face, click on the vegetable itself.
4. Repeat the process until your silly face is completed.
5. Laugh a lot!

Try this:	Highlights:	See also:
Print and save images of your creations to develop an Apple Corps Art Gallery!	This site offers great graphics and is easy to play. This is a good starting point for a younger Internet user.	Mr. Edible Starchy Tuber Head http://winnie.acsu.buffalo.edu/potatoe/

http://www.rahul.net/renoir/monster

Overview:

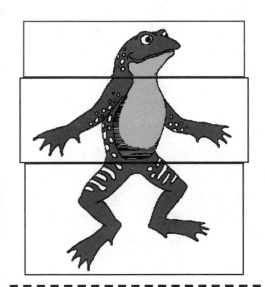

Visit this simple yet entertaining site and have fun creating your own animals and monsters. Creatures have three sections from which to choose: a head, torso, and legs. It is your job to decide which animal you wish to use for each of these parts of the monster, whether it is a frog, bird, dinosaur, or wacky creature. Then you simply click on the head, torso, and legs of your choice and, magically, a new monster is created.

This is a great activity for the young Internet user who can click and create while combining the parts in a variety of ways!

Try this:

After you create several creatures, print the pictures and brainstorm names for your characters.

Highlights:

This site uses CGI scripting and works fine with slow modems.

This simple activity provides great entertainment for young children.

See also:

Build-a-Rocket

http://www.rahul.net/renoir/rocket/

http://www.billybear4kids.com/

Overview:

Come to Billy Bear's Playground and join in the fun with thousands of other Internet users. This colorful and graphically packed site is so popular that sometimes 5,000 people visit in only one hour!

It's practically impossible to go through the entire site in only one visit, so take the opportunity to return to this page time and time again. In fact it may be helpful to browse through one section a visit. Some sections to try are listed below:

- Clipart
- Animal Scoops
- Fun & Games
- Holidays
- Post Office
- Story Books
- Show & Tell

A very popular feature of this site is the holiday portion. Visit Billy Bear on almost any holiday (New Year's, Valentine's Day, St. Patrick's, Easter, Pesach, Mother's Day, Father's Day, Fourth of July, Halloween, Thanksgiving, Christmas, Hanukkah, Kwanzaa, and birthdays. Also find holiday games, holiday downloads, print & play activities, crafts, e-cards, and online coloring pages!

- -

Try this:

Use Billy Bear's *Clip art* to create your own picture book.

Print personalized animal stationery of kangaroos, kaolas, lions and a host of other creatures at *Animal Scoop*.

Highlights:

Need birthday party help? Go to *Holidays* and find balloons to color, a personalized birthday certificate, birthday stationery, and game ideas for your upcoming event!

Graphics, colors, activities—that's what you'll find here.

See also:

Rebus Rhymes: Mother Goose and Others

http://www.EnchantedLearning.com/Rhymes.html

There is one Rebus Rhyme for every letter of the alphabet. This is very rewarding for beginning readers.

BOOWA & KWALA

http://www.boowakwala.com/

Overview:

Travel around the world in a hot air balloon with Boowa and Kwala. Each month these cute critters take you to a new country in their search for Kwala's family. Click on the arrows, and at each new destination they will teach you a song and offer interactive games to play. This highly graphic site uses Flash and has lots of animations, sounds, and music.

Note: Some loading time is required, but even that can be fun at this site! Shockwave plug-ins are required.

- -

Try this:

At *Games Galore,* go to the *Land of Hats.* Mix and match the hats, faces, and bodies.

Highlights:

Find colors, animations and songs extraordinaire!

The site is available in French and English.

See also:

Theodore Tugboat Online Activity Centre

http://www.cochran.com/theodore/

©Nickelodeon. Used by Permission.

Blue's Clues at Nick Jr.

http://www.nickjr.com/bluesclues/home.tin

Overview:

At Blue's Clues, a play-along program for preschoolers, figure out the problem of the episode by observing Blue's paw prints. Download pictures, go to *Blue's Boutique*, and check out *Extended Learning Activities*. Young kids will enjoy this playful site filled with colorful sights and sounds.

Other Nick Jr. characters found on this site:

- Little Beat
- Allegra
- Gullah Gullah
- Franklin
- Eureka

Try this:

Go to *Recipes for Extended Play* and learn to make a newspaper hat.

Go to *Blue's Shockwave Game Collection* and play the game of the week.

Highlights:

Great graphics, games, and fun can be found here.

Additional information for teachers is available.

See also:

Webtime Stories

http://www.kn.pacbell.com/wired/webtime/

Welcome to Jan Brett's Home Page

© 1999 Jan Brett

http://www.janbrett.com/index.html

Overview:

The Hat, The Mitten, Armadillo Rodeo—these are some of the beloved books written and illustrated by Jan Brett. At this site you can view pictures of Hedgie, the rabbit, the goose, and her other famous cast of characters. With a color printer, you can print your very own life-size masks of these loveable animals and put on a play for your friends and parents. Some other activities available at this site:-

- Fun projects you can make
- Coloring Pages
- Piggybacks for Teachers
- Hedge-a-Gram
- Send a Postcard
- Books by Jan Brett

If you know a teacher or librarian, Jan has a special teacher's pack available for free. Just write her at the address listed on this Web site.

- -

Try this:

Click on *Activities*, and then on *Fun Projects You Can Make*. Select *Learn to Draw an Armadillo*. Follow Jan Brett's directions and create your very own armadillo!

Do you enjoy baking? Try the Hedgehog Cookie recipe for a rainy-day treat.

Highlights:

Send an e-mail letter to Jan Brett, and she'll write back with a monthly Hedge-a-Gram.

This site is exceptionally colorful and attractive and is quick to load.

See also:

Children's Storybooks Online

http://www.magickeys.com/books/index.html

http://www.pilkey.com/

Overview:

Remember the Dumb Bunnies? Just in case you don't remember who they are, Dav Pilkey is the author of these hysterically funny characters. To continue with this author's sense of humor, indulge in his site and choose from a wealth of possibilities, including the all-time favorite, *Dav's Page O' Fun.*

Click on *Fun 'N Games* and paint a coloring-book page, using the "watercolor" paints. Wander over to *Print 'N Play* for *Tuffer Stuffer,* a place loaded with searches, mazes, and connect-the-dots games; or read about The Adventures of Captain Underpants on the Flip-O-Rama. These are just a few samples of what can be found at this playful Pilkey page.

Try this:

Go to *How 2 Draw* and follow drawing instructions for a Dumb Bunny.

At *Fold 'N Fly* follow instructions for folding a "Pilkey-Powered Paper Pilot Pug Plane"!

Highlights:

The activity level at this site ranges from preschool to early elementary.

Boring Teacher Stuff is included!

See also:

Story Hour at the Internet Public Library

http://www.ipl.org/youth/StoryHour/

http://www.coloring.com/

Overview:

Coloring.com is a favorite site for young Internet users with a very simple and easy-to-use interface. First, choose a drawing from the following categories:

- Easter
- Other Stuff
- Football
- Halloween
- Thanksgiving
- Animals
- Birthdays

Then follow these directions:

1. Click on the title of a picture.
2. The picture will appear along with a palette of colors.
3. Click on a color.
4. Indicate where you want the color by clicking on a particular section of the template.
5. The page will reload quickly.
6. Repeat the process until the picture is complete!

Try this:

E-mail your colorful creation to a friend or relative.

Experiment with complementary and contrasting colors.

Highlights:

This site provides an excellent way for little ones to become comfortable moving a mouse and creating online!

New colors and templates are constantly being updated!

See also:

Crayola

http://www.crayola.com

http://www.kinderart.com/littles.htm

Overview:

This site is packed with art projects and ideas especially created for little hands. The Activities section includes a wide assortment of free art ideas to bring out that creative spark in every special kid. For some unusual and interesting ideas, go to Aquarium in a Bag, Baggie Paint, Boo-tiful Trees, Feet Treat, Fun with Wallpaper, Glue-In, and Potato People. Then click on the following sections for more fun:

- Art and Craft Recipes—Find simple recipes at the art kitchen.
- Kindercolor—Print original pages to color.
- The Bookstore—Arts, crafts, and cooking are found here.
- The Fridge—Art is submitted by kids.

Try this:

Go to the KinderArt Kitchen and follow the recipe for scented paint. Then use the paint to make a picture of fruit. What a pleasant smelling picture!

Highlights:

These simple yet creative activities are suitable for classrooms or indoor play.

See also:

Idea Box: Early Childhood Education & Activity Resources
http://www.theideabox.com/
Aunt Annie's Crafts
http://www.auntannie.com/

©Public Broadcasting Service

PBS Kids

http://www.pbs.org/kids

Overview:

This Web site is a great entrance into the many pages found on PBS; it features all your favorite characters and friends. Begin your journey at PBS kids Online and then launch into other home pages for Arthur, Barney, Mr. Rogers' Neighborhood, Storytime, Theodore Tugboat, Charlie Horse, and others. Each TV site offers activities, coloring pages, and games, along with the high quality-entertainment you'd expect from public television. With thousands of pages to explore, you'll have loads of learning fun.

Try this:

Forgot the words to a Mr. Rogers song? Learn the words at his song archive.

Browse through Keno's list of favorite-favorite books and choose a few that you'd like to borrow from the library on your next visit!

Highlights:

Click on *Pre-School* to find activities designed for the youngest PS kids. Find animals, reading, music, science and friends!

Teachers: Check out the PBS TeacherSource for classroom resources.

See also:

Children's Television Workshop

http://www.ctw.org/

Seussville

http://www.randomhouse.com/seussville/

Overview:

Meet Sam-I-Am, Yertle, Horton and the Whos, the Cat in the Hat, the Lorax, and all your favorite Dr. Seuss characters at this site. Delve into this zany world and play fun-filled games, prepare tasty recipes, color funny pictures, and enter the trivia contest each month. Kids, you will really enjoy the game link that provides hours of entertainment with its silly list of choices:

- Hooray for Diffendoofer Day! Game
- Sylvester Mcbean's Sneetch Belly Game
- Elephant Ball
- The Lorax's Save the Trees

- The Cat's Concentration Game
- Green Eggs and Ham Picture Scramble
- Horton's Who Hunt

And if all this isn't enough, take a detour to *More Fun* for other surprises!

Note: All games require *Shockwave*.

Try this:

Check out printable games like *Connect the Dots, The Cat in the Hat, What did Marco See?, The Cat's Hat Maze,* and more.

Highlights:

Enjoy delightful fun in a typically Seuss-fashion!

See also:

The Arthur Page

http://www.pbs.org/wgbh/arthur/

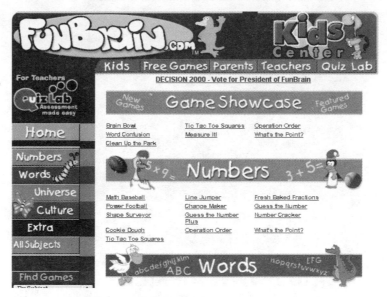

FunBrain.com

http://www.funbrain.com/kidscenter.html

Overview:

This is an excellent site full of wonderful learning games. Children have many choices when they select a game to play, by age, difficulty level, or subject and grade level. Results are posted immediately after the game is completed. You will find games in the following links:

- Numbers
- Words
- Universe
- Culture
- Brain Bowl

Try this:

Check out one game in each of the above links. Choose a different difficulty level for each game.

Highlights:

These games are really cool:
Number Cracker in Numbers.
What's the Word in Words.
Where Is That? in Universe.
Piano Player in Culture.
Kid vs Parent in Brain Bowl.

See also:

Duck Hunt

http://www.ee.duke.edu/~js/ducks.html

Look for the teeny-tiny duck in the pictures.

Tales to Tell

http://www.thekids.com

Overview:

Tales to Tell offers delightful picture stories from around the world. Rhymes, fables, animal stories, adventures, folk and fairy tales, all with beautifully illustrated pictures, are yours to read and explore. Browse through the list of stories in the following four sections:

- Rhymes & Nonsens
- Fables & Animal Stories
- Stories from Everywhere,
- Heroes & Adventure

After choosing a section, click on a story you'd like to read or ask a grown-up to read it to you. You'll find familiar stories like *The Seven Voyages of Sinbad the Sailor*, and *The Straw Ox*, or you'll find stories with unusual names like *Osoon Turkey!*

Try this:

Go to *Kid Stuff*, click on *Sound Off*, and read stories submitted by kids. Then write your own story, submit it to Tales to Tell, and have your very own moment in the literary spotlight!

Highlights:

High-quality links are provided at *Best of the Net.*

If you enjoy stories from long ago and faraway, this site is for you!

See also:

Carol Hurst's children's Literature Site

http://www.carolhurst.com

ZoomDinosaurs.com

http://www.EnchantedLearning.com/subjects/dinosaurs/index.html

Overview:

Zoom Dinosaurs is great for any dinosaur enthusiast! At this site you can navigate through masses of well-organized information, including Dino News, Dinosaur Fossils, Dinosaur Quizzes, and even an illustrated Dinosaur Dictionary with over 500 entries!

Check out *Dinosaur Fun* and try games, puzzles, quizzes, and even vote for your favorite dinosaur!

Try this:

Click on *Dinosaur Jokes* and then tell the jokes to your friends.

Go to *Games, Puzzles, and Quizzes & Activities,* and try the *Scrambled Dinosaur* activity or try *Match the Dino Skull to the Dinosaur* activity!

Highlights:

This site has an easy interface and is packed with delightful dinosaur activities!

Dinosaur information sheets are fabulous references for writing a dinosaur report. Check it out!

See Also:

The Children's Museum of Indianapolis

http://www.childrensmuseum.org/kinetosaur/e.html

Basic Terminology

Bookmark	An electronic marker to a Web page
Browser	Software which allows users to access and browse the World Wide Web (*Netscape Communicator* and *Microsoft Internet Explorer* are examples of browsers.)
Download	The process of retrieving a file from a remote server and transferring it to your computer
E-mail	(electronic mail) A system of sending and retrieving messages from one computer to another
Home Page	Main or introductory page of a Web site
HTTP	(HyperText Transfer Protocol) Coding language used to create hypertext documents on the World Wide Web
HTML	(HyperText Mark up Language) The language used to format Web documents
Hyperlink	(link) A hypertext link or connector which can be in text or graphic form (Clicking on these highlighted words or graphics will transport you to another item.)

Image map	A graphic on a page that contains hyperlinks
Internet	A global network of computers that allows millions of users to exchange and share information.
Net	A short form for the Internet.
Plug-in	An application that allows a graphic browser to complete a task or to view a specific file. (Use plug-ins to view 3-D images, see animations, or listen to audio files. Many games require *Shockwave* and/or *Java*.)
URL	(Uniform Resource Locator) The address or location of a document available on the Internet
Web	A short way to say World Wide Web (WWW)
World Wide Web	(WWW) A part of the Internet system containing hypertext documents that allow for point and click navigation
Web site	A collection of Web pages on the World Wide Web centered around a particular theme

Web Site Collections

These following sites were developed as collections of resources on the Web. Use them to find information on a variety of topics.

B. J. Pinchbeck's Homework Helper

http://school.discovery.com/students/homeworkhelp/bjpinchbeck/

B.J. and his dad started this site to create homework resources on the Web.

Berit's Best Sites for Children

http://www.beritsbest.com/

This is a directory of safe sites for children up to age 12. Sites are rated and listed by subject.

Carol Hurst's Children's Literature Site

http://www.carolhurst.com/

Hurst's site offers a collection of book reviews, books, activities and professional ideas for teachers.

Cool Sites for Kids

http://www.ala.org/alsc/children_links.html

The American Library Association collected and reviewed this list of sites.

The Electronic Zoo

http://netvet.wustl.edu/e-zoo.htm

An extensive list of animal resources is found here.

G.R.A.D.E.S. Archive

http://www.connectedteacher.com/library/search.asp

Classroom Connect handpicks quality education sites.

Kathy Schrock's Guide for Educators

http://school.discovery.com/schrockguide/

Schrock's categorized list of Internet sites useful for teachers and students is quite well-known.

Mega Homework Help Page

http://www.maurine.com/student.htm

Hundreds of good homework sites are found here.

Safesurf Kid's Wave

http://www.safesurf.com/kids.htm

A list of SafeSurf approved sites as organized by category.

Sites for Parents and Caregivers

http://www.ala.org/alsc/parents.links.html

This is another ALA list of excellent recommendations.

700+ Great Sites

http://www.ala.org/parentspage/greatsites/

These are "amazing, spectacular, and mysterious" Web sites for kids from the ALA.

Zoo Links

http://www.ala-net.com/zoos.html

This is an alphabetical list of zoos around the nation.

Favorite Museums Online

Art Institute of Chicago
http://www.artic.edu/

The British Museum
http://www.thebritishmuseum.ac.uk/

The Carnegie Museums of Pittsburgh
http://www.clpgh.org/Carnegie.html

The Metropolitan Museum of Art
http://www.metmuseum.org/

The Louvre
http://www.louvre.fr/

The Montreal Museum of Fine Arts
http://www.mmfa.qc.ca/a-sommaire.html

Smithsonian Institution
http://www.si.edu/

WWW Virtual Libray: Museums Around the World
http://www.icom.org/vlmp/world.html

The Uffizi Gallery in Florence
http://www.mega.it/eng/egui/monu/ufu.htm

Index of Web Sites

My Favorite Web Sites

Name

URL

_____   _____

_____   _____

_____   _____

_____   _____

_____   _____

_____   _____

_____   _____

_____   _____

_____   _____

_____   _____

_____   _____

_____   _____

_____   _____

_____   _____

_____   _____

_____   _____

My Favorite Web Sites *(cont.)*

Name   URL

_____   _____

_____   _____

_____   _____

_____   _____

_____   _____

_____   _____

_____   _____

_____   _____

_____   _____

_____   _____

_____   _____

_____   _____

_____   _____

_____   _____

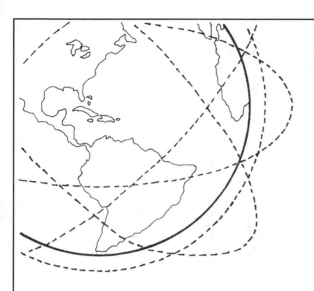

Part II

Internet

Written by Tim Haag

Illustrations by Wendy Chang

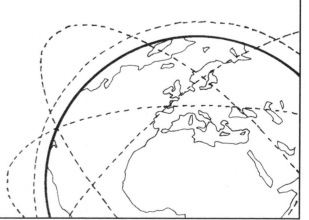

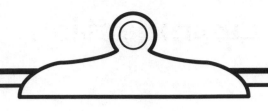

Important Information

Web sites frequently change addresses or become unavailable for myriad reasons. Teacher Created Materials attempts to offset this problem by posting changes of URLs on our Web site. Go to www.teachercreated.com. From the sidebar on the home page, click on URL Updates. Enter a number in the box to find the latest updates. For Part I: Best Web Sites, enter 2000; for Part II: Internet, enter 0621; and for Part III: Computers Don't Byte, enter 0813.

Introduction

The Internet was designed in the 1960s as a network that would enhance military communications. It gained further popularity (and its current name) when the National Science Foundation enhanced its capabilities to facilitate data-sharing among scientists and academicians. The biggest boom to the Internet's popularity, was the development of the World Wide Web. It was introduced at the European Particle Physics Laboratory (CERN) in Geneva, Switzerland, again with the goal of enhancing communication among scientists. However, as the Web's graphical, point-and-click interface developed, people began seeing more and more potential for all, not just scientists. So here we are . . . Welcome to all of you who are reading **Internet**!

If you use this book, you will be joining millions of people worldwide in the communications revolution of the 90s, known as the Internet.

Objectives of this book

This book will help you to:

- explore. Hop on and see what's out there.
- contribute. Be part of this revolution and submit an essay, some fiction, or an opinion.
- learn. This entails a lot. Learn about nature, space, current events, other people. Learn about new interests. Learn where you will most want to "netsurf."

- team up. Collaborate with family and friends. Combine efforts with online acquaintances.
- most of all, have fun!

How this book is organized

In the first half of this book, you will explore the tools that will help you mine the riches of the Internet—electronic mail, file transfer protocol, Usenet newsgroups, Gopher, video, chat, and Telnet. You will take a quick look at the mechanics of using these tools on a daily basis (computer time permitting, of course) by spotlighting a resource that can make them even handier and more valuable than they already are.

Then in the second half of the book, you will become acquainted with the World Wide Web and the numerous sites that can enrich a family's experience in cyberspace. Each site review will include the following:

- a brief overview of that site.
- a suggested activity (often collaborative in nature) to extend the experience beyond the computer.
- site highlights.
- at least one other site related to the site you are already exploring.

Some Added Thoughts Before We Get Started

- The site reviews found in **Internet for Kids** are considered to be safe and educational. If you have a concern about one of these sites please e-mail the author at: haagt@proaxis.com. If there is a change in the author's e-mail address, try looking it up in the Internet White Pages.

- The three major commercial online services—**America Online, CompuServe,** and **Prodigy**—all offer the services and sites mentioned in this book. They are a viable presence in cyberspace, but this book was not intended to summarize their functions and particular interfaces. If you belong to any one of these services, welcome. We are all on this ride together.

- It can be extremely tempting to let the Net sites do the entertaining for us. To an extent, that's fine, but be careful not to let it become another form of channel-surfing. With this in mind, each site review includes a "try this" section.

- In each "try this" section, it may seem as if it is speaking to kids, but most projects are intended to be done as a team.

- Rather than typing in the lengthy URLs look at the "see also" sections, and consider using a search engine to find the suggested site. (In many cases, you can type the URL up to the top domain—usually the character combination ".com"—and then press the enter key. That page may often provide a link to the desired site. From there, you will probably find links to the page

in question.

- Several commercial sites have been included but only if they offer a substantial amount of free activities.

And so we begin . . . and remember, have fun.

Happy, Healthy, and Safe Surfing

Below you will find several tips that will help encourage your students or children to be "safe" online computer users. These tips shouldn't cause you to cast a suspicious eye at your students/kids. Rather, they are points to consider to promote Net surfing as an enjoyable family activity. (Credit for this material goes to the **SafeSurf** Web site.)

1. Is there a room in the home where you can place the computer to encourage more collaborative use? That location will also keep the screen exposed to others in the midst of their daily activities.

2. If you subscribe to a commercial online service, are you using "parental controls" that help filter what your kids can access?

3. Have you tried computer applications such as **NetNanny** or **SurfWatch** to help filter out less-than-desirable content that may be accessible to kids?

4. Are you giving your kids time to "show what they know" in terms of navigational techniques and favorite sites? You can learn a little more about how they use the Internet and they will enjoy the spotlight.

5. Is there a family system of limiting online time?

6. If you sense that some of the content might be questionable, have you considered looking at your browser's history, (the list of sites visited during a given session)? Have you considered reviewing any Web pages that your computer has cached from previous sessions? These considerations bring up the issue of personal privacy, something you can discuss with other family members.

7. Have you reviewed basic guidelines about online behavior, such as:

   - not giving out one's real name, address, and/or telephone number?
   - not assuming that all people on the Net are honest about their true identities?

8. Are you keeping an eye on your telephone bill?

9. Are you acquainted with your kids' online friends?

10. Have you considered signing a parent/child agreement that encourages kids to:

    - contact you if they encounter information that makes them uneasy?
    - not give out their full name, address, phone number, or school name?
    - not meet an online friend in person unless they have checked with you?
    - not respond to derogatory messages?
    - team up with you to set online rules?

Internet FAQ

What is the Internet?

The Internet is a network of connected computer networks. If you have access to one of these networks, you can usually reach many other networks.

What connects all those networks and computers?

Telephones, satellites, and high-speed data links.

How many computers are on the Internet?

More than three million.

How many users are connected on the Internet?

Right now about 32 million people use the Internet, but that number grows by about 10% per month.

What do I need to connect to the Internet from my home?

- The basics first—a computer, a telephone, a modem (connects the phone and computer), and software to facilitate that connection.

- As with most everything technological, there may be exceptions to the lists below, but these are the essentials. **Note:** You can get by with less. These are general guidelines.

- To gain full (a relative term considering the almost-daily advances on the Net) access to the Internet, the rule of thumb is the faster, the more storage, the more RAM, the better.

For users of **Windows** machines:

- 486 or Pentium processor

- eight megabytes of RAM

- 300 megabyte or larger hard disk drive

- color monitor

- mouse

- 14,400 bits per second (bps) modem

- Internet software that includes a Winsock.DLL file

For **Macintosh** users:

- 68040 or PowerPC processor

- eight megabytes of RAM

- 300 megabyte or larger hard disk drive

- color monitor

- mouse

- 14,400 bits per second (bps) modem

- Internet software that includes TCP/IP software

- -

Note: To users of UNIX, OS/2, 80386 Windows machines, 68030 Macintoshes, Amigas, etc., these machines will run on the Internet, as well. You may just need to adjust some of the above requirements.

Internet FAQ *(cont.)*

What is on the Internet that I can use?

Information and entertainment in the form of text (whole books), numbers, video, sound, animation, and graphics.

How do I get to these resources?

Internet tools such as file transfer protocol, Gopher, electronic mail, Telnet, and newsreaders open up these resources to users.

Am I a client or a server?

You (actually, your computer) are most likely a client. Here is a possible scenario: You see a file that you want to download. Through your computer (call it Computer A), you send an electronic request to Computer B to send you that file. Computer B fills that request. Computer A is the client and Computer B is the server.

What is my Internet address?

Your Internet address is also called your e-mail address. Example e-mail address:

haagt@proaxis.com

First is the screen name (haagt), followed by an ampersand (@), followed by the name of the computer through which the e-mail is routed (proaxis is the Internet service provider), followed by the top domain name (com). Top domains indicate the kind of organization where the machine originates; **com** stands for commercial, **org** stands for organization (usually non-profit), **edu** stands for educational, and **gov** stands for government. There are other top domains, but these are the four you will most often encounter.

Electronic Mail FAQ

What do I do with electronic mail?

Its function is almost self-describing by its title. The beauty of e-mail is its immediacy.

When using e-mail, you can send messages that will usually reach their destinations within minutes, often sooner. When using e-mail, friends in Finland are as close as your friends next door. Correspondence with friends is just one use of e-mail. Many documents that you would normally fax are generally quite acceptable via e-mail. Just keep the main function in mind—to communicate. (The next section, which talks about mailing lists, will stretch your e-mail capabilities even further.)

How do I go about sending a message?

Here's the basic process:

1. Open your e-mail software program.

2. Select a command called New Message.

3. Type the recipient's e-mail address (it might look something like this: ebunny@garden.com) where the e-mail form says, :To:."

4. Next, type your message's main theme next to: "Subject:."

5. Then, type your message in the main text area.

6. Finally, click the Send box or use the menu command Send, and it should be a matter of minutes before

ebunny@garden.com receives your message.

Where do you get e-mail software?

- If you have joined a commercial online service, (**America Online, CompuServe, Prodigy,** etc.), your e-mail capability is built into its software.

- If your Internet connection is through a local provider, you probably have two e-mail channels:

1. Your World Wide Web browser. Most browsers are now providing capable e-mail features.

2. Software that came with your account (**Eudora Light** and **Pegasus** are popular shareware choices).

E-mail Tips

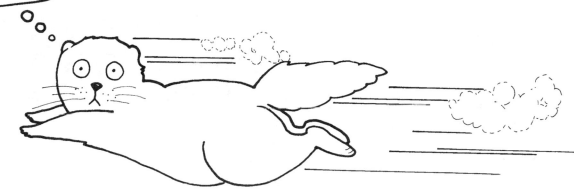

- Whether you send mail from your browser or from your e-mail application, your e-mail address will still be the same.

- Get online, retrieve your messages, and sign off. That way, you save online charges, free up your telephone, and can read and respond to your e-mail at your leisure. When you are ready to send, go back online, send your messages, and log off again.

- Don't plan on memorizing all those obscure e-mail addresses. Most e-mail software packages offer an address book feature where you can keep any e-mail address you want.

- If you have a message you want to send to more than one recipient, use the carbon copy feature. Just type the address(es) next to the "CC:" indicator, enter your message, and click Send.

- Most e-mail applications also let you forward e-mail to others with the click of a button and an insertion of a quick message.

E-mail Shortcuts

Typewritten text does not offer the luxury of facial expressions or body language that face-to-face conversations do. Through the years, users have developed shortcuts to help clarify emotions in e-mail communications..

:-)	happy
:-(	sad
:-C	very sad
:-I	indifferent
;-)	winking
:-D	laughing
:-\	undecided
:-o	surprised
:-@	screaming
}:-(	stubborn
:-&	tongue-tied
:-x	kissing
8-)	smiley with sunglasses
:-8	looking formal (bow tie and all)

BBL	Be Back Later
BRB	Be Right Back
BTW	By the Way
FWIW	For What It's Worth
FYI	For Your Information
<g>	Grin (previous words were a joke)
IMHO	In My Humble Opinion
IOW	In Other Words
LOL	Laughing Out Loud
NBD	No Big Deal
OTOH	On the Other Hand
ROTFL	Rolling on the Floor, Laughing
TIA	Thanks in Advance
TTYL	Talk to You Later

IMHO: Even if you don't use these e-mail shortcuts, this can help you understand those who do.

Netiquette

As with face-to-face interaction, communicating with plain text requires manners, or netiquette (Internet etiquette).

Here are a few points of netiquette you might want to keep in mind as you interact via e-mail, mailing lists, and Usenet newsgroups.

1. Do not assume your e-mail is private. So, do not send something you would not want broadcast on the evening news.

2. Reread your e-mail before sending it. (That includes double-checking the To: box.)

3. Keep your writing short and to the point.

4. When you quote a previous posting (a helpful practice in itself), edit it down to the pertinent points. That will help streamline your message.

5. Consider using a signature when communicating with folks you don't know. A signature may consist of your name, a position you hold, e-mail address, and city.

6. Capitalizing all your text constitutes shouting. Capitalize words only to emphasize an important word or phrase. (An alternative to capitalization: surround the key words with asterisks. That is Shift-8 on your keyboard.)

7. Always check with the original author before you forward any e-mail to a mailing list or newsgroup.

8. Be careful when using humor. Yours may not match the recipient's. Use smileys to ensure that the reader knows you have written with tongue-in-cheek.

E-mail Spotlight: KIDLINK

http://www.kidlink.org/

Multi-lingual. Multi-age. Multi-cultural. Multi-disciplinary. That pretty much sums up KIDLINK. Started in 1990, KIDLINK has used primarily e-mail to involve over 60,000 kids in its number one objective: global dialog.

Why so successful? Let's start with organization. Without it, KIDLINK would not be able to offer kids aged 10-15 such projects as:

- KIDCAFE-INDIVIDUAL (for individual discussions)
- KIDCAFE-SCHOOL (discussions among classrooms)
- KIDCAFE-TOPICS (open-topic discussion)
- KIDCAFE-QUERY (open inquiry discussions)
- KIDPROJ (special projects)
- KIDIRC (KIDLINK's own private Internet Relay Chat channel)

Note: There are separate KIDCAFE discussions for Spanish, Japanese, Nordic, Hebrew, and Portuguese students, as well as English-speaking kids.

To keep all this communication flowing, KIDLINK has set up various KIDLEADER and coordinator discussion groups.

One of the true benefits of KIDLINK is its reasonable cost: $0. To join, students need only answer these four questions.:

1. Who am I?

2. What do I want to be when I grow up?

3. How do I want the world to be better when I grow up?

4. What can I do now to make this happen?

Judging by the questions, you can see KIDLINK's major focus and, with its variety of forums, it should be easy to find your niche. Why don't you add to the dialog and give KIDLINK a try?

KIDLINK™

Mailing List FAQ

Hmmm . . . mailing lists. Am I going to get a lot of electronic junk mail?

First, let's clarify what "mailing lists" are. You might call them "e-mail clubs." Mailing lists cover a variety of subjects and interests. If you see one that interests you, you subscribe to it. Once subscribed, you will receive other members' messages and so will every other member—kind of a blanket mailing.

As for your question about gobs of junk mail—the possibility exists, but it is not common to get spammed (mass mailings of inappropriate messages).

How does everyone on the list get the same message?

When you send a message, you do not send it to each member. Instead, you send it to a main computer whose software (called listserv, listproc, or majordomo) passes it on to other members.

What are moderated mailing lists?

Moderated lists are managed by people who decide what messages are and are not dispersed. If you feel that practice smacks of censorship, you can decide whether or not to join it. If, on the other hand, you think the moderator will help keep out irrelevant or unsavory messages, you may like the concept of moderated mailing lists.

How do I find these mailing lists?

Here are three possible sources:

1. Liszt Directory of E-Mail Discussion Groups (http://www.liszt.com)

2. Publicly Accessible Mailing Lists (http://www.neosoft.com/internet/paml)

3. The Usenet newsgroups news.lists and news.answers.

Mailing List FAQ *(cont.)*

How much mail should I expect?

That depends on the popularity of the list. An active list can net you almost 50 messages a day.

Will I have to read every message I receive?

No, make sure your e-mail software shows the subject lines of the messages in your "in" box. Reading the authors' hints about the mail's content can guide you through that agonizing read it or toss it decision.

Okay, I'm convinced! I want to subscribe to a mailing list. How do I do it?

Follow me:

1. I found a mailing list, called KIDS-EL, about kids in elementary school grades.

2. I opened my e-mail application and selected New Message.

3. I addressed my message to: listserv@vm.ege.edu.tr

4. I left the subject box blank.

5. In the body of the message, I typed subscribe KIDS-EL Tim Haag. The usual format is: subscriber, name of mailing list, first name, and last name.

6. I sent it.

7. In less than a minute, the list's computer had replied and asked for a confirmation of the accuracy of my e-mail address. (Most lists do not require this step.)

8. Following their directions, I clicked reply in my e-mail program and typed OK in an empty body of my message.

9. I sent the confirmation.

10. Again in less than a minute, I received two pieces of e-mail:

    • A confirmation of what I just sent.

    • Introductory information about the list, including the main commands I might need to send to the listserv.

Note: Depending on the list's software, these steps may vary. Altogether, this process took about three minutes.

178

Mailing List Spotlight

http://www.liszt.com/

Overview:

Consider this site a search engine for mailing lists. Liszt proclaims itself as the world's largest directory of mailing lists—over 40,000 listserv, listproc, majordomo, and independently managed lists from 1,201 sites.

To find a mailing list that you would like to join, all you have to do is:

- enter a word or phrase that best describes your interest. (Liszt gives you some search tips.)
- review the search results.
- click on the linked "information" command of the mailing list that best matches your interest.
- read that linked page.
- follow Liszt's advice that, before subscribing, you should get further information about the list by sending the request for more information. Make sure it is to the administrative address, NOT TO THE LIST ITSELF. (A common mistake.)
- wait for the response from the list administrator and decide whether you want to join the list.

See also:

Stephanie da Silva's Publicly Accessible Mailing Lists

http://www.neosoft.com/internet/paml/

Mailing Lists to Try

KIDS Mailing List

A list for pre-college students worldwide.
To subscribe to KIDS, send an e-mail message to:
joinkids@vms.cis.pitt.edu
In the body of the message type:
subscribe kids

Our Children Newsletter

Monthly newsletter that contains articles on parenting issues.
To subscribe, send an e-mail message to:
majordomo@maracomm.com
In the body of the message type:
subscribe ccscnews

Our Kids

Support for parents of children with developmental delays.
owner-our-kids@tbag.osc.edu
To subscribe to Our Kids, send an e-mail message to:
majordomo@tbag.osc.edu
In the body of the message type:
subscribe our-kids

Stay Home Parents

Discussion of the daily aspects of being a full-time parent.
To subscribe to KIDS, send an e-mail message to:
majordomo@lists.sonic.net
In the body of the message type:
subscribe shp-list

Guiding/Scouting

Discussion for parents involved in scouting organizations.
To subscribe to Guiding/Scouting, send an e-mail message to:
majordomo@mail.skl.com
In the body of the message type:
subscribe guiding

Kidsbooks Mailing List

Electronic journal of children's book reviews.
To subscribe to Kidsbooks, send an e-mail message to:
kidsbooks-request@armory.com
In the body of the message type:
please add me to kidsbooks

Pen-pals Mailing List

Another electronic forum for kids.
To subscribe to pen-pals, send an e-mail message to:
pen-pals-request@mainstream.com
In the body of the message type:
please add me to pen-pals

Scout Report

Weekly reports of new resources on the Internet.
To subscribe to Scout Report, send an e-mail message to:
scout-report@is.internic.net
In the body of the message type:
subscribe

Newsgroups FAQ

What are newsgroups?

Newsgroups are discussion groups (numbering over 15,000) that have sprung from Usenet (the Users Network). They are a combination of fact, philosophy, hints and tips, rational opinion, and outright pomposity.

What topics do newsgroups cover?

There are eight main hierarchies to which most newsgroups belong:

comp	computers and technology
soc	social issues
sci	science research and applications
news	updates in all genres of news
talk	discussion of controversial subjects
rec	arts, hobbies, sports, travel, etc.
misc	subjects that do not quite fit in other hierarchies
alt	alternative (often off-beat)

Another hierarchy that might interest you is **k12**, which speaks to grade school issues.

Do I have access to all 11,000?

Probably not. Internet service providers are not required to provide a complete newsfeed. However, you should expect a fairly comprehensive offering in each of the hierarchies.

I have heard that newsgroups cover many subjects that kids should not be exposed to. Is that true?

Yes, it is. Some newsgroups are moderated, but most are not, thus opening the door for very liberal expression and exchange of graphics.

Where can I get more information about newsgroups?

DejaNews (**http://www.dejanews.com/**) is a Web search engine that focuses on Usenet newsgroups. You can also try the NetNews Overview Index (**http://www.asianet.net/engin601.html**).

Newsgroup Tips

- Read your newsgroup's frequently-asked questions (FAQ). This file gives subscribers helpful information and guidance that will help answer questions that you might otherwise post to the group.

- Watch your newsgroup's activities for about a week before you post. Such lurking is acceptable and even appreciated as you get a feel for the group's tone and content.

- Do not follow up articles without using your newsreader's follow-up feature. And, do not use follow-up to post an unrelated article. This will help other readers understand the threads of the group's discussions.

- If your posting does not show up right away, be patient and do not repost the same message. Your input may have to pass through a dozen different systems before it shows up in the newsgroup.

- Your words are there for content, not looks, so try to keep your message as mechanically sound and unformatted as possible (left justify, proper capitalization). Other machines may misread the fancy characters (and even your tab stops) that your computer generates.

- If you wish to emphasize some of your message, rather than using all capital letters (which is interpreted as shouting), surround it with *asterisks* (shift-8).

- To provide readers a clear context for your message, try to quote the pertinent excerpt to which you are responding.

- If you want to rant at those who arouse your ire, e-mail them directly.

- Take the time to learn your newsreader software. It will most likely offer plenty of helpful, time-saving features, but with that power can come occasions where you might click one or two wrong buttons that may result in your embarrassment.

182

Newsgroup Spotlight: Newsreader Software

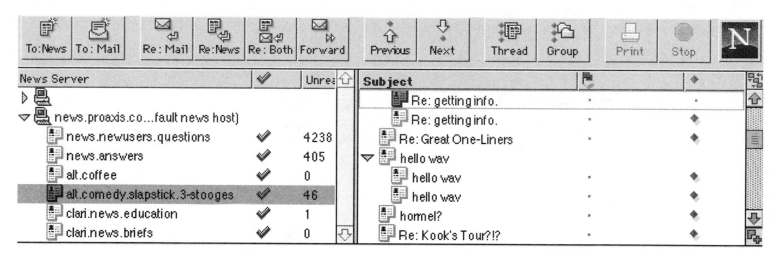

A very helpful piece of software for the Internet traveler is a newsreader, such as **Newswatcher** for the **Mac** or **News Xpress** or **Free Agent** for **Windows** machines.

Newsreader software does the following (and more):

- Shows you what newsgroups are available.
- Lets you subscribe to newsgroups.
- Loads and displays newsgroup articles.
- Organizes the articles.
- Lets you post articles to newsgroup discussions.

Most Web browsers provide their own newsreaders. In Netscape, do the following:

- Under Windows, select Netscape News.
- Under File, select Open News Server.

- Enter name of news server. (Your provider gives you that information.)
- Under Options, select Show All Newsgroups.
- To read a newsgroup, click on its name.
- To subscribe, click in the checkmarked column.
- To reply, use the Re: buttons.
- To start a new thread of relevant discussion, click the Thread button.

Newsgroups to Try

(To read these newsgroups, type news: into your Web browser's location indicator, followed by the name of the group—found in the left column.)

alt.good.morning	some interesting upbeat connections among the members
clari.news.briefs	regular news updates
clari.news.goodnews	something uplifting when the world seems completely crazy
clari.local.state name	just fill in your state's name and get briefs from that area
rec.arts.startrek.current	all about the latest iterations of the sci-fi classic
rec.arts.movies	the world of cinema
rec.pets	dogs, cats, and the like
rec.sport.football.college	NCAA and NAIA football
rec.food.recipes	need an injection of creativity in the kitchen?
rec.food.cooking	more of the how-to than the above list
rec.backcountry	get out of the city with help from this group
rec.crafts.textiles	needlepoint, quilting, knitting, etc.
rec.games.misc	overall look at games of all types
rec.games.video	narrowing the focus of games
rec.gardens	lilies drooping when they should be the talk of the block?

rec.puzzles	need a little brain-strain?
rec.scouting	troop leaders and other interested adults voice their opinions and offer insights
rec.baseball	curve balls, basket catches, peanuts, and Cracker Jacks
rec.basketball	slam-dunks, playoffs, MVPs, and contract hassles.
rec.hockey	from the land of the Stanley Cup, Zambonis, and missing teeth
rec.travel	bargains and tips for those on-the-road
misc.fitness	news and tips on exercise
misc.education	good overview of schooling, students, and teachers
misc.kids	kids and their behavior
misc.kids.computer	software, hardware discussions for kids and parents alike
misc.jobs.offered	looking for a new position?
misc.invest	hints and tips on where to put your money
misc.writing	discourse on issues and genres of writing

Chat FAQ

How do people chat on the Internet?

For most people, chatting is simply exchanging typed text among those present in an electronic chat room. In most cases, all those present can read others' comments on the screen, movie-script style. Expect future technologies, though, to enable more and more users to readily hear and even see each other online while chatting. (The section on video covers more of that technology.)

What do I need to chat on the Internet?

Here are three options you currently have:

1. Use chat rooms on a commercial service.

Services like **America Online** offer a multitude of chat rooms, either private or focused on specific topics. With the click of a few buttons, you are ready to enter into conversations that range from real estate to relatives.

2. Find Web sites with chat rooms.

Parent Soup (featured on the next page), ParentsPlace (http://www.parentsplace.com/), and Nye Labs Online (http://nyelabs.kcts.org/flash_go.html) offer live chat rooms. Because they require no extra software, the latter two might be good sites to break into Internet chat, but sites that do require downloading and installation of chat applications are worth consideration, as well. Once those steps are completed, Web chat is as effortless as that on the commercial services.

3. Use the Internet Relay Chat.

The Internet Relay Chat is certainly a viable option, but behavior and content on many IRC channels are much more, shall we say, free-wheeling. For you to use IRC, you will need to:

- use a separate piece of software, such as Ircle for the **Mac** and **mIRC** and **Wsirc** for the **PC**.
- learn commands to effectively converse online.
- sift for a channel (chat group) that focuses on your desired subject matter and whose participants behave appropriately for children. You do have the option to set up your own channel and then invite your chat partners.

Chat Spotlight: Parent Soup

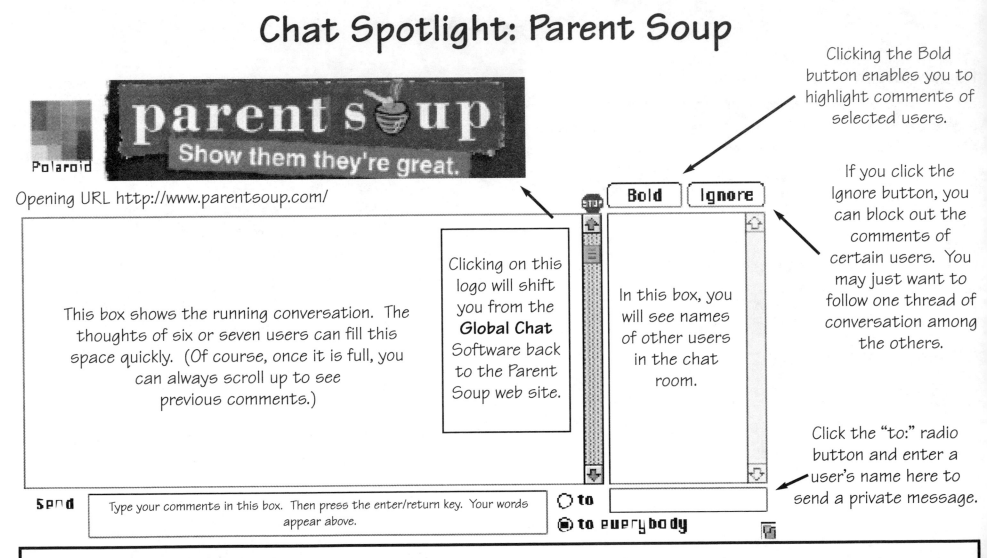

Clicking the Bold button enables you to highlight comments of selected users.

Opening URL http://www.parentsoup.com/

Bold **Ignore**

If you click the Ignore button, you can block out the comments of certain users. You may just want to follow one thread of conversation among the others.

This box shows the running conversation. The thoughts of six or seven users can fill this space quickly. (Of course, once it is full, you can always scroll up to see previous comments.)

Clicking on this logo will shift you from the **Global Chat** Software back to the Parent Soup web site.

In this box, you will see names of other users in the chat room.

Click the "to:" radio button and enter a user's name here to send a private message.

5end Type your comments in this box. Then press the enter/return key. Your words appear above.

○ to
● to everybody

With this spotlight and screen shot of the Parent Soup chat room, you can see how simple real-time conversation on the Internet can be.

(**Note:** Parent Soup says that the **Global Chat** software provides the best results in these chat rooms, though the following programs have also been successfully tested: **Homer, Ircle, Netscape Chat**, and the **SunOS IRC** client.)

Telnet FAQ

What is Telnet?

Telnet (The Teletype Network) is another Internet protocol. It allows a user's computer to connect to a computer at another location.

Once I connect to that other machine, what can I do?

Your computer can use that machine's resources as if they were your own. You can search for information, download files, access a Gopher server, or connect to an interactive environment (more on this later).

Why don't I hear that much about Telnet?

The World Wide Web, with its point-and-click navigation and multimedia capabilities, is the preferred method of finding resources. Telnet is a slower, text-based Internet tool that requires users to type in commands.

Can I run Telnet from my Web browser?

Yes, but make sure you tell your browser where your Telnet application is. You do that by following this one-time process:

1. Select Options—General Preferences.

2. Click the Applications tab.

3. Click the Browse button.

4. Locate your Telnet program and double-click it.

(**Note:** These are directions for Netscape Navigator)

Once I install my Telnet application, how does it work within my browser?

Links to Telnet sites are embedded in various Web pages. When you click the links, they open your Telnet program and connect you automatically.

What if I want to use my Telnet program on its own?

Here is a sample Telnet session using NCSA Telnet. Most **Windows**-based Telnet programs run similarly.

1. Double-click the NCSA Mosaic icon.

2. Under File, choose Open Connection.

3. Type in the Telnet address (in this case, books.com—a large online bookstore) and, within seconds, you are there. (Depending on the site, you may automatically receive a welcome and directions or you may need to log in under a special name. Often the term guest is successful. Sometimes simply pressing the enter key works.)

4. In the case of books.com, enter your name, compose a password, and you are in.

Telnet FAQ (cont.)

What else does Telnet offer parents and kids?

Telnet offers another form of interactive entertainment, but that is going to mean a few more Internet acronyms. Ready?

Let's try MUD (multi-user dimension), MOO (MUD-object oriented), and MUSE (multi-user simulation environment). These are all forms of interactive adventures along the order of the early versions of Zork. Text-based virtual worlds is another apt description.

How are these Telnet adventures different from commercial interactive adventure programs?

- Telnet adventures are text-based rather than graphics-based.
- Other characters in the adventure are people who have connected to the same computer and are interacting with you in real time.
- The adventures can take place in settings which are dreamed up by the players.

(**Disclaimer:** The more advanced commercial computer games become, the more possible it is for players to create their own worlds. Just take a look at the popular **Sim** series from Maxis Software.)

Let's take a look at **MicroMuse**, an entertaining text-based virtual world that invites young and old alike.

Telnet Spotlight: MicroMuse

Let's take a look at **MicroMuse**, an entertaining text-based virtual world that invites young and old alike.

When you arrive at Cyberion City, the largest space city in the solar system, fire up your imagination, and limber up your keyboarding fingers. After all, these are the tools that will carry you through your adventures in this cylindrical settlement. (Picture a narrow tin can, 45 miles [72 km] long, lying on its side.) There are no animation and no 3-D graphics. Just text. But it is what MicroMuse participants do with those keyboard characters that makes this corner of the Internet unique.

Upon entering Cyberion City, you meet an online tutor that leads you through the visitor trail where you learn the basics of communicating in this virtual world. The tutor is a very special feature, as it is patient and makes a novice feel at home during a somewhat uncertain experience.

To give you an idea of how you interact in this setting, here are a few of the basic commands:

- look	view your surroundings
- continue	move further
- page	address/greet another participant
- pose	express some kind of body language
- who	find out who else is available for interaction
- whisper	send a private message to a participant in same room

Once you have completed the visitor trail, you can, with a

mentor's assistance, register for further adventures in MicroMuse.

What else makes this place special?

- a sincere emphasis on mutual respect among users
- friendly mentors
- interesting exhibits, such as The Mission to Mars, The Narnia Adventure, and Professor Griffin's Logic Quest.
- citizens' ability to build their own worlds within Cyberion City
- beautifully-composed descriptions of the environment. For a full description of Cyberion City, point your browser to:

   gopher://gopher.musenet.org:70/11/muse

How to reach MicroMuse:

Open your Telnet program and open the following connection: michael.ai.mit.edu. Log on as guest and follow the prompts for more information.

Video FAQ

Isn't video a bit beyond the capabilities of my computer?

As with chat, video on the Internet is becoming increasingly accessible to the home user. To play back **QuickTime** video, Apple provides **QuickTime** as an extension and a Netscape plug-in for Mac users and as a helper application and/or plug-in for **Windows** users. To play back MPEG (Motion Picture Experts Group) video, there is **MPEGPLAY** for **Windows** and **Sparkle** for the **Mac**. Finally, to view the popular AVI (**Windows**) video format, Microsoft provides its own video utility, **MS Video**.

By the time you read this, however, helper applications may have given way to the previously-mentioned plug-ins. They automatically load with your browser to play video on the fly. There are several Web pages dedicated to updating users on the latest plug-ins. Look them up with your favorite search engine.

What do I need for my computer to receive live video?

For a real-time video connection, you will need the following:

1. a 28.8 bps modem (You can get by with a 14.4.).

2. a SLIP, PPP, ISDN, or direct connection to the Internet.

3. software such as CU-SeeMe or Connectix's VideoPhone.

4. a 16-level grayscale monitor (most color monitors are capable of this).

5. your video partner's IP address to type in when choosing the connect command.

6. a connection to a reflector site (if conferencing with more than one computer).

What do I need to send video from my computer?

1. Items 1-4 above.

2. A camcorder with NTSC-1 vpp output or a Connectix QuickCam. (You have a choice between color or grayscale.)

3. Video digitizing software.

Video Spotlight: Contex VideoPhone

Connectix VideoPhone offers inexpensive videoconferencing, and more, for the occasional user.

For $149, the company supplies **Windows** and **Mac** users with the grayscale QuickCam (a black-and-white digital video camera) and the **VideoPhone** software. In addition, **Windows** users receive **Talk Show Lite**, a shared whiteboard application for easy exchange of data, while **Mac** users get Apple's **QuickTime** Conferencing extensions for a similar purpose.

To get up and running with **VideoPhone** on a 28.8 modem, you will need **Windows 95** running on a **Pentium 75** (or faster) chip. If you are a **Mac** owner, you will need a 68040 or **Power Mac** running System 7.5 and an ISDN or faster connection. (At this writing, Connectix was at work on a version that would enable 28.8 users, as well.)

Let's look at this product's advantages:

- The price is right.
- There is no need for an extra power outlet. It plugs into the PC's and **Mac's** parallel and serial ports, respectively.

- Extra video capture hardware is not required.
- The **VideoPhone** software is not limited to just the QuickCam. It works well with other video input devices, black-and-white or color, though a digitizer would be required.
- QuickCam software includes **QuickPICT** to take easy snapshots, the ability to arrange and frame those images, and **QuickMovie** to create **QuickTime** and **Windows** AVI format movies.
- Connectix provides excellent customer support.

Some reservations you might have:

- The hardware requirements may be seen as a bit steep but, considering the amount of data being processed, any capable videoconferencing package needs respectable processor speed and bandwidth.
- The images are somewhat jerky.
- There is lag time between actions and their on-screen appearance.
- QuickCam's own microphone is adequate, but you may find your own system's sound capabilities better.

World Wide Web FAQ

What is the World Wide Web?

The World Wide Web, the most popular and interactive corner of the Internet, is based on millions of hypertext documents that deliver text, graphics, sound, animation, and video.

What do you mean by hypertext?

Hypertext is a document form that allows users to point-and-click (rather than type commands) to follow author-embedded links to other documents. In other words, if you click on a link, you end up with another, usually related, document.

How do I know what to point-and-click?

On virtually all Web documents, underlined pieces of text signify links to other documents. Many Web page graphics are also links. Here is a guideline for finding hypertext links: Run your cursor slowly over a Web page. If it changes from the normal arrow shape to a pointing finger, you have found a link.

Is the World Wide Web just a read-listen-and-watch kind of medium?

Some users are quite content with these capabilities. However, the Web can be quite interactive. You can buy and sell products and services via Web pages, as well as offer feedback to online merchants, chat (text-style) in real-time with users thousands of miles away, or create and print out maps. Trust me, that is just a sampling of the Web's capabilities.

Who owns the Web?

As with the rest of the Internet, no one really owns the World Wide Web. In a way, we all do. We can all contribute to it in one way or another, with the most obvious contribution being one's own Web page.

How do I create a Web page?

If you were to create one yourself, you would probably want to learn some basic HTML, which stands for hypertext markup language, the main programming language of the World Wide Web.

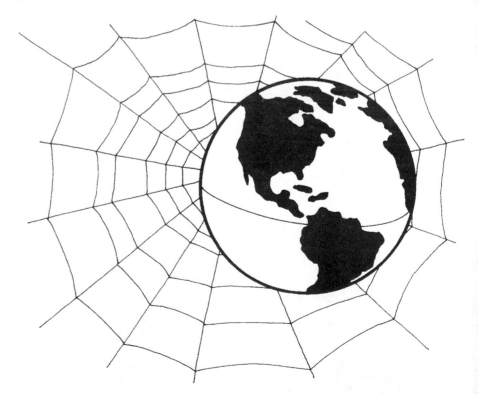

World Wide Web FAQ (cont.)

Me? A computer programmer? My microwave clock still registers 0:00.

First of all, HTML can be written with any simple word processor. Second, there are plenty of good HTML and Web page authoring guides online and in print. Third, HTML programming is similar to the formatting conventions in many of the DOS word processors, such as the earlier versions of WordPerfect. You do have another option, however.

If it is an easier method, tell me more.

You can try commercial software such as Adobe's PageMill and SoftQuad's **HoTMetaL** or shareware such as **HTML Web Weaver** or **HTML Assistant**. These programs offer menu commands and buttons that let you bypass much of the typing required to create an attractive Web page. And, with a few button-clicks, these programs let you view your work as you create it.

Are there any other options in creating a Web page?

You can pay someone to create a page for you. More and more HTML-savvy writers are offering their services. That includes high school students who can design with the best of them. Just make sure you have a general idea of what you want included on the page. Remember: These people are designers, not specialists in whatever content you choose to include.

Okay, so if I choose to dive in myself, what design tips can you offer me?

I'm glad you asked that. Follow me to the next page . . .

Web Page Design Guidelines

1. Content, clarity, and color.

2. Smooth navigation. Make sure visitors to your site can move about your site easily.

3. Give readers something of value. Make it obvious and easy to access.

4. Keep the length of your pages manageable.

5. If you are creating a long page, be sure to add a short list of anchors at the top of the page. (Anchors let readers skip right to the desired location.) Similarly, at the bottom of the page, add a button that takes readers directly to the top. (See guideline #2.)

6. Give your readers options, especially a non-graphical version of your page for those with text-only browsers and those who want to get to your information without awaiting the loading of graphics.

7. To provide reasonable waiting times for users with slower modems, keep your graphics small. Thumbnail images that users can click for larger versions are a popular way to go. (See guideline above.)

8. Offer some form of interactivity.

9. Use a variety of media. A page with just text can be drab, while a page with just graphics can overwhelm your other content. Almost daily, multimedia features are becoming easier for authors to include and for users to access.

10. Links are what hypertext are all about. Use them. Your page should be a launching pad for your visitors' further exploration.

What to Expect from Your Web Browser

You will be spending hours with your Web browser, so you should make sure it helps rather than hinders your exploits on the Internet.

At the very least, browser software should do the following:

- let you keep a list of favorite sites to visit. (The terms hotlist and bookmarks are often used in this context.)

- make it easy for you to organize those bookmarks into folders and into an order that suits you.

- allow for easy navigation, subject to the whims and mind-wanderings of most users.

- offer nearly seamless integration with other Internet components such as FTP, electronic mail, Gopher, and Usenet news.

- make downloading of files a simple process.

- let you easily retrace your current session's path (or history) through the sites you have visited (i.e., links you have followed).

- work hand-in-hand with helper applications and plug-ins that facilitate your computer's handling of video, sound, graphics, and files of various other formats.

- make the creation of Web pages workable with a little guidance from books or tutorials. (i.e., It shows your work as you progress. This is called **WYSIWYG** [What You See Is What You Get], pronounced WIZZYWIG.)

Netscape Navigator, the various versions of **Mosaic**, and **Internet Explorer** are currently the most-used browsers on the market. While you are Web-browsing, keep informed of their latest versions, usually available for downloading at several FTP sites on the Net.

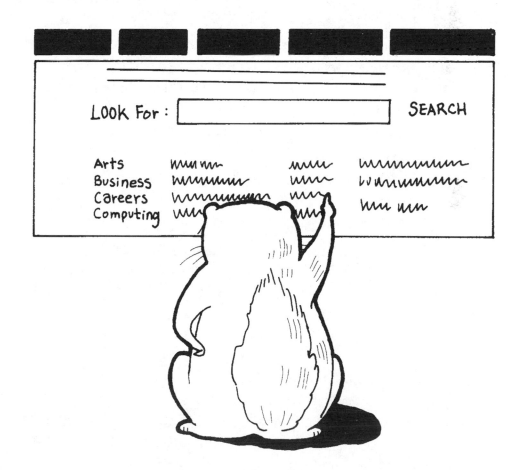

Other Browser Tips

- Have a clear idea of what you want from the Web. Otherwise, you will have wandered far and wide without finding nearly as much as you originally wanted. (Either way, it will be fun.)

- To customize how Web pages and your mail and newsreader screens appear, explore your choices under Options-Preferences.

- Information can be copied from Web pages and pasted into your word processor documents (for your own reference, of course). You can even send whole Web pages via e-mail.

- Interested in using a graphic from a Web page? Aim your cursor on top of the image and press your mouse button. (**Windows** users: your right mouse button). Your browser should offer options on copying and saving the selected graphic. You can do the same with links.

- You can get some guidance in HTML authoring and Web page creation by selecting Document Source under View.

- Take some time to view other options in General Preferences under Options. You can also customize your browser's mail and newsreader appearance and capabilities.

- If your bookmark list is uncontrollably long, use the Find command to seek out the desired Web site. This step will not necessarily help in all cases, especially if you have not taken the time to give comprehensible names to each bookmark. (To supply your own names, click Window, then select Bookmarks. Did you notice your top-of-screen menu choices have changed? Under Item, select Edit Bookmarks. You now have a dialog box where you can rename your bookmark.)

- Go to Window and select History. You now have a window showing the sites you have visited during the current session. Some users prefer to keep it open on a convenient portion of the screen and double-click the previously-visited sites for quicker navigation.

Web Spotlight: Netscape Navigator

⬅o Back	o⇨ Forward	🏠 Home	🔄 Reload	🖼 Images	⇨ Open	🖨 Print	🔭 Find	● Stop	N

Go To: [   ]

What's New?	What's Cool?	Handbook	Net Search	Net Directory	Software

Take a closer look at browser software with the help of this screen shot of Netscape Navigator's control center. This discussion centers around Netscape because it is the browser of choice for over 70% of Web users. (**Note:** At the writing of this book, there is an advanced test version of **Netscape Navigator 3.0**. By the time this book is published, 3.0 may well be the version you are using. After this discussion, you will find a page showing the new Netscape control center.)

Your own browser may have a bit of a different look and feel, but it should offer most of the same capabilities. Let's start at the top and work our way down.

The Toolbar

Back and Forward let you move in those directions among the pages you have visited during your current session.

Home takes you to whatever page you have chosen to greet you when you start up your browser. (The author changes his home page about once a month.) Changing your home page is a matter of finding the URL of your preferred site and typing it into the Home Page Location box in Options-General Preferences.

Reload displays and updates the current Web page you are visiting.

Images lets you load graphics onto your page. For many Web users, this button is rarely used since they let the browser automatically load images. Others, however, turn off the autoload option for more rapid page-loading. If you are interested in seeing the graphics on a page, simply click the Images button and all the attractive GIFs and JPEGs will take over where the placeholders were.

Web Spotlight: Netscape Navigator *(cont.)*

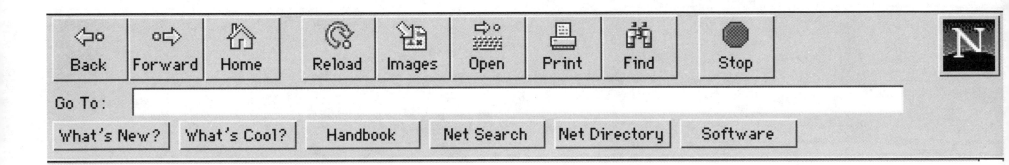

When you click the next button, Open, you get a dialog box that lets you visit a site by entering its URL. (Typing the URL into the location indicator will accomplish the same task.)

The Print button prints the current Web page.

The Find button directs Netscape to search the current Web page for a word or phrase that you have defined.

Finally, the Stop button will halt any connection you have initiated. Use it when a site seems unresponsive to contact and you don't want to wait for the dialog box that tells you the site is too busy. You can also click Stop when you are in a rush, the desired Web site's layout is done, and the necessary links have appeared. (Try not to make a habit of this, however, as only fully-loaded pages remain in the disk cache, allowing for quicker visits in later sessions.)

Location Indicator

Between the directory buttons and the tool buttons lies the location indicator, which tells you that page's URL (uniform resource locator, that is, where on the Internet you are currently interacting). More than likely, you are at a Web site, meaning the URL starts with the letters http. However, you may have landed at an FTP site (ftp://) to download a shareware game, for example, or a Gopher site (gopher://) to view some weather images. If you want to move elsewhere on the Web and your current page does not offer the desired link, you can type a new URL in the location indicator, press enter, and you are on your way.

Web Spotlight: Netscape Navigator *(cont.)*

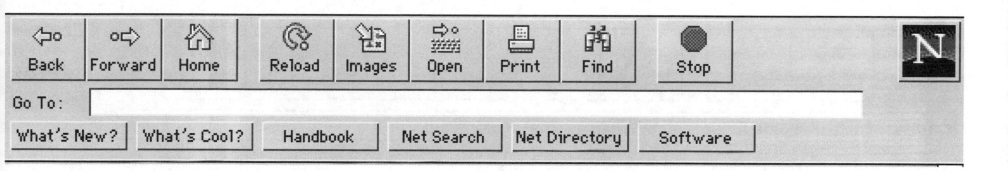

The Directory Buttons

At the lower left corner is the What's New button. Click on this and you get an update on the latest and greatest sites to show up on the Web.

The next button, What's Cool, tells you about Web sites that combine interesting content with a certain flair in their interface and eye appeal. These first two buttons alone could tempt you to stretch your list of bookmarks well off the screen.

The third button from the left, Handbook, takes you to Netscape's online user manual for those tough questions that your own intuition cannot answer.

Net Search follows. With this button, most of the often-used search tools, such as Yahoo, Lycos, Web Crawler, Excite, Alta Vista, and Deja News, are one click away. (There are plenty of others and you will probably have your own favorite.)

Clicking on Net Directory produces online directories (call them subject trees, if you wish) that will help you explore the Internet by topic.

The last directory button, Software, allows Netscape users to download the most recent versions (including test versions not yet ready for commercial release) of their various applications.

A Peek At: Netscape 3.0

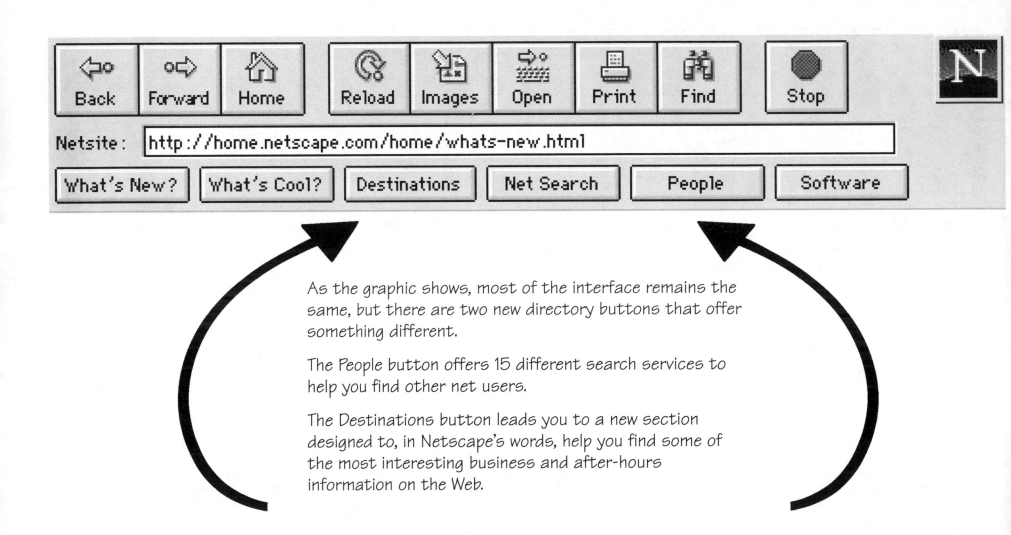

As the graphic shows, most of the interface remains the same, but there are two new directory buttons that offer something different.

The People button offers 15 different search services to help you find other net users.

The Destinations button leads you to a new section designed to, in Netscape's words, help you find some of the most interesting business and after-hours information on the Web.

During Those Inevitable Lulls on the Web

There will be times when Web pages crawl rather than leap onto your screen.

Don't torture yourself! Try these nearly painless alternatives to the mesmerizing routine of point-click-and-wait-and-wait-and-wait.

1. Open a second browser window and search for more sites and information.

2. Start up a low-memory game (save the major portion of your RAM for your browser) that you can easily switch to for some quick and easy entertainment.

3. To sharpen your navigating skills, keep an easy-to-read Internet tips and tricks book nearby.

4. Write a quick letter to friends or family on a low-memory text editor. (Later, when you are offline, paste the text into your favorite word processor to customize with graphics and your favorite fonts.)

5. Have a healthy, non-sticky, non-greasy, non-drippy snack within reach.

6. Blink. And blink some more. That helps keep your eyes moist and eases strain.

7. Slowly roll your eyes in complete circles in both directions. This aids your eyes during longer Web sessions.

8. Leave your chair and stretch.

9. Finish that math work sheet that is due tomorrow .

10. Clean your room. (Here is perfect opportunity to break a big job into a series of little ones. Amaze yourself with how much you can get done in a minute or two, especially when you know that a new, image-filled Web site awaits you when you are done.)

Rough Surfing on the Web

Friendly as most Web browsers usually are, you may still face some messages that are a bit, shall we say, brusque?

First of all, do not blame your browser. There are, after all, several variables at work as you weave your way toward the Web's countless resources.

Here are a few of those messages that greet most users at one time or another: (These examples come from Netscape, but other browsers will display similar messages):

"Netscape's network connection was refused by the server: (name of server). The server may not be accepting connections or may be busy. Try connecting again later:"

Expect to see this fairly self-explanatory message more often than the others, especially from the more popular sites during normal working hours of a day.

"Netscape is unable to locate the server: (name of server). The server does not have a DNS entry:"

- Double-check how the URL was entered. A minor typing error can throw off the whole connection process.
- Check to make sure you are still connected to your Internet provider.
- The computer you have tried to access may have taken a permanent vacation.

"403 Forbidden:"

The system administrator has placed a restriction on the document's access. Such restrictions are often placed on adult-oriented material.

What do you mean you're busy? So am I!

Rough Surfing on the Web *(cont.)*

"404 Not Found:"

The URL was not correctly entered or the desired document was removed from the server.

"This site has moved:" and "These pages have moved:"

No big deal. Links to the new locations should accompany these messages.

"A network error occurred while Netscape was receiving data. Socket is not connected:"

Probably a short-term problem that you did not cause. Try connecting again in a few minutes.

"The information you have submitted is not secure:"

No need to worry as long as you do not pass out credit card numbers or other private information. The words not secure mean that data passed on this server can be easily intercepted and read.

"Please log in . . .:"

You will probably need some kind of password. Information on how to register for this site usually accompanies this request.

A Look At Search Engines

Once you are on the Web, try out a variety of the many search tools offered. You will likely find one that will become a favorite, for awhile at least. (You may want to consider changing about once a month, for reasons such as speed and the relevance of hits—the references that the search tool returns.)

For most of us, simply typing in one or more words into the one-line text field and clicking the search button will get us most of what we need. But for those instances where that is not the case, here are a few search tips that will help you track down that desired data or Web site.

1. Start your search in your mind at first. Try to narrow your subject enough so the search engine can return reasonably relevant hits. For example, for information on Willie Mays, enter his name rather than San Francisco Giants.

2. Unless capitalization matters, stick with lowercase characters.

3. Punctuation is usually ignored, so Willie Mays is the same as Mays, Willie and Mays Willie.

4. Consider bookmarking a page of your search engine's results for quicker return to information you might need a day or two later.

5. Explore the advanced options that most search tools offer you.

A Look At Search Engines *(cont.)*

You have a wide selection of search tools on the Web. New features are cropping up daily and are becoming interchangeable among the tools. Here are a few of the more familiar names and at least one strength of each. Try them all and see which ones you prefer.

Search.com: This links you to search sites in, as of this writing, 20 different categories—a total of 250 search engines. It also lets you create your own personalized search page.

Infoseek: Infoseek offers a great deal of flexibility to your hunt as it can search Infoseek Select Sites, numerous categories, newsgroups, e-mail addresses, Reuters News, and Web FAQ files.

Lycos: PC World magazine recently rated Lycos best of the top search engines in both quality of information and relevancy of results.

Alta Vista: Alta Vista's creator claims that it searches the largest Web index. It won C-Net's award for best search engine, so it definitely does something right.

Yahoo!: This subject tree offers you chances to narrow your search by clicking on its comprehensive selection of categories. It also offers its own kids' version and has recently teamed with Vicinity Corporation to offer close-up neighborhood maps.

Excite: Excite lets you search the Web, Web site reviews, Usenet newsgroups, and classified ads.

DejaNews: You enter the subject and DejaNews scours relevant Usenet postings (newsgroupies' views). It is the largest tool of its kind.

Web Site Reviews

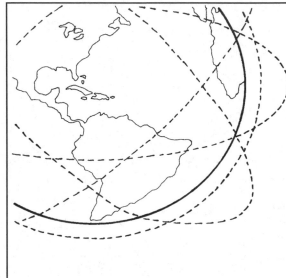

And now, for a look at our selected Web sites.

These are meant to be a springboard for you own explorations and extended activities.

Have a good time!

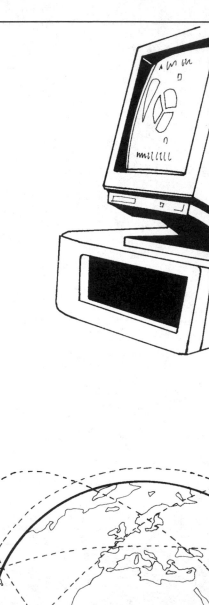

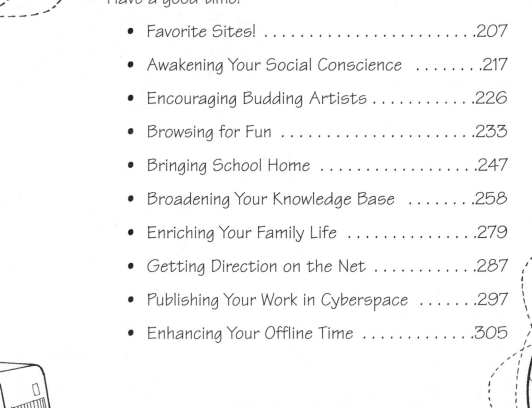

Favorite Sites!

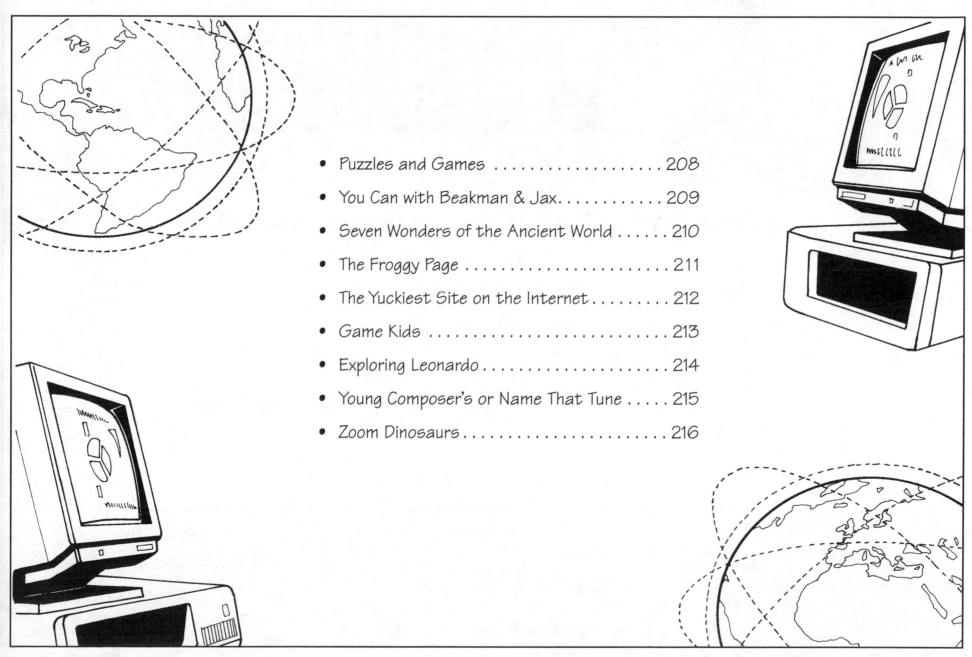

http://www.cyberkids.com/Games/Games.html

Overview:

This is a favorite site for kids who love games, puzzles and mazes!

Play a variety of interactive games such as:

- Alien Assembly
- Concentration using Egyptian Hieroglyphics
- Hippie Hockey
- Lockdown

- Music Match
- Pinball
- Why Do Birds Marry?

Note: You need Shockwave to play most of these games.

Try This:

Play Alien Assembly and create your own alien by choosing alien body parts using the "New" button.

Highlights:

- Games and puzzles are very creative and have interesting graphics.
- Have hours of fun at this site!

See also:

Learn2 Play Checkers

http://learn2.com/05/0501/0501.html

http://www.beakman.com/

Overview:

This is a companion site to the popular TV show "Beakman's World." *You Can* has answers to your questions and interactive science demos. It also has links to other terrific World Wide Web sites. Using *You Can*, you can find out what is coming up in future editions of *You Can* with Beakman & Jax on the TV show "Beakman's World." Many of the images are really buttons you can click to see what happens. Some of the buttons are secret , so you will have to explore for yourself.

Try this:

Brainstorm a list of questions like, "Why is the sky blue?" or "Why is a diamond so hard?" Then follow the *Answers to Your Questions* link to find out the why's.

Highlights:

- There is an abundance of funny questions.
- If they don't have an answer to your question, simply send an e-mail and check back later.

See Also:

AskERIC

http://ericir.syr.edu/

The Seven Wonders of the Ancient World

http://pharos.bu.edu/Egypt/Wonders/

Overview:

This is a cool site to give kids an understanding of the Seven Wonders of the Ancient World.

Try this:

If you are studying Egypt in school, use this site to learn about the building of the Great Pyramid at Giza.

Highlights:

- Go to the clickable map and check out the location of the Seven Wonders.
- There are many useful and interesting of links in the Forgotten Wonders section.

See also:

The Great Wall of China

http://pharos.bu.edu/Egypt/Wonders/Forgotten/greatwall.html

http://frog.simplenet.com/froggy/

Overview:

Do you like frogs? If you do, visit this site! Everything having to do with frogs is here including:

- Froggy Pictures
- Froggy Sounds
- Froggy Tales
- Songs of the Frog

- Scientific Amphibian
- Famous Frogs
- Net Frogs

Try this:

Click on the frog icon with the saw and take part in a virtual frog dissection. (This is not for the tender-hearted!)

Highlights:

- Froggy sounds give you a sample of the different sounds frogs make.
- Many froggy graphics can be found at this site.

See also:

The Lily Pond

http://www4.ncsu.edu/eos/users/e/ebl atham/www/home.html

http://www.yucky.com/

Overview:

Welcome to the yuckiest, most disgusting and easily the funniest site on the Internet. First, click on the "Gross/Cool Body" button and find out why you burp, sweat, vomit, have bad breath, zits, pus, and more! Then go to the "Bug World" button and find out everything you always wanted to know about roaches!

Try this:

Go to "Club Yucky" and try out "Yucky Science" or "Edible Science."

Try creating a "Yucky E-card" and read the poems "Ode to a Worm" and "Worm Hate!"

Highlights:

- Kids will be roaring with laughter at this site!

- Lots of special effects are included at this site, but they are too gross to be mentioned here. Try them for yourself!

See Also:

The Virtual Body

http://www.medtropolis.com/vbody/

http://www.gamekids.com/

Overview:

Game Kids is a gathering place for kids of all ages to learn and exchange noncomputer games and activities. Each month, selected games and rhymes, activities, and recipes will be selected from around the world for you to download, print out, and play. You are invited to submit your favorite games, stories, poetry, artwork, photographs, and recipes.

Try this:

Tired of kick ball and soccer? Use this site to find other great physical education games that are kid tested and approved.

Browse through Nail Party Games for some new inspiration!

Highlights:

- Write a description of your favorite game and submit it to Game Kids.

- Lots of creative ideas can be found here.

See also:

Game Kids Teens

http://www.gamekids.com/teenp1.html

http://www.mos.org/leonardo/

Overview:

This is a very cool site to explore. Experience the creations of one of the most famous painters of the Italian Renaissance; Leonardo Da Vinci. Although he is best known for his paintings, Leonardo conducted dozens of experiments and created futuristic inventions.

Take the opportunity to visit four different sections at this site:

1. Inventors Workshop
2. Leonardo's Perspective
3. Leonardo: Right to Left
4. What, Where, When?

Try this:

Visit the Leonardo Right to Left page, and then try to write your signature in cursive from right to left. This is quite challenging!

Highlights:

- After exploring The Inventor's Toolbox, try going to Gadget Anatomy and see if you can correctly choose which machine parts match the gadgets displayed.
- Many aspects of Leonardo's genius are covered at this site.

See Also:

Da Vinci's Inventions

http://www.lib.stevens-tech.edu/collections/DAVINCI/inventions/

http://www.youngcomposers.com/

Overview:

This is a great site for aspiring musicians. Musical compositions are submitted to this site and when you click on "New Releases" or "Earlier Works" you will find a list of pieces available for your listening pleasure!

Music is listed by category:

- Baroque/Classical
- Modern
- Romantic/Impressionist
- Choral/Religious
- New Age
- World Music
- Jazz
- Rock/Blues

Note: You need Javascript and frames for this site.

Try this:

Click on "Play Music Match" and then name that tune! Listen to music by famous composers and see if you can identify the composer who wrote each piece.

Highlights:

This site offers numerous musical works from which to choose.

See Also:

Popular Midi Music

http://tinpan.fortunecity.com/meatloaf/890/pop_midi.htm

You will enjoy many hours of listening pleasure with numerous well-known songs listed here.

Zoom Dinosaurs

http://www.EnchantedLearning.com/subjects/dinosaurs/

Overview:

Zoom Dinosaurs is great for any dinosaur enthusiast! At this site you can navigate through masses of well-organized information including Dino News, Dinosaur Fossils, Dinosaur Quizzes, and even an illustrated Dinosaur Dictionary with over 500 entries!

Check out Dinosaur Fun and try games, puzzles, quizzes, and even vote for your favorite dinosaur!

Try this:

Click on Dinosaur Jokes and then tell the jokes to your friends.

Go to Games, Puzzles, and Quizzes and try the Scrambled Dinosaur activity or try matching the dino skull to the dinosaur activity!

Highlights:

- This site has an easy interface and is packed with fun dinosaur activities!

- Dinosaur information sheets are fabulous references for writing a dinosaur report. Check it out!

See Also:

The Children's Museum of Indianapolis

http://www.childrensmuseum.org/Dino.htm

Awakening Your Social Conscience

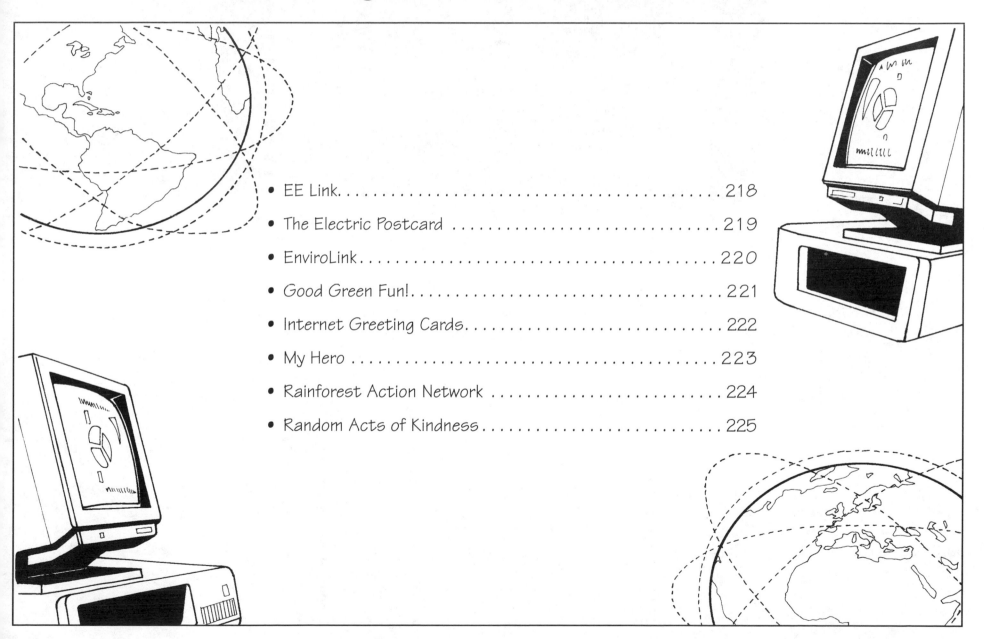

http://eelink.net/

Overview:

A project of the National Consortium for Environmental Education and Training, EE-Link is a clearinghouse of activities, links, and documents whose chief purpose is the enhancement of environmental education. One of EE-Link's strengths is its expanded table of contents, which helps you capitalize on its wide array of topics. You can also use its search engine to find information on acid rain, clearcutting, and erosion.

Try this:

Using EE-Link as a chief source of ideas, create a calendar of earth-friendly activities that your family can try throughout the year.

Highlights:

- This is a great site to bookmark as a reference for science curriculum.
- The search engine was helpful in finding information on acid rain, clearcutting, and erosion.

See also:

Environmental Studies
http://users.bergen.org/~aast/AAST/Projects/atoe.html

The Electric Postcard

http://postcards.www.media.mit.edu/Postcards/

Overview:

Brighten someone's day with a card from this site.

It couldn't be simpler . . . and less expensive.

- Just show up at the site and go to the Postcard Rack to browse images in the following categories:
  - Photography
  - Paintings
  - Contemporary Art
  - Science
  - Graphics
- Select your image.
- Fill in the necessary to: and from: information and type in your message.
- Preview your creation.
- Send it.
- There. You have just made someone feel special.

- - -

Try this:

- Try a little HTML to embellish your card with a graphic of your choice. Electric Postcard will point your way.

- Send a friendly card from a friend's computer so you will not be identified. Sign it with a few ?s.

Highlights:

This site offers a choice of over 150 images from which to choose.

See also:

The DPPlus Electronic Postcard Shop

http://cards.dpp.net/cards/postcard.htm

http://envirolink.org/

Overview:

The words varied, interesting, and comprehensive spring to mind when visiting this site. The home page leads you to places where you can chat, watch live video conferences, view art works, search their library, and get updates on environmental news at places like the World Species List and the Animal Rights Resource Site.

This site's design is very consistent with its "earthish" concerns. The webmasters also did a nice job of giving visitors options for faster navigation throughout this site.

With its clearinghouse of educational materials, this site should be a great starting point for many student projects.

Try this:

- Keep a week-long running tally from the Vital Signs component.
- Make up a work sheet of related math problems that you can bring to class.

Highlights:

- Learning from the Vital Signs component.
- Visiting the EnviroArts Gallery.
- Try the Library to get background information on organic gardening.

See also:

Homepage of the Global Recycling Network (http://clinet.fi/grn/)

Good Green Fun!

Good Green Fun!

http://www.efn.org/~dharmika/

Overview:

A "clear green" musical message for youth and adults alike. With honors from the Parents' Choice Foundation, the song-stories of Good Green Fun! are based on botanist and ecologist Dharmika Judith Henshel's travels in Oregon and Central America.

Not to be confused with The Good Green Fun Tropical Marketplace out of Florida, this site gives you the feeling that Henshel is much more intent on spreading her global awareness message for the sake of the message rather than sales. For example, she offers a free tape to contributors of activities related to her main themes. And from those ideas, she is currently developing a Good Green Fun! Forest Ecology Curriculum.

- -

Try this:

Write your own poem or song with inspiration from Dharmika's own lyrics, which you can read and hear online.

Highlights:

Download a sound sample of Wandering in Wonderland.

See also:

The Ecology Channel (http://www.ecology.com/)

Rainforest Action Network—Kids Corner (http://www.ran.org/ran/kids_action/index.html

http://www.tenn.com/igc/lettershort.html

Overview:

Help save a tree and send an electronic greeting card.

Performance Electronics, the sponsor of this site, lets you do just that. The steps to create a card are quite simple:

First, choose from one of 23 background colors, five text colors, and 25 pictures (ranging from wolves to Batman to a bald eagle).

Second, type your message, the recipient's e-mail address, and a password needed by the recipient. Third, when you are happy with your message and design, click Notify Recipient and off it goes at no charge. (You do have the option to back up and reformat your card.)

- -

Try this:

Send a card to an online acquaintance. But try to think of someone who wouldn't normally expect one from you.

Highlights:

There are similar sites on the Net. This one is good because of its simplicity and flexibility.

See also:

Blue Mountain Arts

http://www2.bluemountain.com/

http://myhero.com/

Overview:

This site has a great concept—in its words, "celebrating the best of humanity."

My Hero does a nice job of showing heroes as people in every walk of life. In keeping with that ethos, users are encouraged to share the heroes in their lives. With this invitation, My Hero really makes visitors feel that their lives count.

At this site, users will read of special people in the following categories:

- Family Hero
- Business Hero
- Science Hero
- My Hero's Hero
- Teacher Hero
- Peacemakers
- Sports Hero
- Angels
- Lifesavers
- Animal Hero
- Poets
- Artist Hero
- Explorers

Try this:

- What is your definition of a hero? Look for people at this site that meet your hero requirements.
- Set up your own heroes gallery and notify people of their inclusion in your hall of fame.

Highlights:

Try the "Hero Chain," where visitors tell about their heroes, whom we then get to meet. Then that second group of heroes tell us about their heroes and so on . . .

See also:

Celebrating Our Heroes

http://www.pathfinder.com/Life/heroes/index.html

http://www.ran.org/

Overview:

Not everyone may agree with The Rainforest Action Network's stance on environmental issues, but that does not mean there isn't plenty to learn and see at this site, including the Kids Corner, which:

- shares answers to kids' most frequently-asked questions about this issue.
- tells about the people and animals of the rainforest.
- features a helpful glossary.
- provides a list of resources for teachers and students.
- sponsors an art contest to find the best 13 pictures to use for each year's Kid's Calendar.

The Rainforest Action Network also supplies a helpful search engine to find pertinent material within their archives and serious ecologists will appreciate Tribal Links—an environmentalist's dream list of links.

Try this:

- Be ready for the next Earth Day. Read **8 Steps for Kids to Take,** then make a photo story of you and/or your friends following these and other eco-tips.
- If you are so inclined, consider having the whole class join as an individual.

Highlights:

Take the rainforest quiz. Here is one fact you will learn by taking this quiz. Over 24 U.S. oil companies have explored for or extracted oil from the Amazon River Basin.

See also:

The Audubon Society

http://www.audubon.org/

National Wildlife Federation

http://www.nwf.org/nwf/

http://www.ReadersNdex.com/randomacts

Overview:

This is truly a "feel-good" site on the Web.

If you have not read any of Conari Press's books, then spend some time at this site. It should revive your faith in your fellow humans and perhaps inspire you to "join the revolution."

Plan to visit and revisit this site for some reminders that not only are we blessed, but we have the power to make others feel that way too.

Try this:

Search your newspaper and follow TV news for new stories of random acts of kindness. Submit them to this Web site.

Highlights:

The "kindness" stories from Web visitors are a great supplement to the printed series.

See also:

Spreading Kindness (TM) (a site by KKTV, Channel 11, in Colorado Springs)

http://www.rmii.com/kindness/kindhome.htm

Encouraging Budding Artists

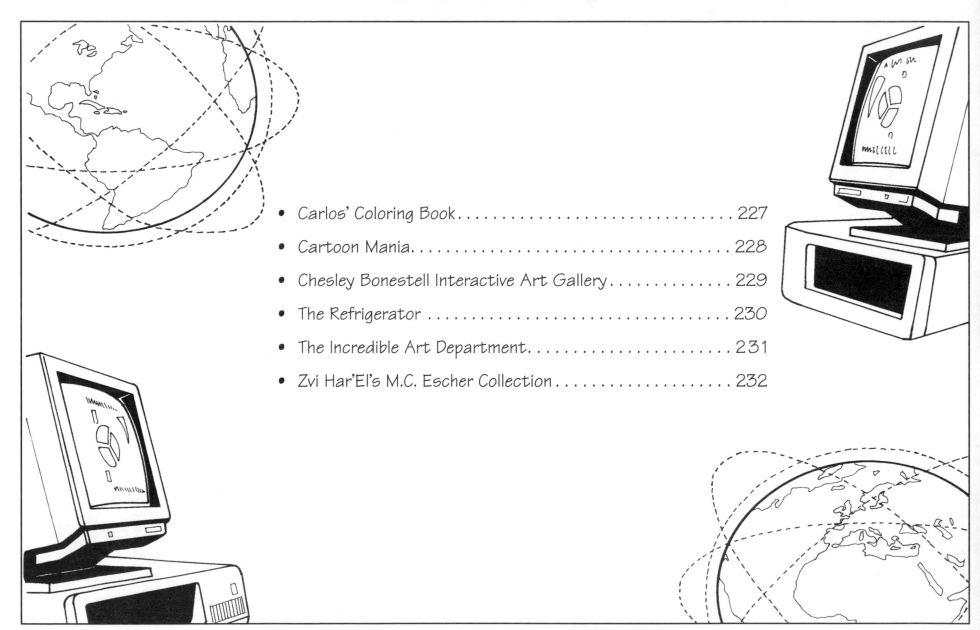

Carlos' Coloring Book Home

http://coloring.com/

Overview:

Above are samples of the templates you can color at Carlos' Coloring Book. Almost all paint programs offer the same capabilities as Carlos' Coloring Book, but if you don't have that software available, this site will do in a pinch. It is just as enjoyable. And with a color printer, you can create your own online art gallery that you created in cyberspace.

A few tips:

- Make sure you have autoload images turned on when you visit.
- Be ready for frequent page reloading.

Try this:

Research and experiment with complementary and contrasting colors.

Highlights:

- Download Coloring Book for the **Macintosh** from this site. (Carlos' site is based on an idea from this computer program.)
- Try the Easter egg template for the Try this: activity.

See also:

TrippyHippy's Coloring Book

http://trippy.shano.com/colors.phtml

CARTOON MANIA

http://worldchat.com/public/jhish/cartoon.html

Overview:

This is the cartoon drawing course for children of all ages, claims cartoonist/illustrator Jerry Hish. Pulling it off via the Web once again shows the promise of the Internet as an educational tool.

Hish takes his students step-by-step through the process of drawing a lion, an elephant, a gorilla, and an alligator. Drawing each new animal presents his students with new techniques. For an added personal touch, he closes each lesson with a pertinent riddle.

Hish also encourages his students to add their own personal flair to each practice piece.

Try this:

Practice! Practice! In the process, discover and develop your own favorite cartoon characters. Then, when you are ready to unveil them to the world, send samples to Cartoon Mania for a gallery exhibition.

Highlights:

So many kids attack drawing with a "why bother erasing" attitude. His approach is to build the picture in steps, as well as his frequent reminders to draw lightly at first to allow for easy revisions.

See also:

TCrayola

http://www.crayola.com/index.html

http://www.secapl.com/bonestell/top.html

Overview:

Chesley Bonestell could see into the future! That is the impression you get after visiting this site, which shares 23 of Bonestell's visions of the earth, Mars, Jupiter, the moon, and the stars. Take the time to follow all the links, to learn about a man who, when not relatively "earthbound" with architectural projects (i.e., the Golden Gate Bridge and the Chrysler Tower) and motion picture endeavors (i.e., **War of the Worlds**), was rendering his perceptions of worlds beyond.

- -

Try this:

Go to the site below in a separate browser window and compare Bonestell's work with the images here:

http://pds.jpl.nasa.gov/planets/

Highlights:

The supplemental text provided just enough information about Bonestell without being engulfed.

See also:

Cybertown Art Galleries

http://www.cybertown.com/artgall.html

http://www.artcontest.com/

Overview:

The Refrigerator's weekly art contest is quite simple. Kids 18-and-under submit their work via United States mail. The site's producers narrow the field to five contestants, post the work on their pages, and let Web visitors vote on their favorite, as well as give a reason for their selections. The winner's work is then displayed at the top of the Web page for a week and, when replaced by the next winner, inducted into the Refrigerator's Hall of Fame.

Try this:

Get adventurous with your art. Try a sand painting:

1. Draw a picture. (Keep shapes simple.)
2. Spread glue on the inside of each shape.
3. Lightly sprinkle sand on the glued areas.
4. When the sand is dry, spray paint it. Protect the other shapes by walling them off with sheets of cardboard.
5. When finished, enter the contest.

Highlights:

- This site has a convenient section for visitors' feedback.

- Take the time to visit the Hall of Fame for inspiration from past winners.

See also:

Making a Splash with Color

http://www.thetech.org/exhibits_events/online/color/intro/

The Incredible Art Department

http://www.artswire.org/kenroar/index2.html

Overview:

This site is packed with fun things to do. Go to the Art Room to view interesting creations and works of art. Then check out Art News, Art Stuff, Lessons, Cartoons, an Art Site of the Week and more!

Try this:

Create your own gallery of cartoons. When you have finished, copy/paste each image into your own graphics program.

Highlights:

Once you enter "Art Stuff" click on links and then Artists. See if you can find your favorite artist on the list!

See also:

A. Pintura, Art Detective

http://www.eduweb.com/pintura/

Zvi Har'El's
M.C. ESCHER COLLECTION

http://gauss.technion.ac.il/~rl/M.C.Escher/

Overview:

Zvi Har'El, a senior lecturer in the department of mathematics at the Technion, Israel Institute of Technology, has collected over 60 images created by the Dutch artist Maurits Cornelis Escher.

The site is fairly straightforward with its catalog and collection, so just sit back and either load the images all at once or turn off your autoload function and pick the images you want to view. If you choose the latter, click on the image placeholder once to get the thumbnail image, then again to get the full-screen image. (**Note:** Try not to do this in the middle of the afternoon, this is the Web's busiest time. Things load somewhat slowly during this time.)

- -

Try this:

Turn off Auto Load Images in your browser and, using just the titles of his works, take a quick guess as to how the piece of art appears. Then click the graphic icon once to get a thumbnail version of the work. Compare your guess with the actual work.

Highlights:

There may be two schools of thought to this: You may like being engulfed by Escher's work and this page does just that. Or you may prefer to view a few images at a time.

See also:

World of Escher

http://www.town-square.net/h/astayton/escher/index.htm

Browsing for Fun

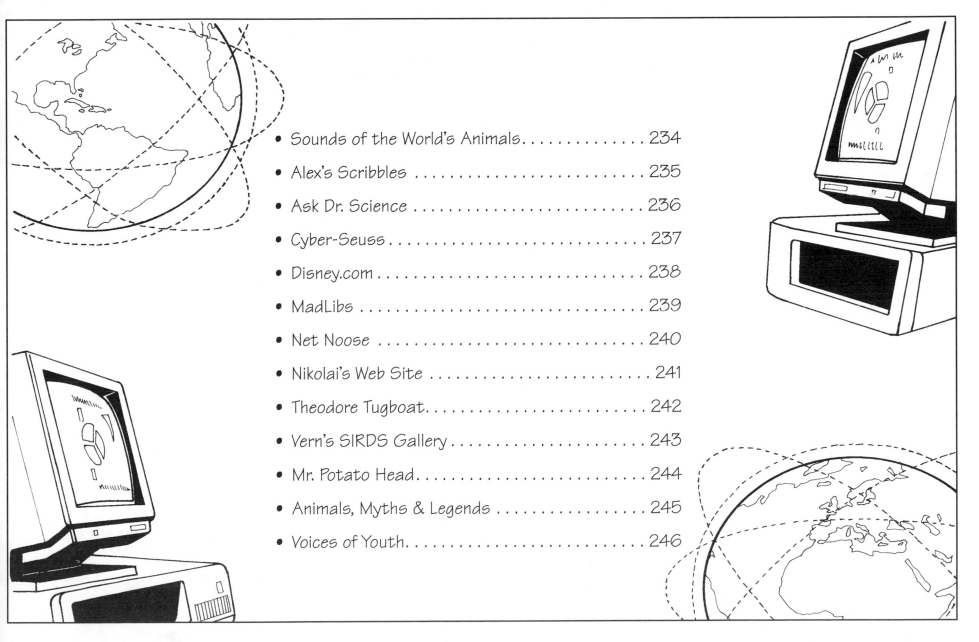

Sounds of the World's Animals

http://www.georgetown.edu/cball/animals/animals.html

Overview:

What does a bird say? It's pip in Danish, tweet-tweet in English, and chunchun in Japanese. How about a rooster? It's cocorico in French, ake-e-ake-ake in Thai, and chicchirichiii in Italian! Have fun at this site learning how people all over the world describe the sounds animals make in over 20 languages.

Try this:

Play a game with your friends. Choose an animal from the site and then take turns guessing what sound the animal makes in different languages.

Highlights:

- This site has a simple menu. Choose sounds listed by the animal or by the language.
- Also included for young readers: Spelling Sounds of the World's Animals.

See also:

What Says a Cow?

http://www.musiknet.se/onomato poetica/frame.asp

Alex's Scribbles

http://www.peg.apc.org/~balson/story/

Overview:

Parents and kids: If you want a clear idea of what you can do when you team up on a Web site of your own, visit Alex's Scribbles. Both Scott (dad) and Alex (son) Balson have shared their creativity and, in so doing, offer a fun and interactive site for a wide audience. Koala Trouble, the series of stories by six-year-old Alex, takes the reader through several adventures of Max the Koala.

But the Balsons do not stop there. They want you to help Max take a worldwide tour. How? Just write your own stories about him. But make sure you use your own home region as the setting for your adventure. (Check with the site's webmasters for further details.)

- -

Try this:

If you have a multimedia program like **HyperCard** or **HyperStudio**, create your own interactive stories.

Highlights:

Read the readers' e-mail. This is excellent proof of the Web's ability to reach many through the efforts of few.

See also:

The land of Amy and Daisy

http://coastnet.com/dhouston/Amy.html

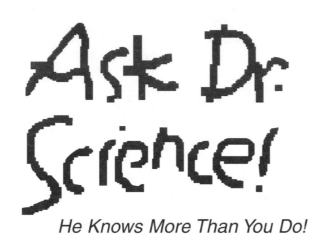

He Knows More Than You Do!

http://www.ducksbreath.com/

Overview:

Dr. Science is here to tackle questions that have perplexed people for years, but modern science shies away from—vital topics like, "Why do we have gums?" and "Why are there duds at the bottom of a bowl of popcorn?" Parents: Occasionally, Dr. Science deals with topics that might require your presence. Peruse the archives every once in awhile to stay in touch. And always remember: Dr. Science knows more than you do!

Try this:

- Using Dr. Science as your inspiration, concoct and publish your own theories about puzzling scientific phenomena.
- Send in your own theory to Dr. Science and ask his opinion on it.

Highlights:

Try joining his mailing list. You will receive Dr. Science wisdom daily.

See also:

Ask Dr. Internet
hhttp://promo.net/drnet/

http://www.afn.org/~afn15301/drseuss.html

Overview:

You can tell a true fan of Ted Geisel created this site. It not only leads us to Dr. Seuss stories, but delves into the author's life and early writings, as well. The site also points us to Seuss graphics, other worthy Web pages dedicated to the world of Dr. Seuss, and an interesting link to "a real shocking reality."

Tip: Take the time to e-mail this site's webmaster. Like this site, he is a lot of fun.

Try this:

- Be an informed voter. Read **How the Grinch Stole Christmas**, follow the link to The Great Grinch Debate and cast your ballot for the character you liked the most.
- Write a rhyming sequel to any of Dr. Seuss's classics.

Highlights:

- Entering your vote in the Great Grinch Debate.
- Visit the Grinchnet.
- Look for a list of Dr. Seuss stories online.

See also:

Seussville (Publisher Random House's Dr. Seuss site):
http://www.randomhouse.com/seussville/

http://www.disney.com

Overview:

As one might expect from the world of Disney, this is a multi-faceted site. However, many of the facets are commercial. With that in mind, immediately click the Fun button. (The words "Don't click here" should easily catch your eye.) Once there, you can find a large number of video and sound clips, photos, Mickey's Treasure Trove of Trivia, coloring book pages, puzzles, and a chance to download or play online the Great Stories Big Game Challenge.

- -

Try this:

Make sure you register; it is free. Without registering you cannot enter any of their contests and sweepstakes. You have the option of registering the whole family at once.

Highlights:

- You might want to learn about effects animation.
- This site has a very helpful search tool that can yield up to 100 results.

See also:

Universal Studios Hollywood

http://www.mca.com/unicity/

http://bexley.k12.oh.us/hs1/games/netlibs/index.htm

Overview:

How about a nice injection of nonsense into your day? They are MadLibs and they are here at Net Stop for your entertainment and learning. The resulting silly stories make you laugh and, along the way, reinforce grammar and expand your vocabulary.

The process is simple: The site prompts you for specific nouns and other parts of speech. You answer the prompts. The site inserts your responses into a prewritten story and sends back the result. How else can you explain the story about the three bears who went to Tanzania to find escargot for lunch, only to have a young girl invade their cottage and eat all their bibb lettuce?

Try this:

Create your own mad libs. Write your story. Take out some verbs, nouns, and adjectives. E-mail your list of story blanks to Net friends. They fill them out and return the responses. You fill in their answers and send back the new story.

Highlights:

- Try the random mad lib for a real surprise.
- Follow this site's link to Manuela's Recipes for some delicious variety from your kitchen.

See also:

Madlibs

http://www.mit.edu/storyfun

http://home.netscape.com/people/nathan/netnoose/index.html

Overview:

While browsing Netscape's own "What's Cool?" section you will find NetNoose. It is the old game of Hangman, and it is now in cyberspace.

A simple game, yes, but alluring when you want to pass a little time and still feel like you are challenging yourself. It is educational and entertaining.

- -

Try this:

- Compare the time it takes to solve a puzzle at each level.
- Find an opponent and adapt this game to "Wheel of Fortune" rules.

Highlights:

This game will allow your kids to work on their spelling and at the same time have fun.

See also:

BU's Interactive WWW Games

http://scv.bu.edu/Games/games.html

http://www.nikolai.com/nikolai.htm

Overview:

If you want to create puppets, concoct some interesting recipes, print out patterns to build your own little town, or follow interactive stories (complete with an online glossary), this is the site to visit.

Our hosts, characters in the software program Nikolai's Trains, also offer a workbook of interesting activities in math, geography, word play, and reading.

Try this:

Play Nikolai's Memory Game. (Make sure your images are autoloading before you start.)

Highlights:

Try the wallpaper patterns to decorate your system's desktop, as well as icons of Nikolai and his friends.

See also:

Microsoft Kids Network

http://www.msn.com/

http://www.cochran.com/theodore/

Overview:

Web sites like Theodore Tugboat's have brought viewers much closer to TV personalities, whether real or imagined. At this site, you will get a closer look at the Canadian series characters (there are more than 30) and we can learn the inner workings of the show's main setting (The Big Harbour).

You can also request a postcard from Theodore himself and you can download a page from the site's online coloring book.

Finally, you can connect to a very important part of Theodore's location: Berit's Best Sites for Children.

Try this:

Flush out an idea for a new character for the show. (How will it relate to the other characters? How will it be introduced to the show?) E-mail your ideas directly to Theodore. (He wants to hear from you.)

Highlights:

Try participating in an illustrated and interactive Internet version of a Theodore Tugboat story.

See also:

Gargoyles

http://trio.simplenet.com/Jebgarg/jeb garg.shtml

Vern's SIRDS Gallery

http://www.sirds.com/

Overview:

Have you gotten your daily dose of single image (random dot) stereograms today? If not, visit Vern's SIRDS Gallery. This collection of very interesting art pieces is privately maintained by Vern Hart, and he welcomes your contributions.

SIRDS are colorful works of art that contain hidden 3-D images. You find them by defocusing your eyes.

The site does a nice job of letting you view thumbnail images first to give you a hint of what the image is. Click it again and you will get a colorful graphic that will have you straining to look closer.

Try this:

Follow the links to find a program that will help you create your own SIRD. Two programs that will help you create a SIRD are:

(1) **Macintosh—Random-dot-stereograms**

(2) **Windows—Minding**

Highlights:

Follow the link to the SIRDS FAQ file. It will give you seven techniques for finding those elusive 3-D images.

See also:

Stereograms

http://cvs.anu.edu.au/andy/sis/sis.html

Gareth and Peter's SIRDS Pages

http://www.ccc.nottingham.ac.uk/~etzpc/sirds.html

http://www.fun1st.com/index.html

Overview:

Designing potato faces is a timeless activity. Give this site a try. It gives you good instructions, but be patient; you will be contacting the site every time you make a change to your vegetable.

Try this:

With friends, save and print images of your creations and develop an art gallery devoted to the tuber (potato).

Highlights:

Try using replacement heads, which include celebrity heads, for the faithful potato.

See also:

Mr. Edible Starchy Tuber Head

http://winnie.acsu.buffalo.edu/potatoe/

Animals, Myths & Legends

http://www.planetozkids.com

Overview:

Come visit Oban the Knowledge Keeper and discover his collection of games, activities and folklore from around the world. This site seeks to discover common themes occurring in different cultures while stimulating children to find out more about the myths and legends of their own country and other cultures.

Try this:

Go to the playroom and try Oban's Brain Torture crossword puzzle. Then, try doing a word search or travel to another playroom in the Internet universe!

Highlights:

Find a legend or myth about an animal from your country, write it in your own words in an e-mail, and send it to Oban. He'll put some of the legends he receives on his page!

See also:

HappyPuppy.com (It's All Games!)

http://www.happypuppy.com/

Voices of Youth

http://www.unicef.org/voy/

Overview:

Voices of Youth is a hip-looking, but practical site for kids sponsored by UNICEF as part of its 50th Anniversary celebration. At this site, you can take part in an electronic discussion about the future of children. Discuss ways in which the world can become a place where the rights of every child are protected from violence and exploitation.

Go to the Meeting Place and discuss your views about the following current global issues:

- Children and Work
- The Girl Child
- Children's Rights
- Children and War
- Cities and Children

Try this:

At the meeting place, explore the lives of children at work through stories and photographs. Take the children and labor quiz, and then give your opinion about the results.

Highlights:

This site can be accessed in French, Spanish and English.

It is packed with valuable information and is designed in a clear, logical sequence.

See also:

Free the Children

http://www.freethechildren.org/

Bringing School Home

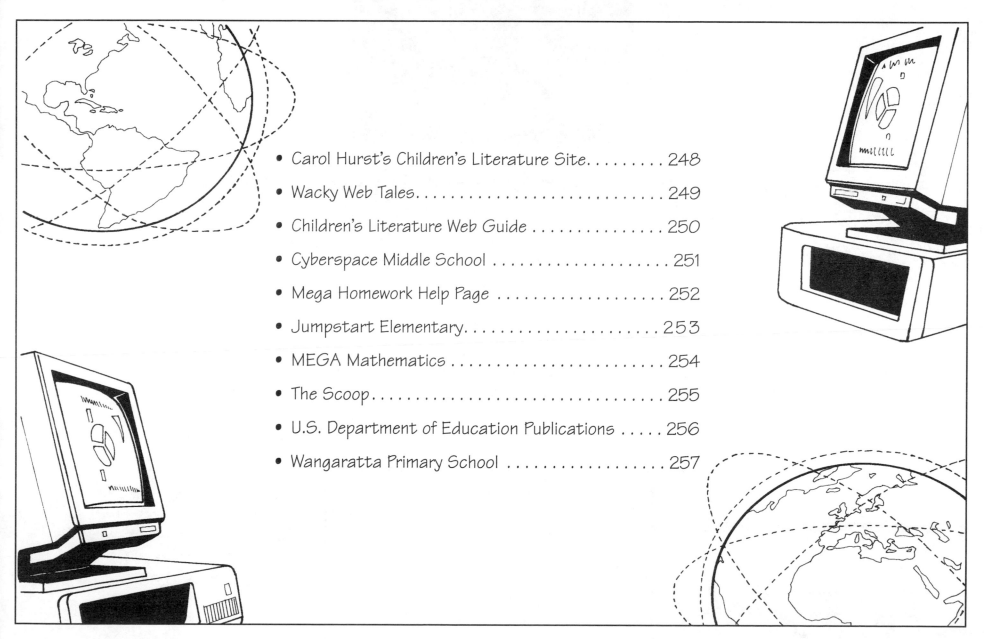

Carol Hurst's Children's Literature Site

By Carol Otis Hurst and Rebecca Otis

http://www.carolhurst.com/

Overview:

The concept at this site is simple and to the point:

Find a book you would like to read. Read a review of the book in the All Reviewed Children's Books section, and then decide if you would really be interested in reading this book. If you are, go to the library and check it out. If not, continue through the book reviews on the site and find a book more suited to your interests! Books can be located by title, author, type of book, and grade level.

- -

Try this:

Do you have a book report due? Use the book reviews at Carol Hurst's Children's Literature Site to spur your own ideas. Try a pros and cons report based on your view and others' views of the same book.

Highlights:

Carol Hurst's site provides a search tool that lets you search by title, author, publisher, or any word. (A veritable Web-based card catalog.)

See also:

Scoop: Children's Book Review Newsletter

http://www.Friend.ly.Net/scoop/

Wacky Web Tales™

Choose one of the tales below to create your own funny story.

http://www.eduplace.com/tales/

Overview:

At this zany web site, select nouns, verbs, adjectives and other types of words to fill in the blanks and create funny stories! There are over 150 stories to try, and you can even submit a tale of your own to add to the collection.

Try this:

At the Kids' Clubhouse, try a "Brain Teaser." You'll find these entertaining and quite challenging!

Highlights:

Try the Fun Stuff Activites Center in the Kids' Clubhouse.

Use the Outline Maps in the Social Studies Center for your next country report.

See also:

Ready To Learn
http://www.libertynet.org:80/community/whyy/rtl.html

http://acs6.acs.ucalgary.ca/~dkbrown/index.html

Overview:

Links—numerous, focused, and valuable—are what stand out at this site. Parents, teachers, writers, and kids can use this site, which is far from just a collection of pointers to other pages.

The site's developer, David Brown of the University of Calgary, encourages art and written submissions from kids, sends us to some well-developed sites for online children's stories, and links us to children's literature associations, discussion groups, research guides, and additional family-related sites.

- -

Try this:

- Read one of the online stories and submit a piece of art related to it.
- Follow a link to other kids' writing and send the authors a letter or a piece of art related to their stories.

Highlights:

- Try following the links for contemporary online children's stories to books (some even illustrated) by Ludwig Bemelmans, the author of **Madeline**.
- Reader's Theatre scripts can be found online and ready for use in the classroom.

See also:

Vandergrift's Young Adult Literature Page

http://www.scils.rutgers.edu/special/kay/yalit.html

Cyberspace Middle School

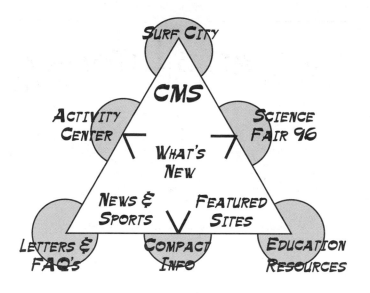

Cyberspace Middle School

http://www.scri.fsu.edu/~dennisl/CMS.html

Overview:

Cyberspace Middle School connects kids and teachers from grades 6-9. One of this site's strengths is its well-conceived set of links to interesting and fun sites. Most visitors would be quite pleased to just wander through this site, follow the CMS's Surf City links, bookmark some sites, and log off.

There is much more, such as its Science Fair component, which offers a help desk, hints for selecting and completing a project, and worthwhile links to more science activities.

- -

Try this:

- Submit an item for their News and Sports from Around the World section.
- Glean some great ideas for science activities.

Highlights:

- Take a look at the "Lift the Planets" activity. (You will need 318 pennies for this one, so save up.)
- Consider using this site for your next classroom science fair.

See also:

The European Schools Project

http://www.esp.educ.uva.nl/

Mega Homework Help Page

http://www.maurine.com/student.htm

Overview:

Okay, kids, let's try out this scenario: You have to do a report on Emily Dickinson's life and works and it is due tomorrow. As "unrealistic" as that dilemma may sound, the Web is here to help you out with The Mega Homework Help Page, whose subject-oriented links point you to a variety of helpful resources. Many of the links are fairly high-level, but if you hunt-and-click enough, you are bound to find some material that is sure to impress your teacher.

Try this:

Use the Mega Search feature and check out the top 2,500 virtual reference sites by subject area.

Highlights:

Along with the more advanced resources, The Mega Homework Page offers links to younger kid's sites.

See also:

Information SuperLibrary(tm)

http://www.mcp.com/137135001568875/

http://www.knowledgeadventure.com/home/

Overview:

Versatility is one of many strong points at Jumpstart Elementary, brought to you by software developer, Knowledge Adventure. This first-ever 3-D learning environment provides activities at five different levels—from toddler through second grade.

The developers' creative design will lure you to fully explore the site. During your visit, make sure you click on the field trip button which will lead to several exciting options:

- Dr. Brain Thinking Games
- Favorite Games at the Kids Space
- Kids Encyclopedia

Try this:

- What activities at this site could you recreate for a school project? Classic Concentration would be a good start.
- Act as tour guide to Jumpstart Elementary for a younger child.

Highlights:

Try the letsfindout.com feature. This searchable index is a great homework helper. Search for any subject from A-Z in this encyclopedia designed just for kids.

See also:

Kidworld

http://www.bconnex.net/~kidworld/

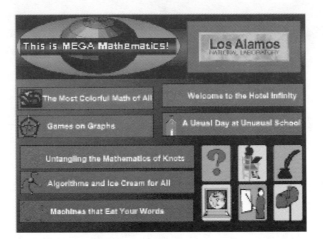

http://www.c3.lanl.gov/mega-math/index.html

Overview:

Finding out why there is so much mathematics involved in the simple act of coloring is just one of the revelations at MEGA Mathematics. Each of the site's main sections (The Most Colorful Math of All, Games on Graphs, Untangling the Mathematics of Knots, Algorithms and Ice Cream for All, Machines that Eat Your Words, Welcome to the Hotel Infinity, A Usual Day at Unusual School) has its own imagemap which supplies a visitor with a veritable mini-course on the subject.

Aside from the site's comprehensive and quality organization, MEGA Mathematics makes math truly interesting.

Try this:

Investigate the section called Games on Graphs and teach the outside games Squelch and Pop or Toss 'N Sort to your teacher.

Highlights:

- The Map Coloring Activities are very intriguing, especially the Making a Two-Colorable Map activity.

- MEGA Math also uses helpful hypertext to define important terms.

See also:

Clever Games for Clever People

http://www.cs.uidaho.edu/~casey931/conway/games.html

http://www.friend.ly.net/scoop/

Overview:

The Scoop offers kid activities, book reviews, and links to other popular sites for parents, teachers, and kids. As of this writing, there is plenty of value here, but future plans for The Scoop (an interactive reading adventure, a readers' top ten list, a chat room, and interviews with authors and illustrators) will substantially enhance this site's value.

- -

Try this:

Use the reviews to guide you on your next trip to the library.

Highlights:

Go to the illustrated instructions on building a bird drinking fountain and the Egret, one of the models from the book **Best Ever Paper Airplanes** by Norman Schmidt.

See also:

Internet Public Library Youth Division

http://www.ipl.org/youth/

U.S. Department of Education Publications

http://www.ed.gov/pubs/parents.html

Overview:

Its how-to orientation on school topics can benefit new and old teachers alike, as well as its primary audience—parents. The main topics are quite comprehensive.

Helping Your Child:

- Learn Math
- Learn to Read
- Learn History
- Get Ready for School
- Improve in Test Taking
- To Write Well

- Use the Library (also a Spanish version)
- Learn Science (also a Spanish version)
- Learn Geography
- Succeed in School
- With Homework
- Learn Responsible Behavior

Another plus is effective lesson/activity plans that accompany each topic. Continue reading below this main section, as there are other helpful links you may want to follow.

Try this:

Do not keep this information to yourself. Do you know a PTA newsletter or home school parent who could use it? Pass it on.

Highlights:

Here is a way to keep your kids academically involved during vacation, by using this site's Summer Home Learning Recipes (courtesy of the National Education Association).

See also:

The Digital Classroom

http://www.nara.gov/education/

Wangaratta Primary School

http://www.ozemail.com.au/~wprimary/wps.htm

Overview:

Let's visit the Wangaratta Primary School from Victoria, Australia. The activities here offer an interesting, interactive look at the country. To begin, you can make a sugar glider kite and a hopping kangaroo. Then, print out a drawing of a rainbow lorikeet and move on to the Aussie animals wordsearch. There is still more to learn. So, even if you are out of school, check this site out.

- -

Try this:

Visit, then e-mail Matthew Slater, Wangaratta's resident "Net Guru." Then just await his response.

Highlights:

Listen to the kookaburra, the Australian bush bird.

See also:

The Perth Zoo

http://www.perthzoo.wa.gov.au/

Broadening Your Knowledge Base

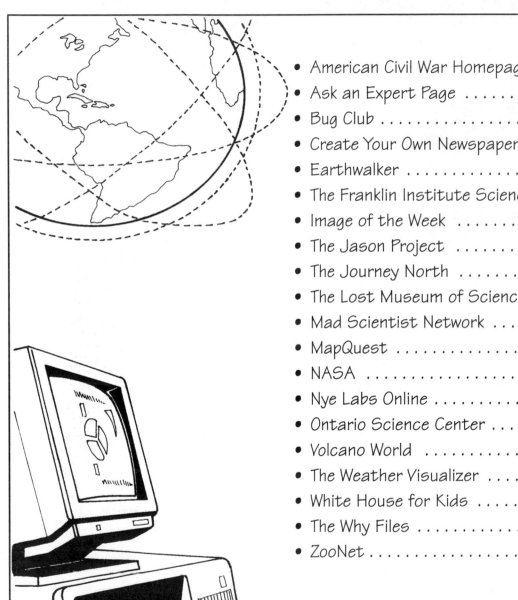

American Civil War

Homepage

http://sunsite.utk.edu/civil-war/

Overview:

You really do not have to take a side to enjoy this site. With its far-reaching links, the American Civil War Homepage should satisfy history buffs from all corners of the United States.

- Delve into the personal side of the war by reading letters and diaries written during that time.
- Look up soldiers' names in the combatants' rosters.
- Remind yourself of the chronology of the war with this site's helpful timelines.
- Embellish a school report by linking up with the various roundtables of Civil War historians.

Your options abound.

Try this:

- Create a photo album and supply your own historically accurate captions.
- Compare daily life in your town with that of people living during the time of the Civil War.

Highlights:

- There are an abundance of images from the Civil War.
- The maps that this site provides weave the importance of geography of regions into the story of the Civil War.

See also:

The Smithsonian Associates Civil War Studies

http://www.si.edu/tsa/cw/one-day.htm

http://njnie.dl.stevens-tech.edu/curriculum/aska.html

Overview:

Experts are scattered across the Internet. However, this page brings together dozens of them to help educate you on subjects from animal care to geology to the Amish. It is quality information at the right price, and it almost always arrives in a reasonable amount of time. If you cannot find what you are looking for, this page offers links to yet other experts' pages.

- -

Try this:

Do you have a question? Involve a friend. Guess your own answers to the question. The person with the closest guess gets to ask the other to do him/her a favor. Make sure you e-mail a thank-you to "your" expert.

Highlights:

Asking questions to experts in the field of your question. For example, asking a professional mover about moving costs and tips before moving to another state.

See also:

Internet Public Library

http://www.ipl.org/

WELCOME
to the
Bug Club
on the World Wide Web

http://www.ex.ac.uk/bugclub/

Overview:

Whether you like bugs or not, they are everywhere and they are here to stay. Even on the Web. Because the Bug Club treats insects as pets, it does a nice job of making them interesting and, for the squeamish, perhaps even tolerable. To start, visitors can learn plenty from the care sheets and use the built-in search engine to extend that learning beyond this site. Even with most of the pages under construction, including the Clickable Bug Hunt, this is a site worth visiting.

By the time this book is in your hands, though, you will most likely be playing entomologist with your mouse at the ready.

Try this:

Visit the Pen Pals List. Find a teammate to create your own care sheet on a bug not yet covered by this site.

Highlights:

The Bug Club's 17-page newsletter could have been a site by itself. Bee lore, build-a-bug, and a puzzle page are just a few of its features.

See also:

The Wonderful World of Insects

http://www.insect-world.com/

(This site has been developed by the Bug Club's creator, Gordon Ramel.)

http://crayon.net/

Overview:

This site truly delivers what it promises—a user-customized newspaper—its services are free, and you get an informative, up-to-date product.

CRAYON offers a variety of foreign publications, such as the Daily News from Iceland, and it lets users customize their papers in just a couple of steps.

Some tips:

1. Closely follow the directions on how to save your newspaper.
2. Be sure to place your paper toward the top of your hotlist.
3. Decide ahead of time whether or not you want your graphics displayed. If they are autoloaded, this could slow down your access time considerably.

Try this:

- Follow one news story and compare its coverage in three vastly different sources.
- Design a separate paper for a friend.

Highlights:

This site has a superb variety of news and entertainment links.

It has an excellent frequently asked questions file.

See also:

Yahoo! News Summary

http://www.yahoo.com/headlines/current/news/summary.html

http://home.earthlink.net/~earthwalker1/

Overview:

Planning on circumnavigating the world? If so, check out this site and read about Dave Kunst's incredible journey. Marvel at the man's endurance and determination in the face of adversity.

To get more details on the trip, be sure to follow the link to the Campus Press article.

Try this:

- Do you need a writing project for school? Visit this site and then write a story through the eyes of Drifter the dog or Willie Makeit, the donkey.

- E-mail Dave and try to arrange a Web chat between him and your family or class.

Highlights:

See the photos of his journey.

See also:

An Appalachian Adventure

http://www.news-observer.com/AT/ATmain2.html

http://sln.fi.edu/tfi/welcome.html

Overview:

Versatile—that is the best word for Franklin Institute Science Museum's site. With its demonstrations, its inQuiry Almanack, and its publications library, it makes science a fun and interesting pastime. It also does an excellent job of providing extra goodies not directly related to science, such as its World Wide Web Workbook (a primer for those new to the medium).

Try this:

Suggest to your teacher the idea of a resident science student. (Get to know Franklin Institute's very well so you will be clear on the concept.) When your teacher gives the okay, offer to be the first to play the role.

Highlights:

The resident student who provides a younger person's point of view toward science and technology.

See also:

The Museum of Science, Boston

http://www.mos.org/

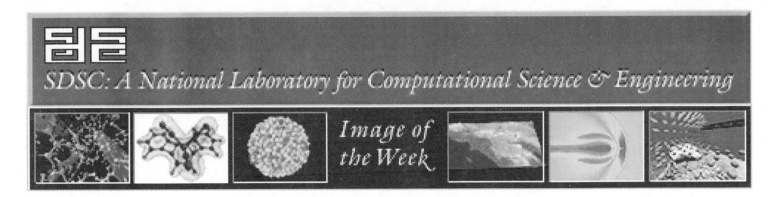

http://www.sdsc.edu/IOTW/

Overview:

The San Diego Supercomputer Center, with the help of contributors, is putting some artistic muscle into its computing chores. And we are the beneficiaries of some intriguing images such as a virtual wheelchair, a triple-helical DNA in a bath of sodium ions, and a VRML (virtual reality modeling language) image of Hurricane Emilia. While you are here, use the browse and search tools to give yourself an informal (perhaps slow-paced) slide show.

Try this:

Paste one of the images into your own paint program and manipulate it with your own tools.

Highlights:

- This site offers lots of information in connection with its images.
- Follow this site's link to the Global Information Infrastructure and you will pick up even more Internet expertise.

See also:

EarthRISE

http://earthrise.sdsc.edu/earthrise/main.html

http://www.jasonproject.org/

Overview:

Because of the Jason Project's impressive selection of activities, you could spend whole days at this site. The Jason Project offers to teachers, students, and scientists first-hand involvement in its various expeditions. Parents and kids will appreciate the vast amount of information, while teachers will like the way the creators link the activities with instructional frameworks and other resources on the Net.

Tip: The various pages are filled with images, so if you want to speed up your navigation, make sure you have turned off your autoload images feature.

Try this:

- Try keeping your own diary of your explorations with and revelations from the JASON project. Make believe you are on the expeditions yourself.

- Follow the link to the Critter Quiz.

Highlights:

Follow their summary of Jason Project VI, Project Earth. The site offers so many details about the project that you will feel as if you area crew member.

See also:

Titanic from Britannica Online

http://titanic.eb.com/01_01.html

The
Journey North

http://ics.soe.umich.edu/JourneyNorth/IAPHome.html

Overview:

At this site, the University of Michigan's Dewey Web weaves literature, culture, meteorology, and ecology into the International Arctic Project, which began in 1994 and ended in the spring of 1995.

Clicking on Arctic Bites offers visitors a collection of fiction and non-fiction to set the stage for the journey. To get a detailed overview of the expedition, you should click the International Arctic Project link. This is where you get to know the travellers and learn about all that went into the preparation and follow-through of the mission. Finally, click on Wild Adventurers to follow a northern migration of wildlife.

Try this:

As with the Jason Project, follow this story as if you were part of the expedition. Then write your own account of the trip. Give yourself daily duties, believable mishaps, courageous actions.

Highlights:

In the Arctic Bites section, the Inuit point-of-view is especially interesting.

See also:

The Arctic Refuge and Its Coastal Plain: Controversy and Debate

http://www.lib.uconn.edu/ArcticCircle/ANWR/anwrdebateindex.html

The Lost Museum of Sciences

http://www.fortunecity.com/victorian/museum/88/lostmuseum.html

Overview:

This site wants you to get lost in its maze of museums. Currently, the Lost Museum of Sciences features a total of 630 links—415 to museums and 215 to related sites. It also offers an organized index. Have fun wandering around.

Try this:

Not only should you enter the World Muse Trivia contests, but you should also send the questions to your teachers, grandparents, classmates, etc. (You can make it a local contest; the winner gets treated to ice cream.)

Highlights:

Try the Find the Exhibit activity. This is a good way to send visitors to a museum that they may not otherwise explore.

See also:

SciEd: Science and Mathematics Education Resources

http://www-hpcc.astro.washington.edu/scied/scnce.html

Mad Scientist Network

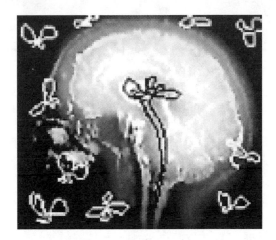

http://128.252.223.239/~ysp/MSN/

Overview:

Talk about covering all forms of science! These informed folks will search high and low, do whatever is needed, to get a satisfactory answer to your question. Along with their ability to seek (and usually find) answers to your submitted questions within ten days, the Mad Scientist Network's easy interface, for visitors, is a matter of clicking on one of the 24 branches of science and browsing the questions currently under discussion. And if you don't find the needed information there, check into the MSN's archives.

Try this:

- Use the MSN to settle a difference of opinion between the scientists in your family.
- Compare the Mad Scientists' answers with information from printed resources.

Highlights:

The Mad Scientists have escaped the laboratory long enough to put together an excellent library, covering 16 branches of science and a link to Pitsco's superb "ask-an-expert" launch pad.

See also:

SCIENCE HOBBYIST

http://www.eskimo.com:80/~billb/

MapQuest

http://www.mapquest.com/

Overview:

For those of you who have trouble getting from point A to point B, MapQuest is the site for you. Visit the TripQuest section and get driving directions to locations all over Canada, Mexico, and the United States.

Just as impressive, the Interactive Atlas supplies 11 different options for customizing maps, and that doesn't count the following points of interest that you can highlight:

- Personal
- Banking
- Recreation

- Education
- Automotive
- Services

- Civic
- Health Care
- Transportation

- Lodging
- Attractions
- Shopping

- Web Sites
- Entertainment
- Dining

So hop in that car, train, or plane, but first arm yourself with a map from MapQuest.

Try this:

- Using Map Quest to get the names of existing establishments, add real-life details to your own historical fiction-writing projects.
- Create your own stories similar to those of an elusive female crime gang leader who stars on a PBS quiz show.

Highlights:

This service is FREE, and they give you your own URL. (It is not easy to remember, but they make sure that once you have registered make sure you bookmark the page for easy repeat visits.

See also:

Mapmaker, Mapmaker, Make Me a Map

http://www.utenn.edu/uwa/vpps/ur/ut2kids/maps/map.html

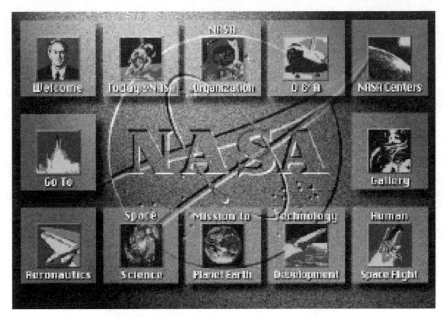

http://www.nasa.gov/

Overview:

Even those of you with more "earthbound" interests will be impressed after browsing through the NASA Gallery. Visitors who were around for that first step on the moon will enjoy a whole section on **Apollo 11**, including audio and video. Beyond that, there are reviews of other missions, visits to the various space centers, a very helpful Go To: page for some navigational help, and payloads of other right stuff.

Try this:

Create your own guess-this-planet game. Use your favorite drawing program to paste an image and some factual hints about a mystery planet. Then quiz a willing contestant.

Highlights:

The question and answer section alone is worth a lengthy visit. It breaks down your questions into subject areas, and you are given a search engine to conduct further investigations.

See also:

An Inquirer's Guide to The Universe

http://www.fi.edu/planets/planets.html

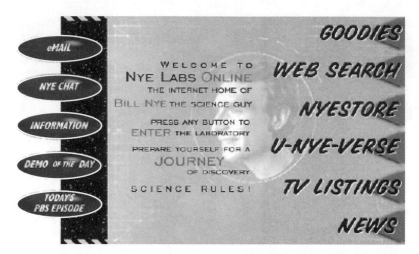

http://nyelabs.kcts.org/flash_go.html

Overview:

Bill Nye has made science enjoyable for young and old alike. He is a bit of a gonzo-scientist whose public broadcasting system shows you wild, entertaining graphics and skits until you give up and admit you have learned a lot within 30 minutes. The Web site is not as entertaining as his TV show, but as Web sites go, this one is still packed with solid entertainment and information. This site does rely heavily on graphics for navigation, so for a more efficient visit, turn off your image-loading option and use the text menus.

Try this:

- Conduct one of Bill's experiments. Then add a variable or two, compare your results, and e-mail them directly to Bill.

- Set up an appointment with other viewers in the Chat Room of Science.

Highlights:

- The U-NYE-VERSE, which offered a helpful episode guide, including a related activity, home experiments, and a memo from Bill.

- Look up the demo of the day.

See also:

The Internet Public Library's Dr. Science
http://ipl.org/youth/scipage.html

http://www.osc.on.ca/

Overview:

If you are at all interested in science, take the tour of the Ontario Science Centre. If your visiting time at the Centre is limited, go straight to The Interactive Zone. Be sure to click on the Web Connections button. This section provides visitors with well-conceived lists of interesting, informative links. The Cool Science section will be especially helpful.

Try this:

Need a refresher on conducting a science experiment? Work with the Interactive Zone activities and break them down into a problem-hypothesis-observation-conclusion format.

Highlights:

With the help of Sound Machine (a helper application) and an Interactive Zone activity, do a comparative study of three heart sounds—one after a heart attack, one with a murmur, and one that is healthy.

See also:

Museum of Science

http://www.mos.org/

http://volcano.und.nodak.edu/

Overview:

For most, Volcano World gives all the information you would need about volcanoes. And if you do need more, Volcano World will link you to other sites erupting with geologic facts.

This site has a great orientation toward graphics—enough to keep your interest and to inform but not so many that page-loading would make you lose interest.

Make sure you check out the "what's new?" section. Volcano World's developers do a nice job of keeping us updated on often unexplored content. Further enhancing includes an on-site search tool and the ask a volcanologist feature. When you are finished here, you will be bubbling over with information about volcanoes.

Try this:

If kids in your class have questions about volcanoes, you can look up answers in Volcano World's already asked questions section. If the answer is not there, you can submit the question.

Highlights:

The Kid's Door will lead you to such things as virtual field trips, kid's art, volcano quizzes, and Volcano World's search tool.

See also:

Stromboli Online

http://www.ezinfo.ethz.ch/volcano/strombolihomee.html

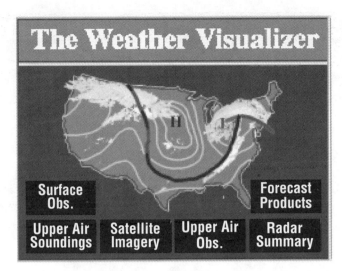

http://covis.atmos.uiuc.edu/covis/visualizer/

Overview:

At the Weather Visualizer, you can create weather maps to your own liking. You can select specific regions you want to view, among numerous other choices which include the kinds of images you want to access, such as radar, satellite, and surface readings.

Some tips:

-Keep your autoload images turned on.

-This site requires a lot of your system's resources, so you may not want to stay too long.

-Take the time to review tips on accessing images.

To avoid data overload, keep your requests fairly simple.

Try this:

Compare the readings from your region over a 12-hour period. Save each image and paste them into a graphics document. Observe the changes.

Highlights:

By clicking various links you will receive a personal tutorial on weather. Just click on a term and its helper page pops right up.

See also:

WeatherNet

http://cirrus.sprl.umich.edu/wxnet/states/states.html

http://www.whitehouse.gov/WH/kids/html/kidshome.html

Overview:

The White House for Kids is a good idea, though a bit underdeveloped. The site brings us a bit closer to the first families and the interface is simple, including a clear set of directions on how to follow Socks, your guide, on the tour.

- -

Try this:

Follow the links to Welcome to the White House. Then take the historical tour and view the White House's art collection. While there, listen to some of President Clinton's radio addresses and use them as a basis for a letter to him.

Highlights:

Listen to the stories about the president, vice president, and their wives when they were kids.

See also:

Congress.org

http://legislators.com/congressorg2/main.html

THE Why? FILES
SCIENCE BEHIND THE NEWS   FUNDED BY THE NATIONAL SCIENCE FOUNDATION

http://whyfiles.news.wisc.edu

Overview:

Mission: Bring scientific knowledge out of the labs and lecture halls and into our homes.

Mission accepted and accomplished: The National Science Foundation's Why Files

This site:

- poses, then investigates, intriguing questions. For example, can bacteria come back to life?
- shakes up conventional wisdom. For example, Electric Cars—Are they really as good as they are cracked up to be?

You will be able to use and reuse the Why Files Archives, which offer a helpful search engine and outstanding, hypertext treatments of previously-discussed topics such as Nature's Flypaper and Cross-Species Transplants.

- -

Try this:

Don't miss the Sports section. It leads to several interesting brainteasers.

Highlights:

Visit the Cool Science Images department. They are cool to look at, but this site adds very instructive captions to enrich the experience.

See also:

Science Hobbyist

http://www.eskimo.com:80/~billb/

http://www.mindspring.com/~zoonet/

Overview:

Want an on-demand picture of a kongoni or a gavial? ZooNet is your source. Creator/director Jim Henley calls this site an attempt to provide a single point of entry to ALL ZOOS EVERYWHERE.

This site's strengths lie in the extensive image galleries, including a slide show feature, as well as numerous links to other nature-related sites.

Try this:

Using ZooNet's extensive image galleries and your own graphics program, create a matching quiz of some very obscure animals. Do some research on the animals so you can give your "victim" a hint or two. Then find a friend and have him/her check his/her "Zoo IQ."

Highlights:

- Kids will like Zoospell, where they will be shown a picture of an animal if they correctly spell its name. (Users will need Netscape 2.0 or later to use this feature.)
- Visit the Wolf Pack Picture Gallery which includes 36 links to related sites.

See also:

NetVet

http://netvet.wustl.edu/

Enriching Your Family Life

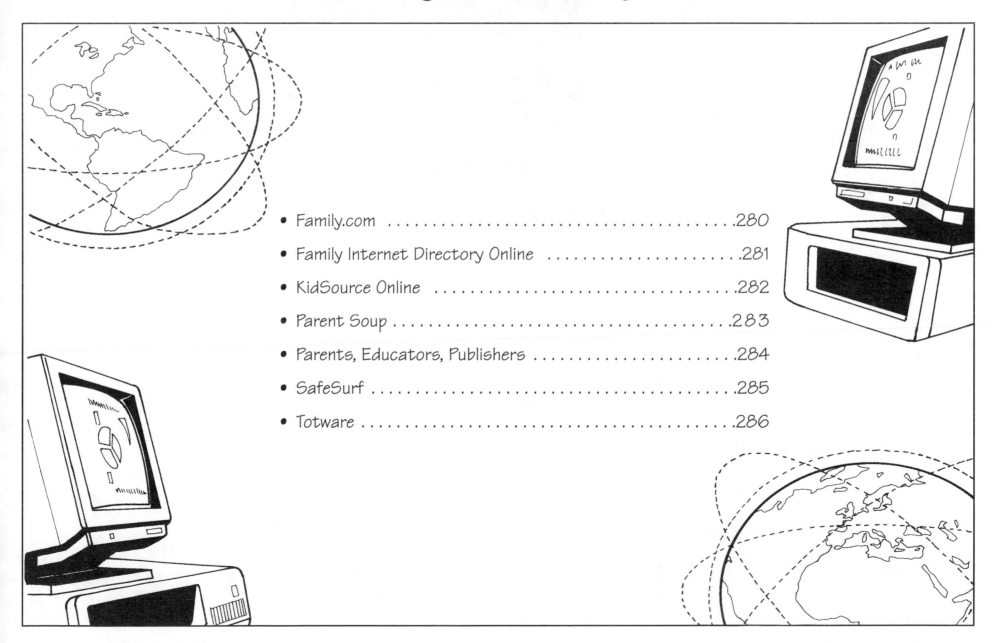

Family.com

http://family.go.com/

Overview:

This site, another winning service from Disney, offers a myriad of reviews and advice columns, helpful to a wide range of family members.

Need help getting kids to develop proper etiquette? No problem. How about some recommendations on toys or parenting books? Those are here too. Do your kids need summer jobs to keep them busy? Simply go to the search function and type in keywords or phrases. You will find interesting articles and advice just waiting for your perusal.

Try this:

Take advantage of Family.com's D'Cards to send electronic greetings to friends.

Click on the activity section and then check out the 365 TV Free Activities arranged by subject.

Highlights:

Try the cookbook with its tips, recipes, and weekly additions.

See also:

http://www.parentsplace.com/

http://www.clark.net/pub/soh/fido.htm

Overview:

One of many high-quality family-focused sites on the Web, the Family Internet Directory Online zeroes in on being the Yellow Pages for parents and kids.

Along with presenting its Blue Ribbon Site of the Day and Leader of the Pack links, FIDO also offers over 300 connections to sites in categories such as parents' resources, art, sports, music, museums, movies, and games. In addition to those expected categories, it features links to teachers' guides, community action, and even sites with more links. Before you complete your first visit, though, sign up for FIDO's newsletter.

- -

Try this:

Follow the Community Action links and see what you can do to contribute to our society.

Highlights:

Take FIDO's CyberTour.

See also:

Children Now

http://www.dnai.com/~children/

http://www.kidsource.com/

Overview:

KidSource wants to be an "information assistant" for those with concerns about kids from age zero to 18, and it follows through quite nicely. It provides a navigable interface to get you where you want to go.

Added features of this site:

- There are 13 pertinent and easy-to-use online discussion forums. The site's forum software even lets registered users add their photographs.
- The site has its own computer donation program.
- There are frequent visitor surveys about child-related issues.

Try this:

Set up your own survey about kid-related issues. Ask kids and parents the same question. Keep the results separate. Then submit your results to KidSource.

Highlights:

Try subscribing to the computers and kids forum. This forum includes 14 separate discussions. The moderator of this forum is the co-author of **The Computer Museum Guide to the Best Software for Kids**.

See also:

International Kids' Space

http://www.kids-space.org/

http://www.parentsoup.com/

Overview:

Parent Soup consists of 14 main "ingredients" that comprise parenting. Its thoroughness and sense of humor make it a joy to visit. One of this site's obvious strengths is its commitment to live chat. On most days, at least six sessions are scheduled, with themes ranging from Singles Support to Military Families to Kids Only.

One of the sites ingredients, called Chill Out, offers 17 relaxation techniques, a cartoon section, and weekly installments of A Mom's Life and A Dad's Life. But there is so much more to this mix. Take the time to share and glean some parenting wisdom.

Try this:

- Search the archives for helpful discussions.
- If you are having a disagreement on an issue, search Parent Soup for either a suggested resolution or for some supportive arguments.

Highlights:

Checkout Parent Soup's free electronic newsletter, Parent Soup News.

See also:

The CyberMom Dot Com

http://www.thecybermom.com/

http://www.microweb.com/pepsite/

Overview:

Parents, Educators, and Publishers (PEP) is brought to you by Warren Buckleitner, editor of the **Children's Software Revue**, and Anne Bubnic, who runs Custom Computers for Kids. They want to help visitors become informed buyers of educational software, and their site offers plenty of pertinent resources to that end.

Buckleitner shares his seven-point software evaluation instrument. PEP also offers an expanded all-star list of top software choices, links to favorite school sites, and, to be expected, plenty of software reviews. Look for even more features (such as a site of the week) in the future.

Try this:

Build a software wish list from knowledge gleaned from this site. Let this list help you prioritize those purchases.

Highlights:

PEP offers a software search tool. You can search by title, publisher, age, category (e.g., early learning or science), and the computer platform you use. It is fast and efficient.

See also:

Classroom Connect:
http://www.classroom.net/

Educational Software Institute Online
http://www.edsoft.com/

http://www.safesurf.com/index.html

Overview:

When you follow the link to the SafeSurf/Kid's Wave site, the following words should catch your eye:

IMPORTANT WARNING: Due to the present structure of the World Wide Web, parental supervision is highly recommended for children surfing the Net.

SafeSurf is dedicated to correcting the situation. We need your support in this effort. You can see that dedication in their own Internet rating standard, a monthly online newsletter, and their Internet Lifeguard, a set of common sense steps toward family-safe computing. For example, consider placing the computer in a "family room" in your home.

SafeSurf-approved sites fall into the following categories: elementary ages, older kids/parents, space stuff, and commercial sites.

- -

Try this:

Do your own sleuthing for kid-safe sites and submit your discoveries to SafeSurf.

Highlights:

- Check out World Village, SafeSurf's favorite site of the month.
- Make a print-out of their Internet Lifeguard.

See also:

NetParents.org

http://www.netparents.org/

http://www.het.brown.edu/people/mende/totware.html

Overview:

Totware is for those parents who would like to find some affordable software for the newcomer to computer technology. The Mende family (now with the help of other visitors' recommendations) list PC and **Mac** programs that do a nice job of introducing kids to the computer.

- -

Try this:

Define your software needs. Then try out the shareware and ask yourself, "Will I get more relative value from a commercial product?"

Highlights:

This site reminds visitors that shareware may be expensive. How? Its immediate cost may seem low, but the program's relative value may be much less than what you pay for a commercial product.

See also:

The Usenet newsgroup

news:misc.kids.computer

Getting Direction on the Net

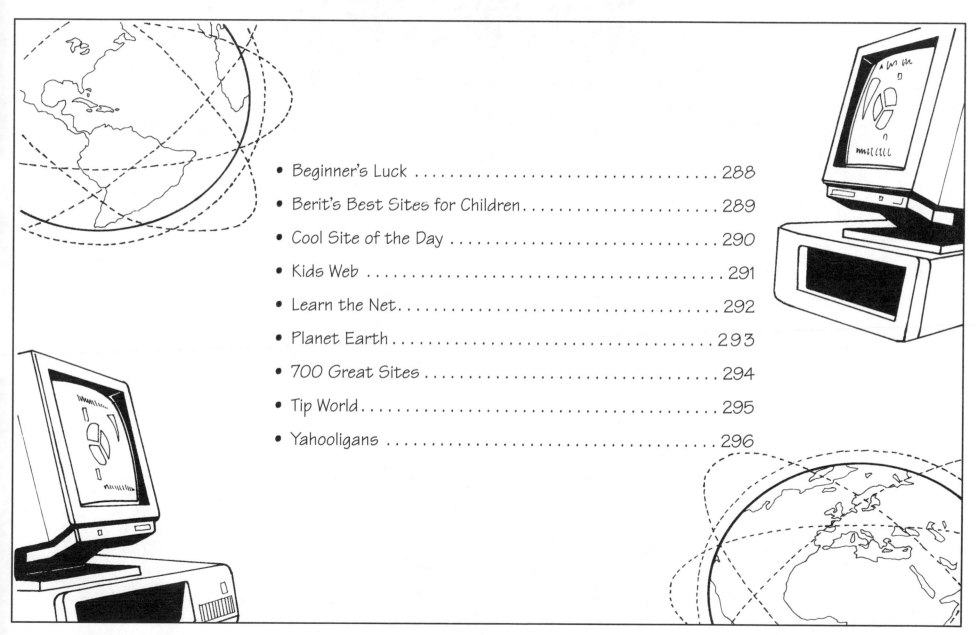

http://www.execpc.com/~wmhogg/beginner.html

Overview:

Part of The Internet Pearls Index, this site is subtitled Helpful Resources for Internet Novices. The site's creator, SoloTech Software, has created massive lists of links (at least 420 of them at this site alone) that are divided into the following categories:

1. Searching the Internet
2. Internet Guides and Tutorials
3. What's New All Over
4. Helpful Computer Magazines on the Web
5. Help with HTML and Web Publishing
6. Backgrounds, Icons, and Images for Your Web Site
7. Good Internet Starting Points
8. Internet Access
9. General Reference
10. Free-Nets
11. Selected World-Wide Web Virtual Libraries

The site is fairly slow to load and reload, but that is the only drawback to this site. The results are worth the wait.

Try this:

Plan to introduce a friend to the Internet. Sift through these lists and choose what you feel are the ten best to show your friend.

Highlights:

You will find excellent sources of tutorials, graphics, and icons for designing your own Web page.

See also:

Search Tools for Mining the Internet

http://www.classroom.com/resource/search.asp

http://www.cochran.com/theosite/KSites.html

Overview:

When users discuss the various Web indices for kids, this set of five Web pages is inevitably mentioned, and always in the most glowing of terms. Berit Erickson, Online Librarian for Theodore Tugboat's Online Activity Centre (also featured in this book), has placed sites in the following categories (followed by two sample sub-categories):

- Just for Fun (Activity Centers, Crafts and Coloring)
- Kids on the Net (Find a Pen Pal, Elementary Schools)
- Creatures Great and Small (Dinosaurs, Creepie Crawlies)
- Serious Stuff (Art Galleries, World Travel)
- And More . . . (Safe Play on the Internet, Other Children's Site Indexes)

Try this:

Berit encourages suggestions, so if you find a winning site, let him know and make Berit's that much better.

Highlights:

Along with the organization and the impressive number of links, he has a 5-point rating system.

See also:

Inforamp Stuff for Kids

http://db.cochran.com/li_toc:theoPage.db

IBM K-12 Links (go to Web Links)

http://www.solutions.ibm.com/k12/

http://cool.infi.net/

Overview:

There are plenty of pointers to new and cool sites. This one has been chosen because of the following:

1. The way the site delves into the issue of "coolness," including the discovery of a new chemical element called "coolium" by one Richard Grimes.

2. The site assures us that Richard Grimes is not dangerous, except to himself.

3. We are encouraged to create coolium ourselves. All we need to do is create something useful, entertaining, surprising, and cognizant of the technological demands on most Webheads' computers.

Try this:

- Visit some sites and consider whether you can use any of their features in something you might create—be it a school report, a work of art, or a piece of writing.
- Make up your "coolness" criteria.

Highlights:

- Visit this site's choices for Cool Site of the Year and Still Cool.
- Check out the Iso-Topically Cool links. There are new ones each week.

See also:

Cool Sites-
http://home.netscape.com/home/

Exploratorium's Ten Cool Sites

http://www.exploratorium.edu/learning _studio/sciencesites.html

http://www.npac.syr.edu/textbook/kidsweb/

Overview:

Kids Web, part of the Syracuse University Living Schoolbook Project, defines itself as a World Wide Web digital library for schoolkids. It does exhibit a stronger academic focus than many of the pages offering links of interest to kids.

In addition, it does a nice job of achieving its main objective: supplying valuable links to material that is presented at most kids' level of interest and comprehension. For those who wish to further research topics, Kids Web offers higher-level links, as well.

The site responsibly warns us that documents accessed from this library are on Web servers all over the world. Links to these computers may be very slow or even temporarily inaccessible.

- -

Try this:

Use Kids Web as your home page for a week and see how well it works as your starting point for searches and browsing. (Just paste its URL in the home page location in General Preferences, under Options.)

Highlights:

- Kids Web offers an extensive list of geography links.

It also offers great reference links. (Similar in quality to the Research-It Web site.)

See also:

4Kids Treehouse

http://www.4kids.com/kidshome.html

Learn the Net

THE ESSENTIAL INTERNET ONLINE

http://www.learnthenet.com/english/index.html

Overview:

For a good electronic overview of the Net, visit this site. It offers a clear orientation to its approach and follows up, section-by-section, with helpful links within the site itself or to other Web sites. Every page also features an easy-to-find link to its glossary of 149 terms.

Learn what the Net's five main sections are:

- Internet Basics
- Digging for Data
- Doing Business
- Web Publishing
- Communicating

Keep this site in mind when you need a quick reminder of what to do with what resource at what site.

Try this:

Along with the Beginner's Luck site, use Learn the Net when you are giving a novice a little introductory overview of life in cyberspace.

Highlights:

Take the time to visit the Web Publishing section and bookmark the Under Construction page. It does a creditable job of helping you plan your own home page before you even touch the keyboard.

See also:

NetLearn

http://www.rgu.ac.uk/schools/sim/research/netlearn/callist.htm

Planet Earth   Home Page

http://www.tidusa.com/IE4_NS4_index.html

Overview:

Talk about a world of information at your fingertips! After a visit to Planet Earth, it is hard not to get smarter. Plus, this site makes it all so easy. You get to choose six ways to explore their virtual library:

- Navigational Image Map
- Museums
- Worlds of Numbers

- Reading Room
- Search Engines
- The Earth 13 Room Floorplan

Make sure you take time to visit the Multimedia Gallery. It offers several interesting links, though the download times for any virtual reality files might be a bit long.

Try this:

- Using trivia question cards, give points if you can find the answer via this site.
- Create your own board game using the Planet Earth Comprehensive Image Map as the board.

Highlights:

Planet Earth's Comprehensive Image Map engulfs you with well-organized links to all corners of the Internet.

See also:

Views of Planet Earth

http://spaceart.com/solar/eng/earth.htm

http://www.ala.org/parentspage/greatsites/amazing.html

Overview:

700+ Great Sites is a colorful site put together by the Children and Technology Committee of the American Library Association. The ALA is very deliberate in making choices, considering essentials such as appropriateness, content, ease of navigation and interactivity.

Try this:

- Visit the other pick-of-the-day sites and compare the choices. (Plan on hotlisting daily.)
- Make your own pick-of-the-day for other friends and family members.

Highlights:

View the sites for girls (Girls Can!) and the compilation of sites in Spanish (Lugares en espanol para ninos).

See also:

What's New? (Netscape's Own)
http://home.netscape.com/netcenter/new.html

Links for Kids' Pages

http://www.adesignabove.com/lcs/kids/kidslinks.htm

http://www.tipworld.com/

Overview:

TipWorld's Web site is streamlined yet very useful. All you do is show up and the site takes care of the rest. Just select one or more of the following tech topics:

- **Windows '95**
- **MS Internet Explorer**
- **Lotus SmartSuite**
- **Netscape Navigator**
- Computer Gossip
- Software Bugs & Fixes
- Shareware
- MS Office
- **Macintosh**
- Cool Web Sites

Then sign up and you will receive a daily tip via e-mail.

- -

Try this:

Compile the tips into a word processing document and make a booklet out of the material. Give a copy of this booklet to a friend.

Highlights:

TipWorld's Netscape tips will keep you up-to-date on customizing your browsing to fit your needs.

See also:

Windows '95 Tips:

http://www.process.com/Win95/win95 tip.htm

http://www.yahooligans.com/

Overview:

"The Web Guide for Kids!," proclaims the home page. The developers have added interesting little kid-friendly touches to this site. For example, there is Club Yahooligans for those who want early notice of the latest what's cool sites, as well as updates on contests and special offers.

Also, Yahooligans invites visitors to be Yahooligans Testers and gives interested parties some guidance with their How We Choose Sites in Yahooligans section.

- -

Try this:

Choose a word from the dictionary. Take turns clicking the Yahooligans random site button. If you find the magic word at that random site, you score a point. First person to five points wins. (Take some time to explore the sites too.)

Highlights:

The developers are intent on quality control of this site.

See also:

Kids' Page

http://www.netguide.com/

Publishing Your Work in Cyberspace

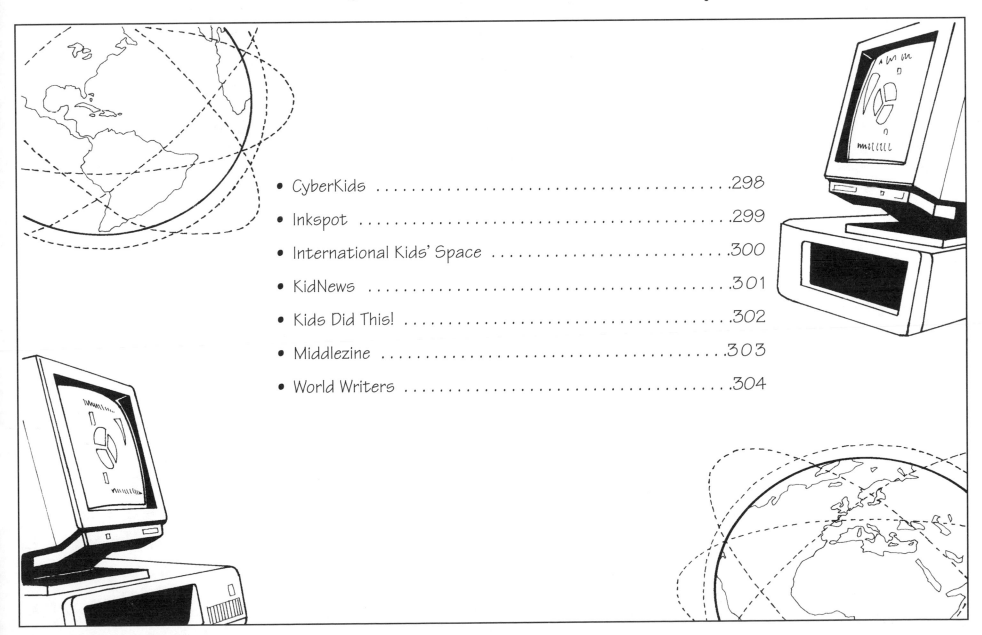

http://www.cyberkids.com/

Overview:

Published by Mountain Lake Software, this site offers kids a multitude of links to places where you can share your wisdom, insight, and creativity. It features CyberKids Connection for some interesting conversation, a section for Young Composers, a Kids Cooking Club, a CyberKids Magazine, an art gallery, and an excellent launchpad to steer you to other sites of interest. This site also connects to CyberTeens, another Mountain Lake site. At the time of this writing, CyberTeens was advertising for persons to translate the site into different languages.

Try this:

- From CyberKids' Launchpad, immerse yourself in art, sports, nature, children's books, fun and games—you name it.
- Using this one as a model, make your own launchpad.

Highlights:

- The Young Composers section features original works by kids from ages 12-16.
- This site offers a link to Starwave, where kids can create and send a Mother's Day card.

See also:

Library of Congress Learning Page

http://lcweb2.loc.gov/ammem/ndlpedu/educator.html

http://www.inkspot.com/

Overview:

Inkspot reaches writers in a variety of ways. It offers classified ads for those who have immediate needs. It also features a search engine for quick and easy reference to items of interest and it shares results of its visitor polls. For example, Inkspot asked the question, "What's the best single piece of advice about writing you've ever read/heard?"

Along with its extensive coverage of writing for children (see below), Inkspot's forte is its extensive list of pointers covering the main writing genres—business, poetry, mystery, journalism, and science fiction, to name a few—and to other pertinent topics, such as writer's block, writing instruction in the classroom, and promotional ideas. Using Inkspot, you will no longer need to subscribe to writing magazines.

Try this:

- Follow the links to the lists of publications seeking young writers.
- Create your own stationery using the site's Writer's Clip-art.

Highlights:

- Subscribe to Inkspot's own free electronic newsletter, Inklings.
- Visit Resources for Young Writers, Inkspot's superb subsite dedicated to kids.

See also:

Arbor Heights Cool Writers Magazine

http://www.halcyon.com/arborhts/ahcool/index.htm

nternationa Kids Space

http://www.kids-space.org/

Overview:

Don't miss visiting the International Kids' Space. Here are just a few reasons:

- The creators of the International Kids' Space have done a superb job of making this site extremely easy to navigate. Imagemaps, floor plans, and jump buttons abound.
- It strongly encourages a large variety of student and school submissions and underscores that encouragement with a very clear message: We Trust Kids!
- This site offers four separate tours, or courses, to acquaint visitors with the inner workings of International Kids' Space.
- Six Kids' Villages await more and more "residents" who supply links to their own home pages.

Try this:

Get your class involved. Classes can participate in the following:
- Kids Gallery
- Class Showcase
- Storybook Chapter III
- Pen Pal Class Box
- Bulletin Board Research Page

Highlights:

A new feature of the Kids' Space is the Parents' and Teachers' Layer, which gives adults a solid background on the site, a message board, and a generous list of activities to augment their children's visits.

See also:

The Shiki Internet Haiku Salon

http://mikan.cc.matsuyama-u.ac.jp/~shiki/

http://www.kidnews.com/

Overview:

"Policeman loses temper," "Learning about animals who aren't loved," and "Good going, Dad!". These are just some of the stories that appear in KidNews.

This site serves as both of the following:

- a source of news you will want to read and consider for your own newsletters or reports. (Just remember to give the author and school credit.)
- a destination for your own kid-related submissions.

KidNews wants to read and share your stories about your school, neighborhood, family—whatever you think kids worldwide would be interested to know. Visit this site to enjoy the candor of the writers and the wide variety of topics they cover.

- -

Try this:

- Browse the Adults Talk section for announcements of interesting new sites for kids, parents, and teachers.
- Browse the Kids Talk section to read some candid views on life among the younger set.

Highlights:

With all the content on this site, the developers have effectively used anchors and news menu buttons to provide easy navigation.

See also:

KidzMagazine

http://www.thetemple.com/Kidz Magazine/

http://sln.fi.edu/tfi/hotlists/kids.html

Overview:

This is part of the very valuable Franklin Science Museum Web site, but it deserves its own page. There are links to kids' contributions in science, art, history, math, language arts, school newspapers, and miscellaneous. This is great browsing material, but it can spark some creativity, as well.

Try this:

- Set up an informal rating system and explore all the work in one subject area.
- Connect with the creators of projects you liked and set up a team venture between families or classes.

Highlights:

Desert View High School's (Tucson, AZ) Where Are You? Research challenge to other students is definitely worth your time. (Follow the miscellaneous links to find it.)

See also:

Web pages set up by (or for) kids

http://www.starport.com/places/forKids/

Middlezine

http://156.63.113.15/middlezine/index.htm

Overview:

Middlezine, a project of Hudson Middle School in Hudson, Ohio, is a very creditable, wide-ranging forum for middle-school age writers worldwide. It actively invites kids' submissions of fiction, nonfiction, poetry, history, adventure, humor, sports, weird humor, reviews, and opinion.

This site provides a very accepting atmosphere for those reluctant to submit, and it does a nice job of celebrating the acts of both writing and publishing.

- -

Try this:

- Read some of the students' work and e-mail your responses or even a sequel. (Make sure the author knows it is a sequel.)
- Visit Middlezine's Poetry Corner.

Highlights:

Middlezine requests a photo of the author with the written piece. It is optional, but adds a nice touch.

See also:

Vocal Point

http://bvsd.k12.co.us/schools/cent/Newspaper/Newspaper.html

http://wwwbir.bham.wednet.edu/wws/wws.htm

Overview:

At the time of this writing, this site seemed to be in its infancy. By the time you visit it, the site will have grown considerably.

Its Ideas for Stories section helps those young writers who need that initial nudge to spur their creativity. Once writers have been given that little prewriting boost and they have cranked out that first draft, they can turn to the Check Your Writing section to review checklists of questions to ask themselves about their work. Once the piece is ready, writers can follow the easy directions to submit. Fame and fortune will be waiting.

- -

Try this:

Submit your solution to the problem of the month in the World Today section.

Highlights:

World Writers is informally following the writing process that schools are integrating into their language arts programs.

See also:

Creative Writing for Kids

http://kidswriting.miningco.com/

Enhancing Your Offline Time

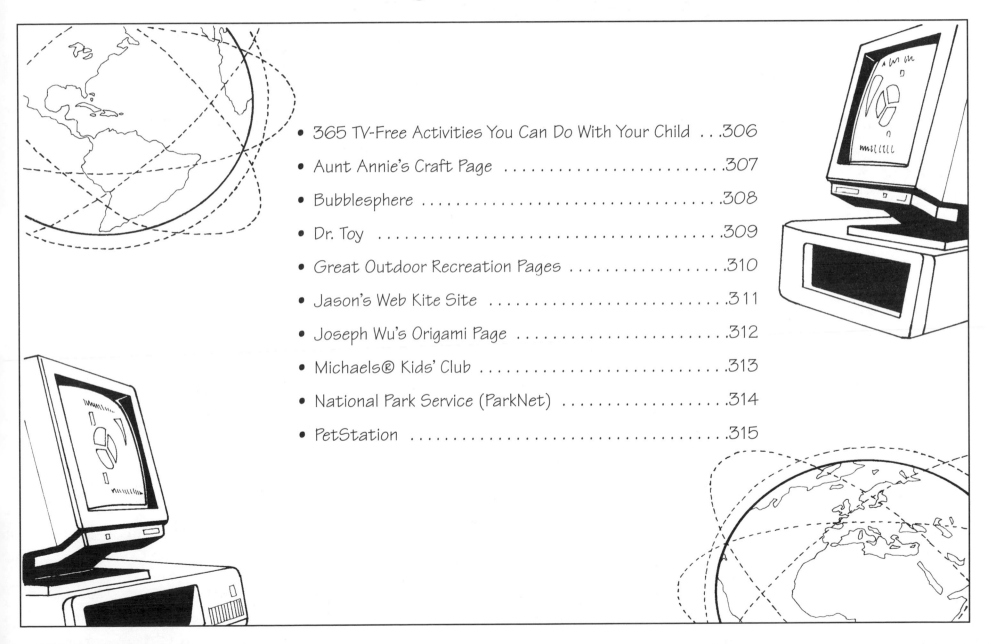

365 TV-FREE ACTIVITIES
YOU CAN DO WITH YOUR CHILD

http://family.go.com/Categories/Activities/Features/family_0401_02/dony/donytv_index/

Overview:

This site will give parents and kids that much-needed break from computer and TV screens alike. The book's categories (seen below), with an average of 23 accompanying ideas, give you a good hint of what is in store for the family when that TV is clicked off:

- Arts and Crafts
- Food Stuff
- Math Numbers
- Outdoor Play
- Tire 'em Out

- Creativity
- Group Play
- Memory
- Household Materials
- Toy Making

- Fantasy Play
- Indoor Play
- Older Kids' Play
- Science
- Words and Language

Try this:

- Share this site's ideas with club leaders, day care providers, and babysitters.
- Follow the link to Have It Your Way. This alone could lead to hours of creativity, fun, and high-quality school projects.

Highlights:

Your Time Only is an excellent section. The fewer materials and preparation, the better.

See also:

365 Outdoor Activities You Can Do with Your Child

http://family.go.com/Categories/Activities/Features/family_0401_02/dony/donytv_outdoor/donytv001.html

http://www.auntannie.com/

Overview:

Decorative cuts, homemade stamps, flexagons—these are just a few of the projects you will find at this site. The sequentially illustrated instructions accompanying each project are enough to get anyone involved in craft projects.

Let Annie's well-organized indices carry you through this site. You are bound to find good ideas for gifts or children's activities.

- -

Try this:

Chalk up some extra credit in math class by completing one of the projects from Aunt Annie's Geometric Playthings Series.

Highlights:

The recipe for Homemade Gooey-gak for Kids is too good to pass up.

See also:

Family Fun Crafts Index

http://www.familyfun.com/filters/mainindex/crafts.html

http://bubbles.org/

Overview:

Professor Bubbles has joined the Web to share all things bubble, the science behind them, the history of bubbles, the technology of bubble-making (including his own inventions), even a Tic-Tac-Bubble game. During your visit to Bubblesphere, take the time to complete the following:

- write to Professor Bubbles.
- follow him on his travels via a nice clickable image map.
- try out his on-site search engine.

- -

Try this:

Can you concoct a great bubble solution? Send your recipe to Professor Bubbles.

Highlights:

- The section, Make Your Own Bubble Tools, will give you some ideas to follow up on a surface tension teaching unit.
- Check out the professor's ultimate bubble solution.

See also:

50 Questions

http://www.ed.gov/pubs/parents/Science/bubbles.html

http://www.drtoy.com/drtoy/index.html

Overview:

At this site, Dr. Toy, an author of 14 books (including **The Toy Chest**), covers a wealth of topics, from The 10 Best Creative Products of 1995 to her prescription for the best use of toys and children's products. Because of her product listings by category, age, and company, you will find it easy to zero in on a product that would fit a given child.

Tip: This site is so extensive it is possible to miss some very helpful features, so make sure you hotlist the index page rather than the welcome page.

Try this:

Follow the links to learn about a product's play quotient and review the list of toys to choose one for the family to share.

Highlights:

Take a look at Dr. Toy's 10 tips on selecting kid's products.

See also:

Planet Internet:Toys and Entertainment

http://www.toysonline.com.au/

http://www.gorp.com/gorp/resource/US_National_Park/main.htm

Overview:

This site really makes you feel as if a travel agent is sitting inside your computer. You get prices, lodging hints, beautiful photos, important phone numbers, and a fine search tool. GORP by no means limits itself to national parks. It offers helpful information on forests, wilderness areas, monuments, even archaeological sites and the "eclectica" feature, adds much more than the hard facts of travel.

All this information helps you shop around and decide ahead of time how you want to spend your time off. And for kids, this is one of those sites that could save them that extra trip to the library for their state reports.

Try this:

Borrow, then place, an image of your choice into your favorite paint program. Use the marquee tool to cut up the graphic into puzzle pieces. Have a friend put it together and guess its location. (Research the location and give hints.)

Highlights:

Use GORP to plan your next trip to a national park.

See also:

The American Wilderness Guide

http://www.worldmind.com/Wild/Parks/parklist.html

Graphic of a kite towing a "passenger" in a buggy.

http://www.latrobe.edu.au/www/glenn/KiteSite/Kites.html

Overview:

At this site, Jason Hellwege of Melbourne, Australia, shares his wide-ranging passion for kites. There is a lot of science involved in kite-flying and Jason takes the time to weave some instruction into an impressive selection of kite images. He also includes some helpful links to other kite pages as well as an FTP site and a kite newsgroup.

Try this:

Study the JPEG kite images. Think of features you can add to the existing models. Send your ideas to this or other kite sites.

Highlights:

- Impressive selection of kite graphics.
- The introduction to kite-buggying (i.e., being towed by a power kite) is extremely interesting.

See also:

Peter's Kite Site

http://www.win.tue.nl/cs/fm/pp/kites/

Joseph Wu's Origami Page

http://www.origami.vancouver.bc.ca/

Overview:

This site has a very clear focus and it offers visitors a true sense of enthusiasm for the art and a sincere interest in sharing as much knowledge as possible about origami. If you want instructions and diagrams, this site has them. If you want beautiful (and fast-loading) images, this is the place to visit. If you want plenty of relevant links, they are here too.

Try this:

- Use two different methods to build the same piece. Compare the difficulty factor and the end-product.
- Design your own work and submit it to this site.

Highlights:

- Try not to miss this gallery of mythical creatures.
- The diagrams provided will help anyone create a creditable work of origami.

See also:

The Electric Origami Shop

http://www.ibm.com/Stretch/EOS/

Michaels® Kids Club

http://www.michaels.com/kids/kid-main.html

Overview:

Michaels® The Arts and Crafts Store, provides various craft opportunities at their locations throughout the country. This Web site lists numerous crafts for kids of ages 5-12.

Michaels® offers a nice variety of projects (31, with more available in the Kids Club Newsletter) and good simple images to show the steps toward each masterpiece. These color images are enough to give us a clear vision of each project, which is exactly what aspiring artists and crafts people need. They need room for their own creativity. Michaels® is also easy-to-use and has a fast moving interface.

Try this:

- Set up your own craft fair based on the ideas you glean from this site.
- How about making extra money from your favorite projects? Find a local craft fair and give it a try.

Highlights:

This site allows you to choose craft projects that anyone can make.

See also:

Crafts for Kids

http://craftsforkids.miningco.com/mbody.htm

United States Department Of The Interior

National Park Service

http://www.nps.gov/parks.html

Overview:

Here is a great place to visit if you cannot get down to your local automobile club. This site fills you in on the finer points of using the parks (e.g., preparing for a park visit), as well as the essentials (e.g., phone numbers, fees, reservation information, etc.). This site lets you search in four different ways:

- by the state map
- by the park name
- by regional maps
- by a theme

The last option seemed like a creative way to reach visitors. Certainly, it would be a question that a travel consultant might pose, but Web sites usually are more concrete in their searches. In this case, the parks service teams up with the search tool Excite to find locations that meet your criteria. **Note:** This page is just a smattering of what the NPS offers on the Web. You might want to start at ParkNet (http://www.nps.gov/) and browse from there.

Try this:

- Use ParkNet to link to Nature Net and Links to the Past.
- Try the Ask a Ranger feature. Submit your question to: nps_web_master@nps.gov

Highlights:

Follow the link to NPS's special travel feature and get the inside scoop on the lesser known parks in the system.

See also:

Grand Canyon

http://www.nps.gov/grca/

http://petstation.com/index.html

Overview:

PetStation blends a lighter touch (departments such as Funny Bones, Pet Photo of the Month, and a kids' talk area rated KG-13) with a more serious side (features like Pet Not, The Pets Bill of Rights, and The Do's and Don't's of Pet-Keeping). To move through the site, just hop on the "e-train" to places like the Dog Domain and Cat Cabana.

Try this:

- Notify your vet or local humane society of PetStation's existence.
- Offer to print out a weekly excerpt (light or serious) for their office, bulletin board, or newsletter.

Highlights:

- PetStation has a well-organized set of over 100 links.
- Acknowledging the groups' different pet-related concerns, the site divides discussion areas into kids, teens, and seniors.

See also:

PetNet

http://www.petnet.com.au/

Acme Pet

http://www.acmepet.com/

Appendix A

Some software programs that can help you access the various Internet services covered in this book:

Chat
Netscape Chat (Mac, PC)
ircle (Mac)
wsirc, mirc (PC)

E-mail
Pegasus (PC)
Eudora (Macs and PC)

FTP
WS FTP (PC)
Fetch, Anarchie (Mac)

Gopher
WS Gopher (PC)
TurboGopher (Mac)

Telnet
NCSA Telnet (Mac)
Telnet (PC)

Usenet Newsreaders
Newswatcher, Netscape Navigator (Mac)
Free Agent, News Xpress, Netscape Navigator (PC)
Video (for sending images)
CU-SeeMe (Mac, PC)

World Wide Web
Netscape Navigator (Mac, PC)
Internet Explorer (Mac, PC)

Other Sites to Visit

World Village
http://www.worldvillage.com/

Cybergirl
http://www.cybergrrl.com/

Creative Kids in Kamchatka
http://www.informns.k12.mn.us/kamkids/

Ralph Bunche School
http://rbs.edu/

Klutz Galactic Headquarters
http://www.klutz.com/treefort

Kid's Window
http://jw.stanford.edu/KIDS/kids_home.html

Interactive Model Railroad
http://rr-vs.informatik.uni-ulm.de/rr/

Piano on the Net
http://www.artdsm.com/music.html

Smithsonian Museum of Natural History
http://nmnhwww.si.edu/nmnhweb.html

The Joe Boxer World Wide Web Playground
http://www.joeboxer.com/

Glossary

America Online—This is one of the largest commercial online services in the world.

Applications—This is a synonym for computer programs.

Archie—This is a service on the Internet that helps us find FTP files.

Bandwidth—This is the maximum data that can be transmitted in a specific amount of time (generally measured in seconds). If data traveled in a pipe, the bandwidth would be analogous to the diameter of the pipe.

BBS—This is short for bulletin board service.

BPS (bits per second)—This is a measure of how quickly data can be sent over communications lines.

Chat—This is the exchanging of typed messages in real time.

Client—This is a computer program that asks for some kind of data (file, software) from another computer (called a server).

Compressed—This is data that has been reduced in size to save space on a disk drive or to save time when it is sent electronically.

Compuserve—This along with **Prodigy** and **America Online**, is one of the largest commercial online services in the world.

Cyberspace—This is a general term given to the universe of computer communications.

Dedicated Line—This a phone line set aside exclusively for one purpose, in this case, an Internet connection.

Dial-in Direct—This is one type of Internet connection. PPP (point-to-point protocol) and SLIP (serial line interface protocol) are the two main types of dial-in direct connections.

Glossary (cont.)

Download—This is to transfer data (usually text, software, or graphics) from a remote computer to your own computer.

E-mail—This is short for electronic mail.

Emoticons—These are human expressions created from keyboard characters. They help compensate for a reader's difficulty in interpreting emotion in printed text. To read most emoticons, turn your head 90 degrees to the left.

FAQ—This is short for frequently asked questions.

Freeware—These are free software programs available at ftp sites throughout the Internet.

FTP—This is short for file transfer protocol, a process for sending and receiving files.

GIF (graphics interchange format)—This is the graphics format most often used for Web page images.

Gopher—This was created at the University of Minnesota (home of the Golden Gophers), an Internet service that offers menus through which users "dig" en route to desired information.

Hits—These are the references returned by search engines.

Home Page—This is the first screen you view when you visit a Web site.

Host—This is a computer with which your computer connects and interacts.

Hotlist—This is a list of Web sites that a user reserves for later and more convenient access. (The term bookmark is also used in this context.)

HTML (hypertext markup language)—This is the programming language of the World Wide Web.

Glossary *(cont.)*

HTTP—This is short for hypertext transfer protocol; it is the set of standards on which the World Wide Web is based.

Hypertext—This is the basic document form of the World Wide Web; it features clickable links to other Web sites and documents.

Image Map—These are found on Web pages, a graphic with different regions that, if clicked, link the user to pertinent Web pages.

Inline Image—This is a Web page image displayed automatically by your browser (unless commanded otherwise).

Internet—This is a worldwide network of computer networks which feature such services as data-sharing, electronic messaging, and online commerce.

JPEG (joint photographic experts group)—This refers to a graphic format that uses the JPEG compression standard.

Link—This is a hypertext connection to another Web site .

Log Off—This is to disconnect from another computer.

Log On—This is to connect to your Internet provider, commercial online service, or other computer network.

Megabyte—This is the amount of memory (1024 kilobytes) that you would need to save a document of approximately 620 pages of double-spaced text.

Modem—This is the device that uses communication lines (usually telephone) to connect one computer to distant computers.

MPEG (moving pictures experts group)—This refers to one type of video that is displayed on Web pages.

Netiquette—This is short for network etiquette, which is acceptable conduct in network communications.

Glossary *(cont.)*

Newsgroups—These are not so much "news" groups as they are subject-oriented discussion groups where subscribers exchange opinions as much as they do facts.

Newsreader—This is a software program that lets you navigate through newsgroup postings.

Offline—This is not being connected to a computer network.

Online—This is being connected to a computer network.

Posting—This is the act of submitting input to a computer bulletin board, newsgroup, or mailing list.

PPP—See Dial-in Direct.

Prodigy—Financially backed by Sears and IBM, **Prodigy** is one of the three largest commercial online services in the United States.

Protocol—This is a set of standards or conventions.

QuickTime®—This is software developed by Apple Computer Inc. to display videos/animations directly on your computer screen.

Real-time—This is live, happening at that moment.

Server—This is a computer that offers services or functions to other computers.

Service Provider—This is an organization that offers Internet access.

Shareware—This is try before you buy software.

SLIP—See Dial-in Direct.

Telnet—This is a service available on the Internet that allows a user to connect to, navigate around, and glean resources (files, documents) from a remote computer.

Glossary *(cont.)*

Upload—This transfers a file from your computer to a remote computer.

URL—This is short for uniform resource locator, which is a fancy name for a World Wide Web site's address.

Usenet (users network)—These provide discussion forums, which currently number over 15,000.

Veronica—This is short for very easy rodent-oriented net-wide index to computerized archives, which is a tool that searches Gopher files throughout Gopherspace for requested information.

Webmaster—This is a person in charge of a given Web site.

World Wide Web—(The Web, WWW, W3)—This is a corner of the Internet highlighted by the millions of hypertext documents that are easily-accessible to users of browser software.

Yahoo—This is one of the more noted search tools on the World Wide Web.

Bibliography

Aboba, Bernard. **The Online User's Encyclopedia: Bulletin Boards and Beyond.** Addison-Wesley Publishing Company, 1993.

Biggar, Bill and Joe Myers. **Danger Zones: What Parents Should Know About the Internet.** Andrews and McMeel, 1996.

Butler, Mark. **How to Use the Internet.** Ziff-Davis Press, 1994.

Castro, Elizabeth. **HTML for the World Wide Web (Visual Quickstart Guide),** Peachpit Press, 1996.

Ellsworth, Jill H. **Education on the Internet.** Sams Publishing, 1994.

Engst, Adam. **The Internet Starter Kit for Macintosh.** Hayden Books, 1994.

Fristrup, Jenny A. **Usenet: Netnews for Everyone.** PTR Prentice Hall.

Haag, Tim. **Internet for Kids.** (Intermediate) Teacher Created Materials, 1996.

Harris, Stuart and Gayle Kidder. **Netscape Quick Tour for Macintosh.** Ventana Press, Inc., 1995.

Hoffman, Paul E. **Netscape and the World Wide Web for Dummies.** IDG Books Worldwide, Inc., 1995.

Johnson, Keith. **Using Gopher.** Que Corporation, 1995.

Keeler, Elissa and Robert Miller. **Netscape Virtuoso.** MIS:Press, 1996.

Krol, Ed. **The Whole Internet User's Guide & Catalog.** O'Reilly & Associates, Inc., 1992.

LeJeune, Urban. **Netscape and HTML Explorer.** Coriolis Group Books, 1995.

Lent, Max. **Government Online.** HarperCollins Publishers, Inc., 1995.

Levine, John R. and Carol Baroudi. **The Internet for Dummies.** IDG Books, 1994.

Levine, John R. and Margy Levine Young. **More Internet for Dummies.** IDG Books, 1996.

Marsh, Merle. **Everything You Need to Know (But Were Afraid to Ask Kids) About the Information Highway.** Computer Learning Foundation, 1995.

Peal, David. **Access the Internet.** SYBEX, Inc., 1994.

Pfaffenberger, Bryan. **The USENET Book.** Addison-Wesley Publishing Company, 1995.

Pfaffenberger, Bryan. **The World Wide Web Bible.** MIS:Press, 1995.

Stout, Rick. **The World Wide Web Complete Reference.** Osborne McGraw-Hill, 1996.

Strudwick, Karen, John Spilker and Jay Arney. **Internet for Parents.** Resolution Business Press, Inc., 1995.

Part III

Computers Don't Byte

Written by Linda Pereira

Illustrations by Karon Walstad

Introduction

Computers Don't Byte has been designed to give children, parents, and teachers a simple way of learning how to use and how to understand the operation of computers. This 160 page book contains information that will help you understand what a computer is, the history of computers, hardware that is available for computers, what is inside a computer, several types of software available for computers, and how to use the many functions computers have to offer. **Computers Don't Byte** will provide you with a basic understanding of how computers influence you as an individual, and society as a whole. Most importantly, **Computers Don't Byte** will serve as an instructional guide in fostering computer literacy and proficiency, and will help to reduce any fears or anxieties you may have about working with computers. Included in this book are several activities that will help reinforce ideas and concepts about computers, as well as provide a stimulating and enjoyable resource the whole family can use.

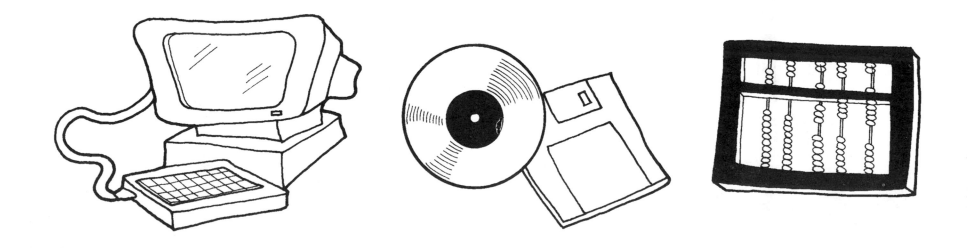

What Is a Computer?

A Computer Is a Machine

A computer is classified as an electronic machine. You can use a computer to help you with your schoolwork, play a game, or even read a book from its screen. It will help you write, solve problems, count numbers, and even draw. A computer works very quickly and accurately; it never gets tired or makes mistakes.

You may think that a computer is very smart, even smarter than the smartest person, but a computer is only as smart as the person who programs it. Computers cannot think, or do anything by themselves. In order for a computer to operate, it must receive instructions from someone like you who can tell it what to do.

Computers come in many shapes and sizes. Microcomputers are the most common types of computers we use at home and at school.

Activity: Gather up some old magazines and look for as many types of machines as you can find. Then cut them out and make a collage of them on a piece of paper.

A Computer Is a Tool

A computer is a tool that we use to help us do our work.

A tool is considered anything used by the hands to help complete a job.

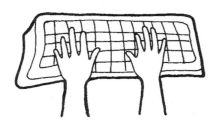

For example, you are sitting at your desk, and your teacher asks you to create a map of the United States. What tools might you need in order to complete this job? You would probably need a **pen** or **pencil** and a **ruler** to get started. Then you could use **colored markers**, **crayons**, or even **paints** for coloring your map. And if you were really feeling creative, you might even use **scissors**, **glue**, and **construction paper**.

All of the words highlighted are tools that you may need or want to use while you complete the job asked of you. A computer is also a tool that you can use to help you complete this task or any other task. Computers can help you write reports for school or letters to friends. They can calculate numbers and help you learn math. You can even create music and art with a computer. Computers can help you learn or do just about anything you want.

Activity: Make a list of all the tools you use throughout the day. Next to each tool, write down how it helps you to do your work.

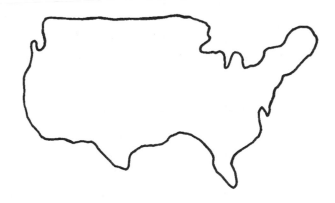

What Can a Computer Do?

When computers are at work, they appear to be very intelligent. Do you think that computers are really all that smart? Well, they may appear that way because of what they can do, but in reality a computer is not intelligent at all. A computer is only as intelligent as the person who programs it. In order for a computer to do a job, it must be given a set of instructions which tell it what to do. Always remember that you are much more intelligent than a computer!

A computer cannot think for itself.

A computer does not have any feelings like people do.

A computer cannot show emotion.

A computer cannot form opinions.

A computer cannot make decisions.

However, once you tell your computer what to do by giving it a set of instructions, it works accurately and quickly. If programmed properly, it will never make a mistake or get tired. A computer is capable of remembering billions of pieces of information, and it will never forget.

Activity: Make a list of all the different things a computer can do for you.

Computers Need Proper Care

Computers must be cared for properly so they will continue to do the work they were designed to do. This will minimize the chances of it breaking down, thus assuring it will last a long time.

Below is a list of things you can do to ensure that your computer will continue to work properly and last a long time.

- Keep it clean. Dust it often or keep it covered.
- Keep it at room temperature, not too hot or too cold.
- Do not eat or drink near your computer.
- Never drop any part of your computer.
- Keep it dry.
- Do not bang the keys on the keyboard. Type gently.
- Do not put anything besides your disk into the disk drive.

Activity: Review the information that came with your computer on proper care and maintenance.

Artificial Intelligence

Have computers already, or will they in the future, take on human-like characteristics? Scientists today are trying to invent machines (computers) that exhibit human intelligence. Such machines include robots and computers which will understand and respond to the human voice. Computer scientists are attempting to improve computers by incorporating into them features associated with human characteristics and intelligence. Who knows what the future will bring?

Artificial intelligence (AI)—is a computer term used when a computer seems to be thinking human-like thoughts.

Activity: Draw a picture of a computer doing something you wish your computer could do.

Computers—Analog or Digital

Computers can be **analog**, **digital**, or **hybrid**.

Analog computers are used by scientists and engineers. This type of computer compares and measures such scientific quantities as temperature, weight, speed, voltage, frequencies, and pressures. Analog computers work with a continuous flow of electrical information. Most analog computers are one-of-a-kind, designed to perform a specific scientific task. In order to use an analog computer for multiple tasks, it must be rewired for the new tasks. These computers can be found in laboratories, hospitals, and places of scientific research.

Digital computers are the computers you most commonly see and use. They take words, pictures, sounds, numbers, and symbols and translate them into numbers. Then they perform simple calculations so you can complete a task. These computers are mass produced and duplicated. They are very useful due to the variety of programs (instructions) used in their operations to suit the needs of their owners.

Hybrid computers are a combination of analog and digital computers and are generally used in the scientific community.

History of Computers

Early Counting Tools

A computer is a machine that works with data and information in the form of numbers. People from the beginning of time, and throughout the years, have invented and continue to invent things that help them count.

Caveman counted with the only counting tools they knew, their fingers and toes. These were considered the first counting tools.

Some of the other counting tools that have been used throughout time have been stones, knots on ropes, and notches on sticks, to name just a few. People used these counting tools to count their possessions and also to keep track of the passing of time.

Activity: Find several examples of early counting tools.

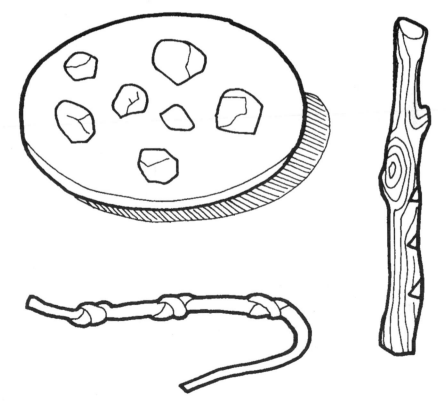

The Abacus

Approximately 4,000 years ago, the Chinese invented the Abacus. It was the first machine used for counting and calculating. It is made of a wooden frame, metal rods, and wooden beads. It takes a great deal of time and practice to learn how to master the use of an abacus. An abacust is a person who is very experienced in using an abacus. Today, the abacus is still used widely in China and other Asian countries to count and calculate, just as we use calculators. Each bead has a specific value. Reading from right to left, the beads in the first column are worth 1, in the second column the beads are worth 10, in the third column the beads are worth 100, etc. Addition, subtraction, multiplication, and division are performed by moving the appropriate beads to the middle of the abacus.

Approximately 400 years ago, the first adding machine was invented. The first calculator was not used until the 1900s.

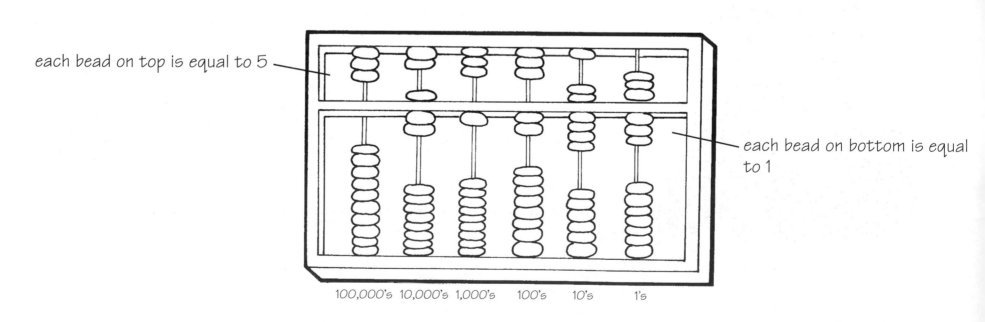

each bead on top is equal to 5

each bead on bottom is equal to 1

100,000's 10,000's 1,000's 100's 10's 1's

The Pascaline

In 1642, at the age of 19, a French mathematician by the name of Blaise Pascal, invented the Pascaline. The Pascaline is known as the first mechanical and automatic calculator. Pascal invented the Pascaline to help make his father's job as a tax accountant easier. The Pascaline was a wooden box that could only add and subtract by means of a series of gears and wheels. When each wheel rotated one revolution, it would then turn the neighboring wheel. On top of the wheels were a series of windows through which the totals could be read. About 50 models were constructed and were made of wood, ivory, ebony, and copper.

Activity: Go to the library to further research Blaise Pascal and his Pascaline.

Blaise Pascal

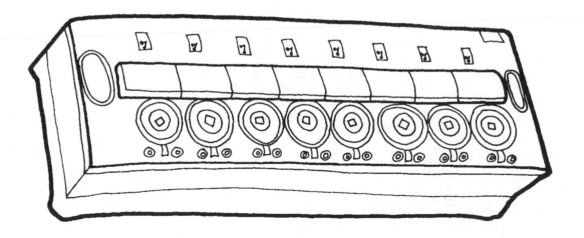

The Pascaline

Gottfried Leibniz

In 1673, German inventor Gottfried Liebniz perfected the Leibniz Calculator. The Leibniz was also a calculating machine, but much superior to that of the Pascaline. It could do more than just add and subtract. The Leibniz Calculator could also multiply, divide, and find square roots of numbers. It too was mechanical and worked by hand. A crank was added to speed up the work of this calculator. It was used by mathematicians and bookkeepers.

Mr. Leibniz believed that it did not make sense for men to spend hours and hours doing mathematical calculations when he could invent a machine that would work much faster. Would you rather add a long list of numbers with a pencil and paper or use a calculator?

Activity: Go to the library and do further research on Gottfried Leibniz and the Leibniz Calculator.

Gottfried Leibniz

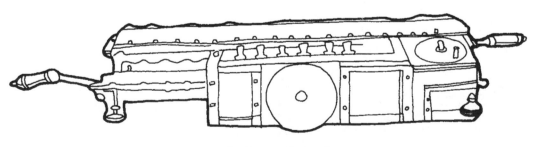

Leibniz Calculator

Joseph-Marie Jacquard

Joseph-Marie Jacquard was a French weaver. The job of a weaver was hard. A weaver had to do several tasks at the same time while making a piece of cloth. He had to string threads over and under other threads, he had to pump a loom with his feet to keep the piece of cloth that he was making moving, and he also had to choose each thread by hand so that the thickness and color pattern of the cloth would be perfect.

In 1801, Jacquard invented the Jacquard loom. It was a weaving machine that was controlled by punched cards. While the loom was being pumped, cards with holes in them were attached together in a pattern through which strings of thread were automatically fed. These cards would feed the right pieces of thread into the loom to make a beautiful cloth.

His invention scared other weavers because it made cloth faster and better than they could by hand. As a result, Jacquard's house and loom were burned down. This violent act did not discourage Jacquard, for he built another loom. Weavers today still use the Jacquard Loom.

Jacquard Loom

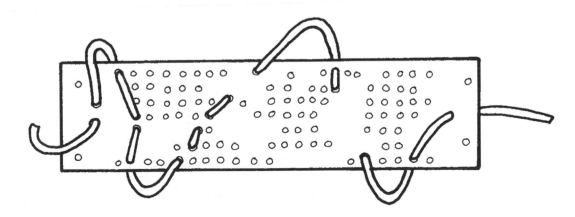

Punched Card

Charles Babbage—The Father of Computers

In the early 1820s, an English mathematician by the name Charles Babbage, designed a computing machine called the Difference Engine. This machine was to be used in the calculating and printing of simple math tables. In the 1830s, he designed a second computing machine called the Analytical Engine. This machine was to be used in calculating complicated problems by following a set of instructions. However, neither of these machines were ever finished because the technology at the time was not advanced enough, and both of his projects lacked financial funding. The computing machines made in the 1900s, and even those today are based on the designs of the Difference Engine and the Analytical Engine. This is why Charles Babbage is known as the Father of Computers.

Activity: Write a paragraph explaining why Charles Babbage is considered the Father of Computers.

Charles Babbage

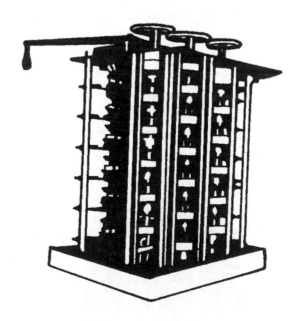

Difference Engine

Herman Hollerith

An American inventor by the name of Herman Hollerith wanted to speed up the work involved in taking the government census. In 1890, 50 years after Charles Babbage's death, Hollerith invented a machine called the Tabulating Machine, using notes that were left by Babbage.

Prior to this invention it took nearly eight years to count everyone in the United States and add up all the information about where people lived, their ages, and what their jobs were. The Tabulating Machine used punched cards to record and sort data or information. Each hole punched meant something. If a hole had been punched, a pin would pass through it to make an electrical contact with mercury in a cup below. This turned motors that moved numbers that counted. Approximately 65 cards could be passed through this computer in a minute, and in 1890 it took only 2.5 years to complete the U.S. Census.

Hollerith did not stop with this one invention. He began a company by the name of the Computing-Tabulating-Recording Company. Eventually this company changed its name to International Business Machines (IBM)—the largest computer company in the world.

Activity: Using the information you have learned, take a census of your neighborhood.

Herman Hollerith

Tabulating Machine

First Generation Computers

Prior to the 1940s all calculating devices were mechanical. Therefore, they needed some type of manual operation in order for them to work. It was not until electronic parts were invented and used that calculating machines became known as computers.

Vacuum tubes were invented during the 1940s and 1950s. They were one of the most important technological developments in the history of computers. They were electronic devices that controlled the flow of electricity in computers, and they looked like long light bulbs. In order to work, they needed large amounts of electricity and they gave off lots of heat.

First Generation Computers, such as the Mark 1, ENIAC, and EDVAC all used vacuum tubes. These electronic computers were developed during the 1940s and 1950s. They contained as many as 18,000 vacuum tubes, weighed more than 30 tons, and took up some 1,500 square feet (135 m²) of floor space. They were able to perform thousands of mathematical problems per minute but were very expensive to build and operate. Because they used enormous amounts of electricity, they often became overheated and broke down. However, each of these early computers led to the development of the computers we use today.

Activity: Draw a picture of a vacuum tube.

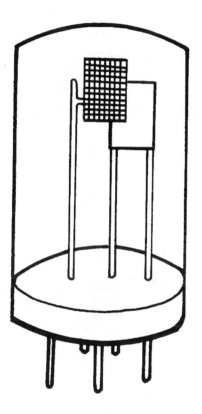

A Vacuum Tube

Second Generation Computers

Transistors, which were developed in 1947, did not replace the big, bulky vacuum tubes until the late 1950s. Transistors were considerably smaller in size and could do everything that vacuum tubes could do. Just like vacuum tubes, transistors control the amount of electricity flowing in and out of a computer. However, they were more dependable because they did not emit the heat that vacuum tubes did. They also used much less electricity and lasted longer.

Second Generation Computers, such as RCA, IBM, and UNIVAC were built from 1959 to 1964, using transistors. These computers were somewhat smaller, less expensive to build, much faster, and more dependable. In 1951, information about the 1952 presidential election was put into the UNIVAC computer. UNIVAC predicted that Dwight D. Eisenhower would win the presidential election less than an hour after the polls closed.

You could not yet buy one of these computers for your home because computers were still too large and too expensive. However, businesses began buying their own computers when they realized that computers could help them do their work quickly and efficiently.

Activity: Find a transistor from any piece of electronic equipment and examine it.

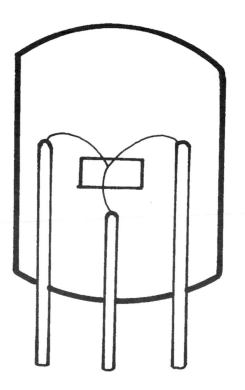

A Transistor

Third Generation Computers

The integrated circuit (IC) was the next great invention in the development of computers. It was invented during the 1960s. Integrated means combined. The integrated circuit combines all the parts a computer needs to run in one small place—a chip. A chip is a very small piece of silicon, which is made from sand. It is about the size of your fingernail. An integrated circuit contains several transistors and other necessary electronic devices in a circuit, or pathway on a chip. This allows electricity to flow throughout the computer.

Third Generation Computers were built in the 1960s and 1970s and used integrated circuits. Mainframe computers contained integrated circuits and were used to meet the computing needs of large organizations and businesses. By the 1970s, minicomputers were designed to meet the needs of smaller companies. Minicomputers were less powerful but smaller than mainframe computers.

Computers were now getting smaller, becoming easier to use, working faster, using less electricity, and were becoming more affordable.

Activity: Find an integrated circuit from any piece of electronic equipment and examine it.

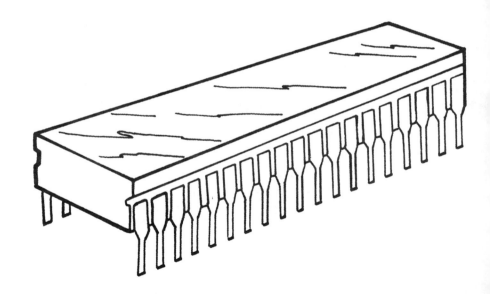

An Integrated Circuit

Fourth Generation Computers

The **microcomputer** is an integrated circuit that contains arithmetic, logic, and control units necessary for the operation of a computer. Microcomputers are also found in household appliances, calculators, toys, video games, and hundreds of other similar devices.

Microcomputers are the personal computers, or desktop computers, we use today. It was not until the 1980s that computers became so affordable and small enough to purchase for use in our homes and schools. The development of microcomputers still continues today. These computers continue to be made smaller, work faster, have more memory, and are most reliable. Today's computer can add numbers in one-billionth of a second, faster than you can blink your eyes! Did you know that a microcomputer is usually used by one person at a time?

Microcomputers have become so small that today one can fit into a briefcase. These briefcase-sized computers are called laptop computers. Did you know that there are more than one million transistors on 1 integrated circuit?

Activity: Go to a computer store and look at all of the different kinds of computers available.

A Microcomputer

Fifth Generation Computers

Fifth Generation Computers are in the process of being invented as we speak. These will be the computers of the future. Do we know what they will look like? Not really, but we can make some intelligent guesses from what we have learned about the evolution of computers.

- They will be smaller.
- They will work faster.
- They should be less expensive.
- They will be more reliable.
- They will do more.
- They will be even more accurate.
- More people will have one.

We have already learned about artificial intelligence. Remember, this is when a computer appears to have human-like qualities. Computer scientists are trying today to invent a computer that will have some of the characteristics of human intelligence, such as the ability to understand language, reason, learn, and make decisions. Do you think that one day computers will understand human voices or maybe even speak to us?

Activity: Write a paragraph titled "How 'Smart' Do You Think a Fifth Generation Computer Will Be?"

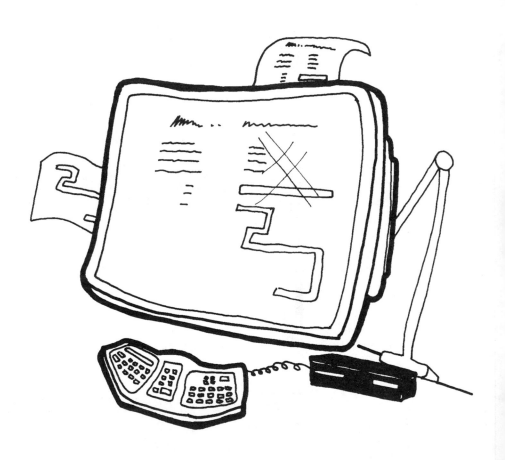

Fifth Generation Computers

Hardware

Parts of a Computer

Computers are made up of many different parts, just like cars. When these parts are not combined with anything else, they are just parts. However, when they are put together with other parts, be it car parts or computer parts, the end result is a complete car, computer, or even a computer system. A computer system is made up of a central processing unit (CPU), a monitor, a keyboard, a printer, etc. Each separate part that can be added to a computer system is called a **peripheral**.

Hardware is all the parts of the computer that you can see and touch.

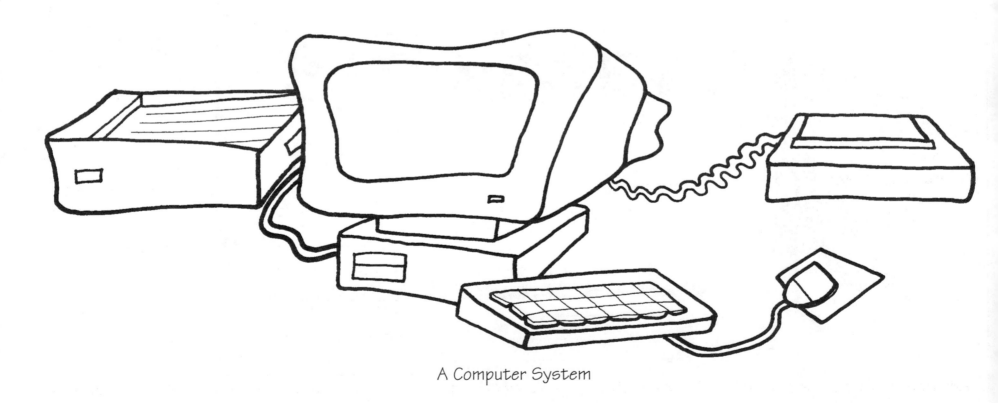

A Computer System

The Keyboard

The keyboard, is a peripheral device that lets you "talk" to a computer. You press the keys on the keyboard to tell the computer what to do.

Dvorak keyboard—In the 1930s, August Dvorak designed the following layout for the keyboard.

' , . P Y F G C R L ?	22%
A O E U I D H T N S -	70% Home Row
; Q J K X B M W V Z	8%

Notice that the letters most commonly used are on the home row keys—the keys In the middle row. It is still used by some people today.

QWERTY Keyboard—This is the keyboard we are most familiar with. QWERTY are the letters on the top left of the keyboard. It was originally designed to prevent keys from jamming on a typewriter, by slowing down typing. In eight hours, a Dvorak typist's fingers travel 16 miles, compared to only one mile for a QWERTY typist.

Q W E R T Y U I O P	52%
A S D F G H J K L ; '	32% Home Row
Z X C V B N M , . /	16%

Activity: Using a piece of 8.5" x 11" (22 cm x 28 cm) cardboard design your own keyboard. Use the above two as examples.

The Keys

There are 101 keys on the standard computer keyboard. We are now going to learn about these keys.

Function Keys—a set of keys on the top row. F1 is usually the key you press if you need help. The use of the other function keys depends upon each individual software program that you are using.

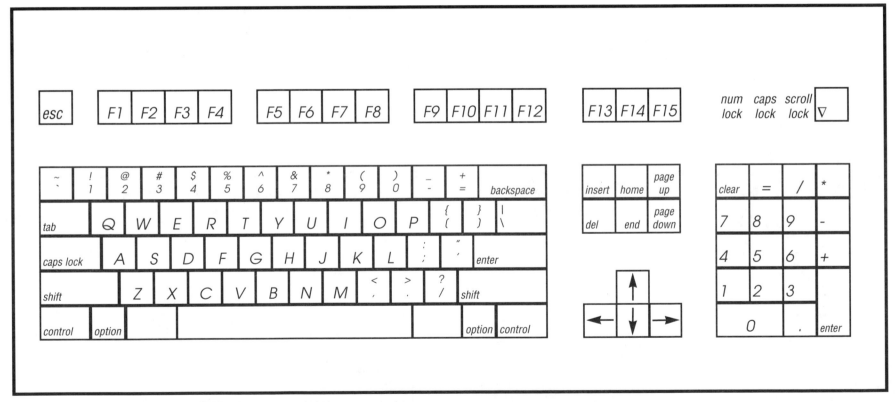

Activity: Practice your keyboard typing.

The Keys (cont.)

Most of the keys on a keyboard are for making letters and numbers. Below are some of the other keys you will see and use.

Enter Key   When you are typing, the enter key is used to tell the computer to start a new line. It also tells the computer to carry out commands when working with a software program. (A command is an instruction that you give to a computer.)

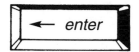

Escape Key   This key is used to exit a screen or a program.

Tab Key   Use this key to indent your paragraph.

Caps Lock   When you press this key, all your letters will be typed as capitals.

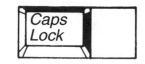

The Keys (cont.)

Arrow Keys   These four keys are known as the arrow keys. They move the cursor around on the screen. A cursor is a blinking box or line that is a place marker on the screen.

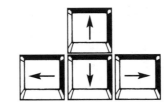

Control and Alt   These keys do not work on their own. They must be used with one or more keys. The commands they make depend upon the software program you are using. For instance:

Ctrl + U = Underline

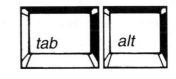

Home   This key moves the cursor to the left side of the screen.

End   This end key moves the cursor to the right of the screen.

Spacebar   Press this key to put a space between the words that you are typing. Can you imagine what it would be like to read a book without any spaces between the words?

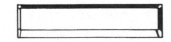

The Keys (cont.)

Backspace Use this key to back up and erase words you have already typed.

Numeric Lock When pressed, this key allows you to use the numbers on the right side of the keyboard, just like a calculator.

+ = add   = subtract

/ = divide   * = multiply

Page Up Use this key to move the cursor up one page or one screen.

Page Down Use this key to move the cursor down one page or one screen.

Insert Use this key to insert a word, sentence, or paragraph.

Delete Use this key to erase anything at the current cursor location.

The Monitor

The monitor looks like a television. It has a screen on which you can see the software program you are using. When you are typing, it displays the words you are typing. If you are using a graphics program, it displays what you are drawing.

The cathode ray tube (CRT) is inside the monitor. The screen is attached to it. You can also find cathode ray tube in your TV.

There are different types of monitors that you can attach to your computer.

- Monochrome monitors display only one color, usually green, on a black or white background. IBM's first personal computers had monochrome monitors.
- Color Graphics Adapter (CGA) monitors display the colors red, blue, and green. These were the first IBM color monitors. The colors were not very bright and not as clear as the ones we use today.
- Enhanced Graphics Adapter (EGA) monitors were able to display up to 16 colors at the same time.
- Video Graphics Array (VGA) monitors display as many as 256 colors at one time.
- Super Video Graphics Array (SVGA) monitors are the monitors we use today. They still display 256 colors, but the colors are much sharper.

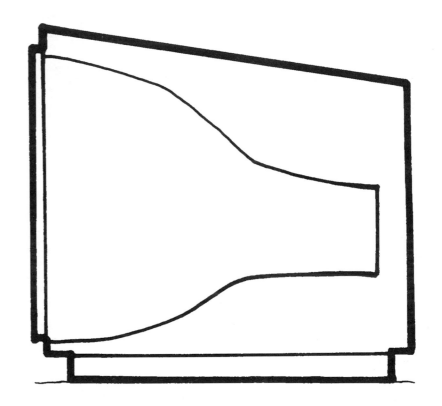

The Side View of a Monitor

Activity: Go to a local computer store and have a salesperson demonstrate some of the different monitors they have available.

Printers

A **printer** is a device attached to your computer that prints information processed by your computer onto a piece or several pieces of paper. A **hardcopy** is that piece of paper that has your printed work on it. Printers vary in size, style, printing speed, output capabilities, and price.

Dots per inch (dpi)—is the measurement of how sharp your print will be. If you have 300 dpi, that means your printer will print 90,000 dots per inch. The higher number dpi, the sharper your print will be.

These are the most common printers.

Dot matrix—A set of pins on the print head hit the ribbon in the shape of the character typed.

Ink jet—A fine jet of ink electrically charged hits the paper and prints each character.

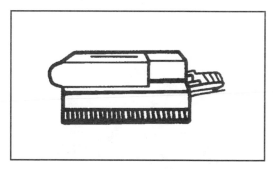

Laser—A laser beam of heat and a drum make black toner stick to paper to make it print.

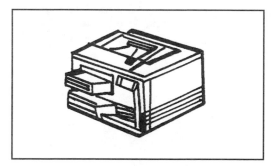

Daisy wheel—This has a round printwheel with all the characters on it. This print wheel is rotated to the right character and then printed.

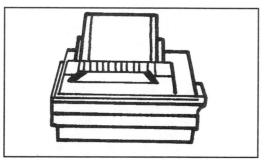

Activity: Go to a local computer store and have a salesperson demonstrate the different printers they have available.

Disk Drives

A disk drive is the part of your computer which reads programs and data from your magnetic disks. Data is information you give to your computer. Once the disk drive reads this data, it copies it into the computer's memory so that it can be used by the computer.

Many computers today have three disk drives in them:

Floppy disk drive—is found on the outside of your computer. This is where you insert your floppy disks. Usually there is only one floppy disk drive, but it is not uncommon to have two floppy disk drives. Most floppy disks today are 3.5" in diameter. However, many people still have and use the older floppy disks, which are 5.25" in diameter. These disk drives are known as the a: drive and the b: drive.

Hard drive—is found inside your computer. It stores and saves everything you put into the computer, even after you turn it off. The hard drive is made of several nonflexible disks stacked together with recording heads. You can put programs from disks onto your hard drive. The hard drive is known as the c: drive.

CD-ROM drive—is also found on the outside of the computer. It is where you insert your CD-ROM. It is known as the d: drive.

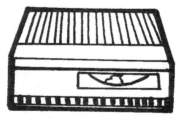

Activity: Carefully open up your external drives and examine the different disk drives.

Mouse

A mouse is an input device used for moving the cursor around on the screen. It must be used on a flat surface or mouse pad. As you move or point a mouse, the cursor moves on the screen.

There are usually two or three buttons on the top of a mouse. When you press or click a button (usually the left button with your index finger), an electronic signal is sent to the computer to select something on the screen. If you continue to hold down the mouse button as you move the mouse across the screen, you are dragging the mouse. This is used to move objects on the computer screen.

Eek! It's a Mouse!

A computer mouse is very similar to that of a real mouse. Look at this diagram of a computer mouse. The corresponding parts of a real live mouse are in parentheses.

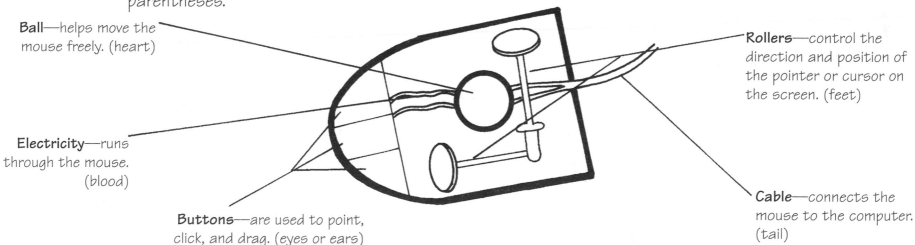

Ball—helps move the mouse freely. (heart)

Electricity—runs through the mouse. (blood)

Buttons—are used to point, click, and drag. (eyes or ears)

Rollers—control the direction and position of the pointer or cursor on the screen. (feet)

Cable—connects the mouse to the computer. (tail)

Activity: Draw your own computer mouse and give it real life features.

Scanners

A **scanner** is a device which you can use to copy a picture or words from a printed page onto your computer screen.

- Scanners can be hand held so you can move the scanner over the printed page.

If you have ever seen a picture on a t-shirt, it is done with a scanner and a computer. The picture is scanned onto a computer screen. Then the picture is printed onto a t-shirt rather than a piece of paper.

- Scanners can also be bigger. You could put your printed page into the scanner. It looks like a small copy machine. These scanners are more expensive than the hand-held versions.

Activity: Go to a local computer store and have a salesperson demonstrate the different scanners they have available. After the demonstration, try one yourself.

Computer-to-Computer Communication

People communicate with one another in a variety of ways. Computers can communicate with one another as well with the use of an attached modem. A modem changes a computer's binary coded digital signals into analog signals that can travel over telephone lines. Imagine being able to communicate with anyone anywhere in the world!

The word **MODEM** stands for **MOdulator/DEModulator.**

1. You type your message on your computer.

2. The modem changes digital signals to analog signals.

3. Your message travels along telephone lines.

4. Your message is received on your friend's computer.

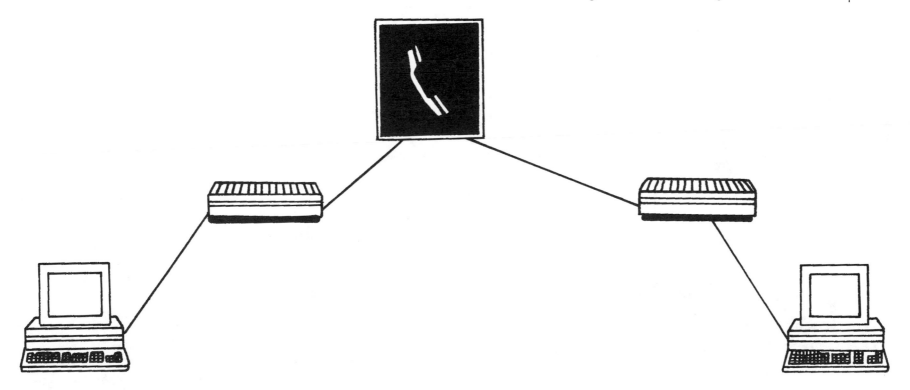

Activity: Locate a computer that has a modem and send a message to another computer.

Inside a Computer

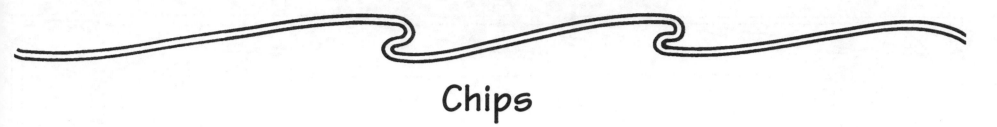

Chips

Chips can be found inside your computer. They carry electronic signals that tell a computer what to do. There are many chips inside your computer. Chips are made from a substance called **silicon**. Silicon can be found in quartz rocks. In chip-making, silicon is purified at very high temperatures and then mixed with other chemicals to make it an ideal semiconductor material.

Chips are about the size of your fingernail. Chips are covered with microscopic electronic circuits which control everything that a computer can do. Millions of tiny pulses of electricity flow through the chips in your computer. These currents of electricity are used by the chips as signals to send and receive messages inside a computer.

Think of it this way. A chip is somewhat like your own brain. Your brain sends messages to your body so that you can do many things. A chip works in a similar way inside a computer. However, there is one really big difference. A chip must be programmed—given a set of instructions—before it can do anything. Chips are programmed by people.

Inside your computer, chips process and compare information, perform calculations, and execute operations.

Chips can also be found in calculators, watches, robots, spaceships, and many other electronic devices and equipment.

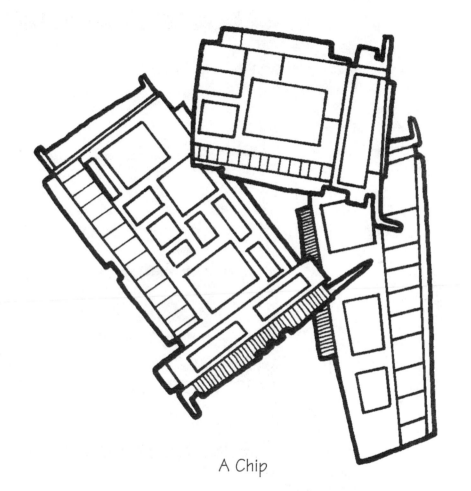

A Chip

Activity: Look around your house and make a list of how many things you can find that have chips in them.

Circuit Boards

A computer is a complex system of connected electronic circuits. A circuit is a set of electronic components that perform a particular function in an electronic system. They are pathways on which electricity flows.

A computer has yet to be invented that can work with just one chip. Therefore, each chip that exists inside a computer must be connected in an orderly way. Chips are arranged on circuit boards inside computers. Circuit boards are made of plastic and come in different sizes. Their sizes depend upon their functions and the number of chips they need to run.

Each circuit board looks like a miniature city. There are metal tracks on circuit boards on which electricity flows. There are also other electronic devices—transistors, resistors, and capacitors—which control the amount and smooth flow of electricity.

Each particular circuit board contains chips which perform a specific function within a computer. Circuit boards are also known as printed circuit boards (PCB's). The more circuit boards your computer has, the more capabilities your computer has.

A Circuit Board

Activity: Have an adult carefully help you open up your computer and examine the circuit boards inside.

Motherboard

The **motherboard** is a large computer circuit board. It is also known as the **system board**. It contains chips, as well as the computer's central processing unit (CPU) and random-access memory (RAM). We will learn more about these on the following pages. Until then, understand that the mother board is (1) the largest circuit board in your computer and (2) the main circuit board in your computer. On your motherboard you will find expansion slots. These slots are spaces that are used to connect smaller circuit boards. For example, if you want to increase the memory of your computer, you can add a smaller memory circuit board to your motherboard.

Think of it this way. Your motherboard is like a loose-leaf binder. If you want to write more but have run out of pages, you simply need to add more loose-leaf pages to your binder. The same is true about your motherboard. Anytime you wish to add something to your computer, you usually just have to connect another circuit board to your motherboard.

When you buy a computer, you should get one that has a motherboard with several expansion slots. This way you will have the ability to add peripherals to your computer.

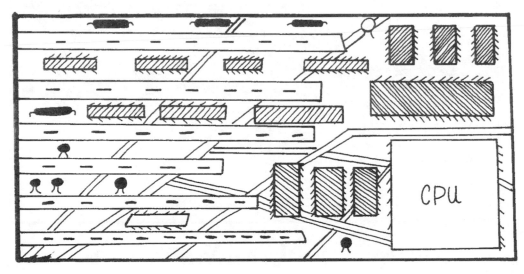

The Motherboard

Daughterboards

Daughterboards are smaller circuit boards that can be connected to the motherboard's expansion slots in your computer. Daughterboards come in a variety of sizes. This depends upon the number of chips they have and the job they are to perform in the computer.

Daughterboards can be added to your computer to provide video, audio, memory, graphics, input devices, and a number of other peripheral devices that you may require. Remember, a computer cannot do anything on its own. It needs chips to tell it what to do, and these chips are found on circuit boards.

Daughterboards are also known as **expansion cards**.

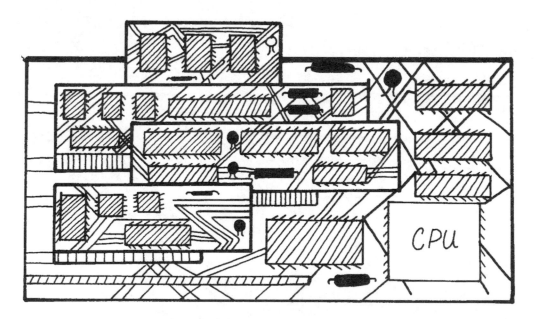

Daughterboards Connected to a Motherboard

Activity: Look inside your computer to see the different daughterboards connected to your motherboard.

Central Processing Unit (CPU)

The **central processing unit (CPU)** is the brain of your computer. It carries out all the functions needed to control the operations within your computer. It regulates and controls the flow of information in and out of your computer. Also, the CPU contains the arithmetic/logic unit (ALU)—where arithmetic and logical operations are carried out—as well as the control unit—which directs the step-by-step operation of all the parts of the computer.

The CPU is the most important chip inside your computer.

The same way your own brain controls everything that your body does, the CPU controls everything your computer does. Without the central processing unit, your computer would not know what to do or how to do it.

Miniaturization and integration techniques have made it now possible to develop a CPU chip called a microprocessor. As a result, we now have smaller, more personal computers.

The Central Processing Unit

Random Access Memory (RAM)

Random Access Memory (RAM) is one of the types of memory chips found inside your computer. It is used to hold programs and data you put into the computer while your computer is in operation.

RAM is the computer's primary workplace. All information or data that you put into RAM only stays there while the computer is turned on. Once you turn the computer off, any information in RAM will be erased and lost forever. Therefore, you must save your data to a disk before turning off your computer if you do not want to lose it.

Think of RAM as a blackboard. Any information a teacher writes onto a blackboard must be copied into your notebook if you want to save the information written on the blackboard. When the teacher is finished, he/she will erase the blackboard, and all the information will be gone. But because you saved or copied the information into your notebook, you will have it forever. The same is true of RAM in your computer. RAM is a temporary workplace inside your computer. You must save your work onto a disk before you turn off your computer, or else your work will be erased and lost forever.

RAM is Like a Blackboard

Read Only Memory (ROM)

Read-Only Memory (ROM) is a permanent memory chip inside your computer. It is installed into your computer when it is first manufactured.

ROM cannot be altered or changed. It is programmed by the manufacturer, and it does not lose its contents, nor can any of its information be erased when your computer is not on.

ROM (pronounced rahm) basically contains all the information the computer needs to tell it how to run and do all that it is supposed to do. For instance, ROM tells your computer how to do various operations:

- how to turn itself on and off
- start-up instructions
- load your computer's operating system
- where your computer can find its disk drives
- how to read information from disks

Do you think you have something like ROM in your own brain? Is there information in your own brain that will never be erased? What about your name? Are you a male or a female? Do you know how to get up out of bed each morning? What language do you speak? I think you can see that ROM is permanent information inside your computer that basically tells your computer what it is and how to work.

ROM Is Permanent Information Inside a Computer

Activity: See if you can list other ways you have ROM chips in your own brain and body.

Bits

A **bit** is the smallest unit of data a computer can process or understand.

A bit is a binary digit.

A bit is either a zero or a one.

Transistors inside your computer act as on/off switches to create the language your computer uses to process data and information.

The information we feed into computers turns into electronic pulses. These pulses are the only language that computers understand. Each electronic pulse is equals either "on" or "off." The "1" is equal to "on" and "0" is equal to "off." Computers use these two choices to process all the information we give them.

Millions of electronic pulses move through your computer every second. Computers are capable of processing thousands of functions in the time it takes you to blink your eye.

1 = ON

0 = OFF

bit = binary digit

Byte

A **byte** is equal to eight bits. A computer only understands binary code—data written as ones or zeros that represent electronic pulses.

When your computer puts together eight bits, it makes one byte, which is the amount of information needed by your computer to produce one alphanumeric character (a letter or a number, i.e., t or 3). A character is any letter, number, punctuation mark, or symbol found on the keys of a keyboard.

We make words using the 26 letters of the alphabet. Your computer makes words using bytes. Remember, a byte is a group of eight electronic signals that represent one piece of information. Inside your computer, electronic pulses move through the circuit boards to the computer chips. In each little chip, there are millions of very small switches lined up in sets. When an electronic pulse reaches a chip, it turns each switch on or off in an exact order. Each letter, number, punctuation mark, and special character on the keyboard has its own pattern of "on's" and "off's" (ones and zeros).

When you type the word "me," the computer turns it into this:

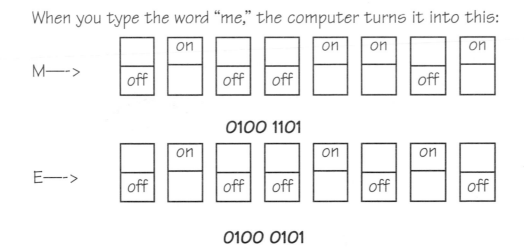

an example of bytes in binary code

Activity: Write your name in binary code (look in any computer book for the binary codes for each character).

Diskettes

A disk or diskette is a reusable storage device that holds information. It is used to save or store completed work from a computer and can also physically transport programs from one computer to another. In order for a disk to work, it needs to be inserted into a computer's floppy disk drive found on the main body of a computer. It should be removed when you turn off your computer but will not be damaged if it is not. However, if your disk is in your disk drive when you turn it on, you will cause an error and possible damage to the disk.

Disks come in a variety of sizes, as well as having a variety of capabilities, but they have all been developed for one purpose—to hold information. There are two types of disks, magnetic and optical. Magnetic disks are what we put into our floppy disk drives. They are round pieces of plastic that are coated with a magnetic substance. Data can be stored in magnetic or nonmagnetic areas. Optical disks, such as CD-ROMs, have their data burned into them with a laser. Disks can be purchased one of two ways—either blank, that is with no information until you put it there, or as commercial software, which have programs already on them.

Activity: Go to a computer store and locate all the different types of disks that are available.

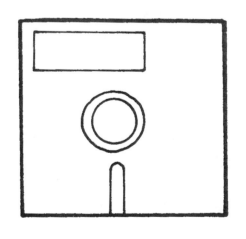

5.25" Floppy Disk

3.5" Floppy Disk

CD-ROM Disc

Laser Disc

5.25" Diskettes

One of the two types of diskettes available today is the 5.25". This was the first type of diskette produced. They are square and actually measure 5.25" in diameter. These diskettes are very flexible. The disk itself is enclosed in a protective plastic envelope. You can actually see the disk in three places—the center, a small circle to the right of the center, and a long oval beneath the center. Be very careful not to touch the disk itself. It is always a good practice to hold any floppy disk by its label so that you will never touch the disk itself. By doing so, you can damage your disk.

These disks can be single-sided (SS), which means you can record your data on one side only, or double-sided (DS), which means you can record your data on both sides. Single-sided disks are not used much anymore.

Disk density refers to the amount of data that can be stored on a diskette. double-sided (DS) disks can store twice as much data as single-sided (SS) disks.

Today, 5.25" disks are being replaced by sturdier 3.5" disks and CD-ROMs.

Activity: Take apart a 5.25" diskette to see how it is constructed. Locate and identify its parts: disk and protective cover.

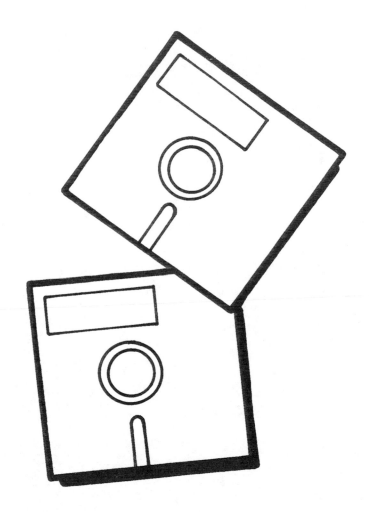

5.25" Diskette

3.5" Diskettes

Most of the floppy disks used in computers today are the 3.5" size. They are rapidly replacing the 5.25" disks. Although they are similar in size, the 3.5" disks have the ability to store and hold more information, as well as being sturdier.

Although 3.5" disks do not appear to be floppy, in reality they are. The disk is still floppy. The protective cover, though, is made of a sturdier and more durable plastic.

All 3.5" disks have write-protection notches on the upper right-hand side. These notches allow you to protect the data you have already saved to your disk, or they allow you to write over it. Audio and video tapes also have write-protection tabs on them.

Think of floppy disks as musical cassette tapes which can record and play back music. Make this analogy to 3.5" floppy disks, 5.25" floppy disks, eight-track musical tapes, and musical cassette tapes.

Activity: Take apart a 3.5" blank disk. Compare it to a 5.25" disk.

3.25" Floppy Disk

Formatting a Disk

When you buy a new blank floppy disk you must format it before you can use it in your computer. A floppy disk must be organized into magnetic bands because a blank floppy disk has no magnetic patterns. Formatting is also known as initializing a disk, that is, dividing it up into tracks and sectors. Sectors are pie-like slices made by lines from the outer edge to the center of a disk. Tracks are rings around a disk.

Formatting your disk is done by the operating system in your computer. Once your disk is formatted, a pattern is established for storage, retrieval, and printing of your data.

Think of your disk as a binder you would use in school. Usually, a binder is divided into several sections so that all your work will be neatly organized and easy to store and locate for future use. Imagine putting your papers in random order. Everything would be messed up. You should also put your name on your binder so you can identify it as your own. Your formatted or initialized disk works the same way.

New blank disks can be purchased formatted or unformatted. Formatted disks cost a little more but will save you and your hard drive time and work.

Activity: Format a blank disk on your computer.

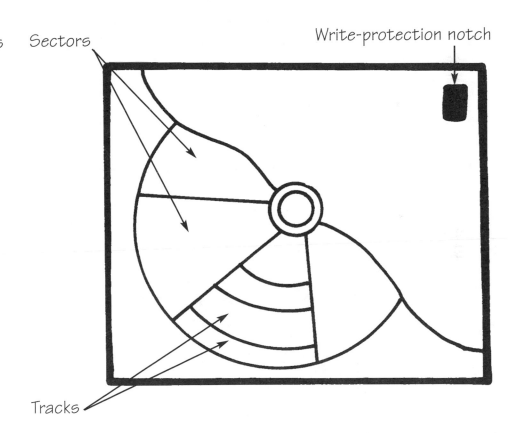

Sectors

Write-protection notch

Tracks

Formatting a Floppy Disk

#3457 Computers Don't Byte!

CD-ROM Discs

A CD-ROM measures 4.5" in diameter. It is used to hold text, graphics (pictures), and stereo sound. It looks like an audio musical CD but uses a different track format for its data. Stereo CDs can be played through a computer's CD-ROM drive, but your stereo system cannot play your computer CD-ROMs because they are formatted differently.

When a computer reads information from a CD-ROM, it does not do so magnetically like your diskettes. Instead information is recorded using a pattern of lands, smooth surfaces, and pits, depressions, on a disk. Your computer uses a beam of light to read the multimedia information on your disk. If the light hits a land, it is reflected; if it hits a pit, it is scattered. Electrical voltage is generated into patterns of 0's (pits) and 1's (lands).

CD-ROMs can be read only by your computer. You cannot write to them. That is why they are called Read Only Memory. However, the technology does exist today where you can write to a CD one time and then read it as much as you want. The technology that is still being worked on is the ability to write-erase-write to a CD over and over again.

CD-ROMs hold approximately 600 MB of data, which is equal to about 250,000 pages of text. For example, an entire set of encyclopedias including text, pictures, sound, and animations can be purchased on one CD-ROM.

CD-ROM

Activity: Use a CD-ROM encyclopedia. You will be amazed at what you will see.

Proper Disk Care

All disks must be cared for properly. If they are not, your disks will become unusable, and you risk loosing all of the data and information on your disks.

Below are some rules to follow so you will be able to protect the life of your disks (i.e., CDs, floppies, laser):

- Handle by the label only—NEVER touch the disk itself.
- Do not touch the metal part of your 3.5" disk.
- Do not bend your disk.
- Do not drop it on the floor.
- Keep it dry and clean.
- Keep it out of the direct sunlight and away from heat.
- Do not keep it in freezing temperatures.
- Never put it on top of your computer, monitor, microwave, TV, or near any magnetic field. Remember, disks are formatted magnetically, and exposure to magnetism of any kind will make "alphabet soup" of the information that was arranged on your disk.
- Never write directly on your disk—Write on the label first and then attach it to your disk.
- Keep all disks stored in jackets, boxes, or cases. Store disks standing upright.
- Hold CD-ROM's by their edges—Never touch the surface of the disk.

Proper Disk Care

Activity: Practice proper care of your CDs, floppies, and laser disks.

Software

Software

Software is computer programs that run on your computer. It is a step-by-step set of instructions expressed in computer-readable language. A common misconception is that software is data—or a collection of facts, calculations, ideas, and instructions that are processed by a computer. Software in reality tells the hardware how to process data.

Try to understand it this way. Think about baking a cake. All the ingredients represent data. The recipe itself, which gives you step-by-step instructions, represents the software.

There are several categories of computer software and several different types within each category. To understand the difference, think about music. There are many different categories of music, (e.g., classical, jazz, pop, rap, country, etc.). Once you have chosen a category of music, such as classical, you then need to choose a composer (Bach, Beethoven, Mozart, etc.). Got the idea?

There are four basic categories of software which you can use on your computer:

1. **Application software**—helps you perform a specific task on your computer.

2. **Utility software**—tells your computer how to run.

3. **Simulation software**—produces a model of a real-life situation.

4. **Educational software**—helps you to learn an educational related topic.

On the next few pages, you will learn more about the many various types of software you can purchase for use on your computer.

Activity: Go to a computer store to find all four categories of software. Then make a list of titles from each category.

1.

2.

3.

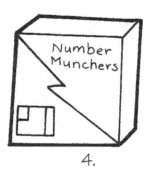

4.

Disk Operating System (DOS)

Remember that a computer cannot think or do anything for itself. It must be given instructions. Therefore, the first piece of software you will need to install onto your computer's hard drive is an operating system called **DOS**. DOS stands for disk operating system; it has its own set of commands that helps you to manage and organize your files in your computer. DOS allows you to format and prepare your diskettes to hold information for you and to arrange your files—a collection of related records. DOS also allows you to change disk drives, that is, tell your computer which disk drive your disk or disc is in so that the computer can read the information on it. DOS allows you to make backup copies of your original disks so that you can store the original disks in a safe place. This only scratches the surface of what DOS is capable of doing. Refer to any DOS guide that you can get from your local library or bookstore for further applications of DOS.

Think of DOS as a file cabinet within your computer. A file cabinet contains file folders in which all records are sorted and filed. You would not be able to find anything if papers were haphazardly placed into each drawer. You would certainly have a mess. DOS avoids this mess within your computer. It allows all files to be neatly sorted so that you can easily access all your files and information anytime you need them.

You can also think of DOS as a Xerox machine within your computer which allows you to make backup copies of your original disks, just as you would with a piece of paper on a copy machine.

Activity: Continue to research the DOS on your computer and see what else it can do.

Windows

Windows is a program many computer users use to manage files within their computers. Where DOS; organizes and runs your computer system, Windows organizes and runs the data and information you input to your computer.

Just because you have Windows does not mean that you do not need DOS, as they are two separate and distinct programs. DOS controls your computer's internal mechanics, while Windows controls DOS. Windows is one of the most popular operating environments for computers, although technically it is not a complete operating system because it requires and interacts with DOS.

If you are completely confused, picture in your mind the dashboard of the fanciest car you can imagine. Windows is that dashboard. Although the dashboard is fancy, pleasing to the eye, and easy to use, it still requires the mechanics of your car for any of the buttons on the dashboard to work. DOS is those mechanics, the workings behind all those buttons on the dashboard.

Many computers today use Windows. In fact, if you buy a new IBM type computer, you will find that Windows is already installed. To learn more about Windows, there are many books that you can read. However, Windows can offer more than one way to perform a simple task. Find out the easiest one for you and stick with it. It is kind of like solving a math problem. As long as you can explain how you got your answer, that is all that matters.

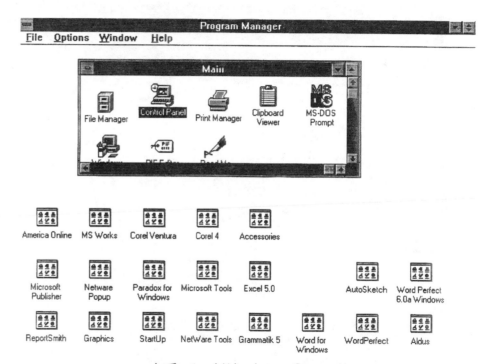

A Typical Windows Screen

Microsoft Windows 3.1 © (screen shot reprinted with permission from Microsoft Corporation)

Activity: Compare using DOS and Windows.

Application Software

Application software programs enable you and your computer to produce useful work. Application programs carry out jobs that you, the computer user, want to accomplish, as opposed to DOS and Windows, which carry out and control the workings of your computer.

This book was written using a word processing program.

Application software packages are capable of the following applications:

1. **Word processing**—Create letters and typewritten reports.

2. **Database programs**—Manipulate, store, record, and retrieve data.

3. **Spreadsheet**—Create and edit rows and columns of numerical data for budgets, financial reports, grades, etc. Spreadsheet programs accurately compute mathematical formulas.

4. **Graphic programs**—Create freehand drawings, as well as create slide shows and animations.

5. **Communication software and electronic mail**—Send and receive data with the use of this special software and a modem.

Remember, your computer is a tool used to do work. Application programs are but one type of software program that is your key into the many wonderful jobs you can do with your computer.

Activity: Make a list of as many different application software programs as you can.

Utility Software

Utility software assists you in maintaining and improving the proficiency and effectiveness of your computer. We have already discussed one of the most common utility programs that computers use—Windows.

Utility software programs are specially created to facilitate and assist the operation and use of your computer for a number of various functions and utilizations.

Think of your computer as a car. Most cars come equipped with standard equipment. However, you can add extras to your car to enable it to have air conditioning, power steering and brakes, tinted and power windows, stereo system, etc. The same is true of your computer. You can purchase additional utility programs which Windows does not provide.

These are some of the most common utility programs:

- screen savers
- virus protection programs
- file compression utilities
- defragmentation utilities
- text editors

The average computer user will be satisfied with a software package like Windows.

Activity: Pick one utility program that you would like to install onto your computer. Learn as much about it as you can so you will know how it will enhance the operation of your computer.

Simulation Software

Simulation software programs replicate real-life situations. They are interactive and set up problem solving situations.

One of the most important contributions computers are making is the ability to perform simulations, especially in the field of science and medicine. Not only do simulation programs help test scientific theories, they reduce the amount of time and the expense of using actual models.

Simulation programs are also being extensively used throughout our schools. Simulation techniques enable students to learn standard laboratory techniques when expensive lab equipment is unavailable. **Operation Frog** is a classic example whereby students dissect frogs on their computer screens. Also, comparisons are made between the organs of a frog and that of a human being. Other popular educational simulation programs are **The Oregon Trail**, **Voyage of the Mimi**, **Where in the World Is Carmen Sandiego**, and **Sim City**, just to name a few of the many wonderful simulation programs in existence.

You can also purchase simulation programs that build cars, planes, houses, remodel your kitchen, and even fly a plane. You can assume the role of a pioneer, architect, detective, pilot, doctor, or scientist as you participate in the model situations presented in simulation software programs.

Activity: Prepare a list of questions you could use with a simulation program. (What would I do. . . ?, What if. . . ?)

Educational Software

Educational software is widely used in schools, as well as at home. You can purchase educational software relating to any subject area and at any grade level. Educational software is exceptionally user friendly. It is easy to use and gives positive and non-judgmental feedback.

One of the most commonly used educational software programs is **The Children's Writing and Publishing Center**. With it, students can create wonderful stories and reports which include both text and graphics.

Many educational software products are of a drill and practice nature—that is, they reinforce what a child has already learned. Popular drill and practice programs are **Money Works, Clock Works, Number Munchers, Word Munchers, Reader Rabbit**, and **Reading and Me**.

Other educational programs actually contain topics from which a child can learn concepts in all subject areas. Some even contain tutorials. Such programs are **Algeblaster, Math Blaster Mystery, CD-ROM encyclopedias, Work Attack**, and **What's My Angle**.

Simulation software packages are very popular educational programs, as well. They allow students to think logically and to develop higher-order thinking skills. The most popular educational simulation programs are **Where in the USA Is Carmen Sandiego, The Oregon Trail, Sim City, Headline Harry**, and **The Amazon Trail**.

Remember, educational software and computers will never replace the role of a teacher. They are only tools used to enhance learning. Computers do no have the feelings, love, care, or concern that can be expressed by teachers and parents and are needed by all children.

Activity: Discuss among your friends everyone's favorite educational program. Ask your teachers or parents if it is possible to purchase and use educational software on the computers in your school or at home.

Entertainment Software

Entertainment software packages are perhaps one of the most popular types of software packages you can purchase to use on your computer. Unfortunately, once you begin playing with a piece of entertainment software on your computer, you may find it addictive.

One of the most popular entertainment pieces of software today is **MYST**. It is an adventure that has delighted many a computer user. Other popular entertainment adventures are **King's Quest** and **Police Quest**.

There are also many popular board games that you can now play on your computer. Trivial Pursuit, Scrabble, Risk, Monopoly, Clue, and Chinese Checkers are a few of the games available.

Many television game shows can also be played on the computer, such as Jeopardy, Concentration, and Wheel of Fortune.

Sports are also very popular forms of entertainment. Games like football, baseball, car racing, and billiards can all be played on your computer.

Be advised that some software can be violent in nature and is not suggested for children. Overall though, the majority of entertainment software is wholesome and enjoyable to use.

Activity: Design an entertainment piece of software that you would like to play on your computer.

Virtual Reality

Virtual reality software creates a life-like illusion. You will feel the experience of actually becoming a part of a computer-generated world. This type of software uses special visual- and audio-generated graphics and sounds which allow you to manipulate the program so that you feel as if you are part of the computer program. It is similar to that of simulation software but more enhanced. Most often a three-dimensional perception will be experienced.

For example, virtual reality software is being used successfully in many different areas. In the field of science and technology, virtual reality software is being used to simulate and practice surgical techniques by doctors and to train and test pilots, astronauts, and aircrafts. Virtual reality software is also being used to design three-dimensional buildings, cars, airplanes, and homes. In the field of entertainment, virtual reality software allows you to experience anything from an active part in a golf tournament to holding your breath as you feel the excitement of skiing down a ski slope.

Virtual reality software is becoming more and more popular. It allows the user to experience real-life situations in an engrossing and exciting way. Each virtual reality software user will travel differently through sensational worlds of wonder and excitement.

Activity: Go to a local computer store and have a salesperson demonstrate virtual reality software, if it is available.

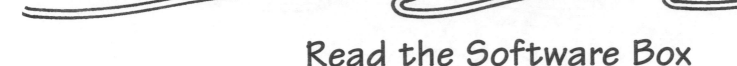

Read the Software Box

When you go into a store to buy a piece of software, or if you order it through a catalog, there are some considerations you must take into account. Most obviously, you must decide upon the type and then the title of the software you are purchasing. You should also note the publisher, date of publication, and a description of the software. This information will let you know whether the software will meet with your goals, as well as whether it will be compatible with your computer system. **Compatible** means that the software program will run on your computer.

On every software box the following information is listed:

- the type of computer it is compatible with
- the size of the disk enclosed—3.5", 5.25", or CD-ROM. You must have the appropriate disk drive.
- the version of DOS needed to execute the program
- the minimum amount of RAM necessary to run the program
- the type of monitor needed—EGA, VGA, or SVGA
- whether it supports a mouse, a joystick, etc.

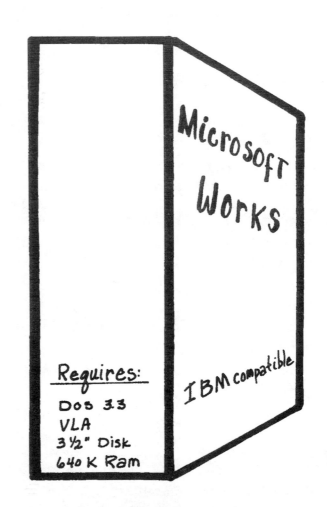

A Software Box

Activity: Examine a software box. Make sure you can locate all of the important information on it.

384

Copyright Laws

Most software is protected by **copyright laws**. This means that you may not make illegal copies of software that you have purchased. Many manufacturers build into their programs copy protection which prevents you from making duplicate copies of a particular program. Some companies allow you to make one back-up copy so that you can store the original disk(s) in a safe place. Sometimes, you will not be allowed to make a back-up copy, but for a minimal fee, you can send away for one.

Different publishers have different licensing agreements. When you purchase a piece of software, in effect you are also purchasing the rights to use that software on your computer. Copyright laws protect software programmers and publishers, just as copyright laws protect authors and illustrators.

It is illegal to copy software and pass it on to a friend or have a friend make an illegal copy of a piece of software for you. Breaking copyright laws is not only wrong but is punishable by imposing fines and jail sentences.

However, there are **shareware** programs that you can purchase. As the name implies, shareware programs can be copied and shared with your friends. They are also inexpensive, but the copyright holder often asks you to send a donation if the program is regularly used.

Public domain software is not protected by copyright laws. It is donated to the public by its creator. You can feel free to duplicate and share these programs with your friends. Public domain software is also inexpensive.

Do Not Copy That Floppy

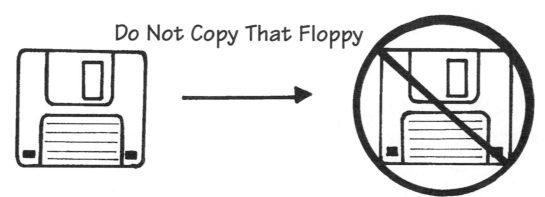

Activity: Research further software copyright laws. Read carefully the copyright laws enclosed with any piece of software you have purchased.

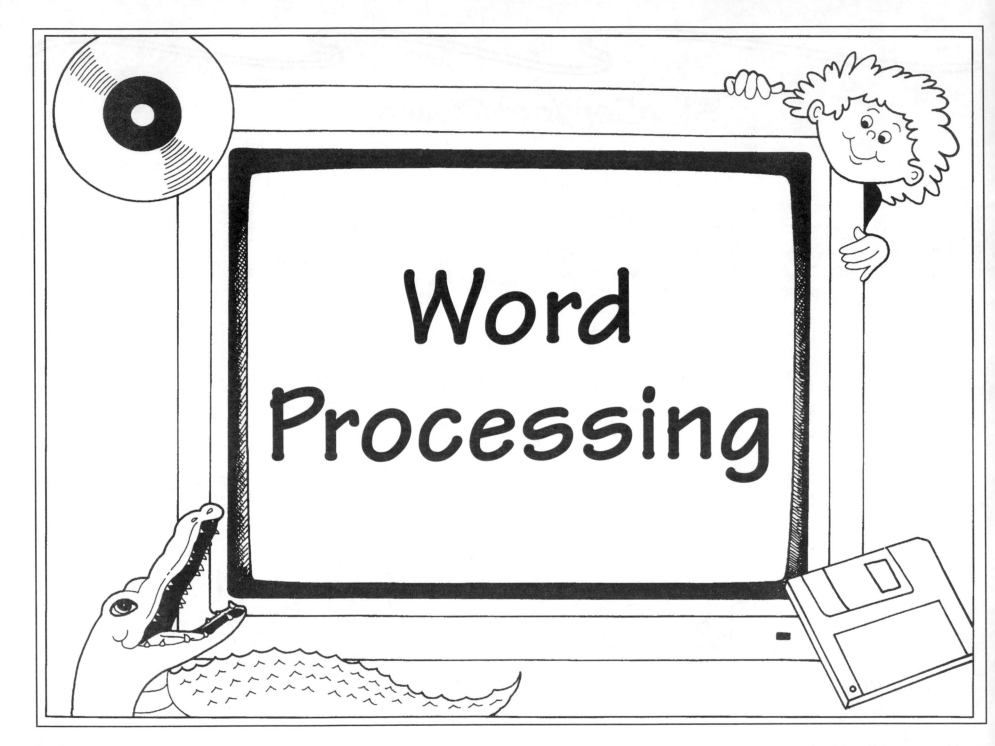

Word Processing

What Is Word Processing?

Word processing is a type of application software especially designed to make the creation of a written document (e.g., letter or report) easier. **Microsoft Word** and **Word Perfect** are two of the most commonly used word processing programs used by computer users today.

So what makes a word processing programs so different from that of a standard typewriter? Well, word processing programs provide you with all the tools a writer needs to create and edit text, check spelling, use a thesaurus, lay out pages, move and cut text, insert words, sentences, or paragraphs, scroll to view text, change character sizes, and boldface and underline text. Also, if you find an error after printing out your document, it is very simple to go back into your document on your computer and correct any problems without retyping anything like you would on a typewriter.

Word processors are user-friendly, that is, they offer you help if and when you get stuck. Many of them come with tutorials, as well, that give you step-by-step instructions before you ever begin.

It may seen complicated now, but word processing software programs give you the opportunity to produce professional looking documents in an easy and efficient way.

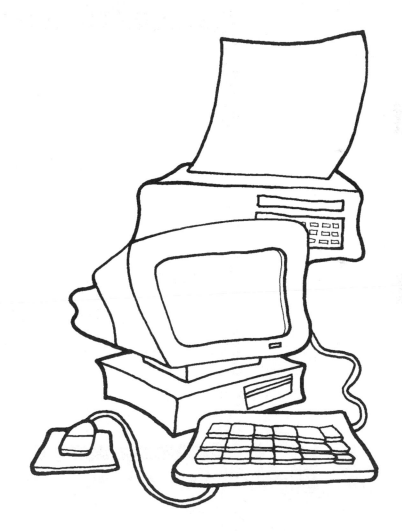

Activity: Go to your library and take out and view a video about a word processing program.

#3457 Computers Don't Byte!

Understanding Word Processing—Characters, Text, and Documents

You may be overwhelmed after reading the previous page about word processing. Hopefully, you are ready to try to learn how to create different documents on your computer, using a word processing program. Before doing this, it will be easier if you understand some of the more important word processing terms.

First, remember that **characters** can be letters, numbers, and symbols that you use on your keyboard.

Text is made up of many characters. It is words, sentences, and paragraphs of information you want to express.

This sentence is an example of text.

A **document** is a completed piece of text. A document can be one page or many pages. It can be a letter, report, poem, list of information, recipe, or any other typewritten file. The printed sheet(s) of paper with your document on it is called a **hardcopy**.

This book your are reading is a document. There are many types of documents that you can create. It is not hard to do, so have fun.

> Each page in this book is a separate document. There are many types of documents that you can create. It is not hard to do.

Activity: Find a poem you like and practice typing it, using your word processor.

Word Processing Terms to Know

There are a few basic word processing terms that need to be clarified before we continue any further into the wonderful world of word processing.

The first is **highlighting text**. Whenever you want to do something special with certain characters in your text, you must first tell your computer which characters you would like to select. It is similar to using a highlighting marker in a book when you want something to stand out that you have written or read. Of course, you cannot use a highlight marker on your computer screen, but there is an easy way to highlight text within your document. The easiest way is to use your mouse. Put your mouse arrow at the beginning of the information you want to highlight, hold down your mouse button, and simply move the mouse over the text you want to highlight. Then, let go of your mouse button. Your highlighted text will turn black or some other color, causing it to stand out on your screen.

If you do not have a mouse, there is another way to highlight text. You still need to move your cursor to the desired location. Then, activate your highlight control and use your arrow keys to highlight your text.

Why would you have a need to highlight text? You highlight text so you can make a change to a character, word, sentence, or paragraph.

Some of the changes that are available using your highlight function:

- **Underline**—place a straight line under a piece of text
- **Center**—place your text into the middle of a page
- **Boldface**—emphasize text by making it visibly darker
- **Italicize**—emphasize text by making it slightly slanted

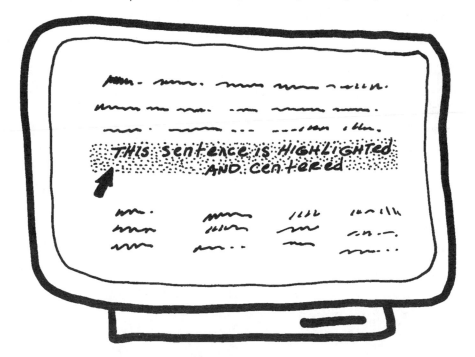

Activity: Learn how to highlight text without using your mouse and practice that function.

Scrolling Text

As you are type down your page, eventually you will come to the bottom of the screen. Did you run out of room? Can you type any more? Yes! Think of your computer monitor as having an endless scroll of paper inside of it. Most people who word process will never reach the end of the scroll. **Scrolling** is the movement of text up or down as a new blank line appears at the bottom of your screen. As your text disappears from your screen, do not worry; it is not lost forever. It has just moved upward and out of sight.

Many times your document will be several pages long. Remember you can use the page up and page down keys to look up and down within your document. You can use the control (Ctrl) key with the home and end keys to go quickly to the beginning and end of your document. Or you can scroll more slowly, using your arrow keys.

As your document scrolls, your word processor will automatically place a page break and start a new page. This is usually indicated on your screen by a little arrow on the bottom left of your screen. You also have the option of placing your own **page breaks** within your document and **numbering your pages**.

Activity: Read over the section in your word processing manual that talks about scrolling and page breaks in your document. Try practicing these techniques.

Setting Up Your Page, Wrap Around, and Tabs

As you type on a keyboard, your characters and text will appear on the screen of your computer. This works much the same way as a typewriter. However, when you come to the end of a line using a word processing program, your computer will automatically start the next line by using the **wrap-around** function. When using a typewriter, you must hit the return key.

When typing your words, they will not run off the page.

Your words will wrap-around to the next line.

When you want to start a new paragraph, there are two things that should happen. First, you need to press **ENTER** key at least once to move the cursor to the next line. Remember that a **cursor** is a blinking line or box that acts as a place marker on your screen. Wherever the cursor appears is where the next character that you type will be placed. The second thing you can do when starting a new paragraph is to press your **TAB** key, **indenting** your paragraph. Using your TAB key moves your cursor more than one space at a time.

[tab] Sam was chosen first to play on the baseball team. Everyone knew how well he could pitch and hit the ball. The coach would always let Sam pitch at the start of the game and when he would get tired, he would put in Johnny.

[tab] In the outfield Christine was the best player, she always got to play the entire game.

Activity: Practice changing and setting tabs.

What Are Margins?

Your page has four **margins**—this is, the number of spaces between your text and the right and left edges of a page, as well as the number of spaces between your text and the top and bottom of a page. Normally, you do not need to change the standard settings for the margins on your page. Standard page settings allow for a 1" margin at the top and bottom of your page and 1.25" margins to the left and right. So why would you want to change your margins? Maybe you would like to fit just one more sentence onto your page and you need just a little more room. What would you do? Well, try changing your bottom margin from 1" to .5". You could also do this to your top margin. Or, maybe you would like to change your left and right margins from 1.5" to 1" to give you more room on your page.

There is usually a ruler on the top of your screen that you can use to view how you need to set your margins, as well as your tabs.

Margins allow you to type text neatly without getting too close to the sides of the page. The dotted lines are imaginary margins.

Margins

Activity: Type a one-and-a-half-page story on your computer, using your word processing program. Then, change the settings of your margins and watch what happens.

Justification and Centering

Here are some other concepts related to word processing that you should understand and know how to use.

When you are using a word processing program, to **justify**, means the alignment of the lines of text along the left margin, the right margin, or both margins.

1. **Left justification** is most common. When text is left justified, it is lined up flush against the left side of the page.

2. **Right justification** allows your text to be lined up along the right side of the page. This would not be common or appropriate for an entire document but might be used for an address on the top right side of a letter.

3. **Full justification** is when your text is lined up evenly on both the left and right margins. Newspapers and magazines use fully justified text much of the time.

4. **Centering** your text means to put your text in the exact center of the page.

A document can have all four types of justification on each page. You can change the justification or center your text by pressing the justification or center command in your word processing program.

Look on the next page to see a sample letter written where all four types of justification were used.

Activity: Learn how to use all four types of justifications with your word processor.

Justification and Centering (cont.)

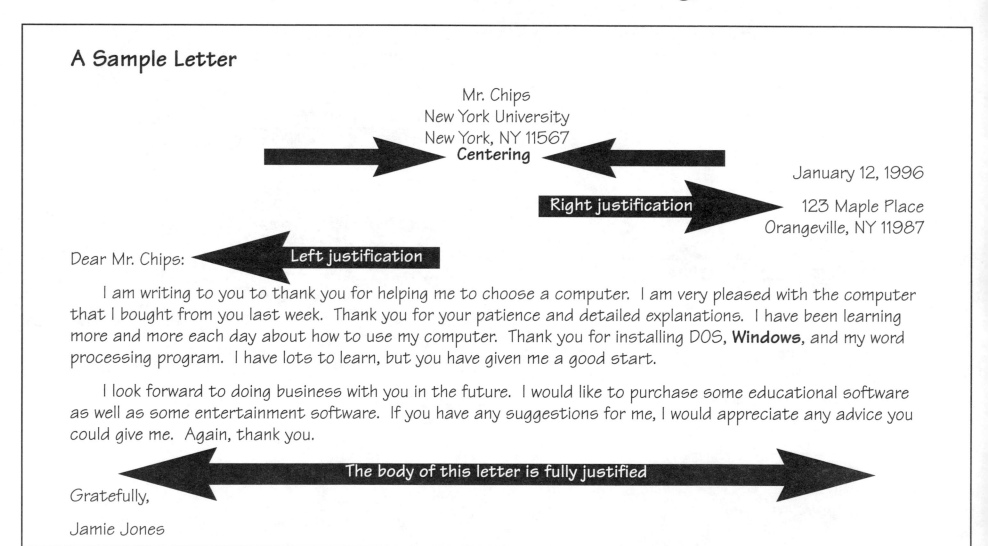

A Sample Letter

Mr. Chips
New York University
New York, NY 11567

Centering

January 12, 1996

Right justification

123 Maple Place
Orangeville, NY 11987

Dear Mr. Chips:

Left justification

I am writing to you to thank you for helping me to choose a computer. I am very pleased with the computer that I bought from you last week. Thank you for your patience and detailed explanations. I have been learning more and more each day about how to use my computer. Thank you for installing DOS, **Windows**, and my word processing program. I have lots to learn, but you have given me a good start.

I look forward to doing business with you in the future. I would like to purchase some educational software as well as some entertainment software. If you have any suggestions for me, I would appreciate any advice you could give me. Again, thank you.

The body of this letter is fully justified

Gratefully,

Jamie Jones

Activity: Try typing a letter on your computer, using the four types of justification.

Editing Text—Inserting

While you are working on your document, there may be a situation where you forget to add a letter, a word, a line, or even a whole section of text. Don't panic! You do not have to type your entire document over again. All you need to do is move your cursor to the place where you need to insert the missing letter, word, line, or section of text.

Insert simply means to add characters to already typed text. In order to do this you need to move your cursor, using your arrow keys or mouse to the place where you want to insert the text. Then just start typing. The text that is already there will begin to move to the right and down to make room for your newly inserted text. When you do this, you are typing in the insert mode of your word processor. Normally all typing is done in the **insert mode**.

By changing a command in your word processor, you can change to another type of insertion mode in your word processor if you desire. It is called the **overtype mode**. In this case, when you type, you will actually be typing over the characters already typed in your document. The characters you type over will be lost, as they are replaced with new ones. It is usually not a good idea to type in the overtype mode because you may forget to turn it off and then lose wanted text.

Both the insert mode and overtype mode of your word processor are toggled by pressing the Ins (Insert) key.

There is a word that was left out and should be added to this sentence.

> There is a word that was left out and should added to this sentence.

1. Move the cursor with your arrow keys before the letter "a" is added.

2. Type the word "be" into your document.

3. Hit the space bar to put a space between the words "be" and "added."

4. Move the cursor to the end of your sentence and continue typing.

5. The word "added" will move down automatically to the next line, as will all the words following it.

Activity: Practice inserting text into your document.

Editing Text—Deleting

In the same manner that you may want to insert text, there may be times when you would like to remove or take out already typed characters, words, sentences, and even paragraphs. To **delete** means to erase text. You can delete text in several ways.

The simplest way to delete text is to use your **backspace** key. The backspace key moves the cursor one place to the left. As the cursor moves to the left, it deletes the character along with it. Each time you press the backspace key, you delete another character. The backspace key is often used when you realize that you have just made a mistake while typing a current passage, and want to correct it immediately. You can also use your arrow keys to move your cursor to a place where you need to delete text. Once your cursor is in place, you can press the backspace key to delete a character, word, or words. You can also hold down the backspace key to make it move more quickly and then delete whole sentences or paragraphs rather quickly. Be careful; once you have deleted the only way to get the text back is by retyping it.

Another way you can delete text when word processing is to use the delete key (Del). Many novice computer users are afraid to press the delete key for fear that they will delete everything in their computers. This is not so. The delete key is only used to remove or erase unwanted text in word processing or any other application software. If you want to use the delete key to remove text, you must first position your cursor to the place where you want to delete your text. It is done the same way as when you insert text. Now you can start pressing the delete key. It is important to note that the **backspace** key deletes text to the left of it; the delete key deletes text to the right of it.

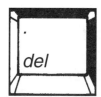

There is no right way to delete text. Both the backspace key and the delete key accomplish the task of deleting text. You will have to experiment on your own and decide which you prefer.

 or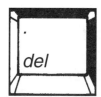

Activity: Experiment on your own word processor using the backspace and delete keys to delete text. Which do you prefer?

Cutting and Pasting Text

Try to remember back to the days when you were in kindergarten. What was one of the things your teacher taught you how to do? How many projects did you complete that included scissors and glue? How many times did you cut and paste? Although you do not have scissors and glue in your computer, you can still accomplish the same tasks with your word processor. Why would you want to do this? You have just completed a six-paragraph report, and after you read it over, you decide paragraph three should be after paragraph four. You certainly do not want to delete one and retype it over again. This is where the cutting and pasting of text is most beneficial.

You can move text around with two simple commands—**cut** and **paste**. Here is how you do it.

1. Move the cursor to the first character of the text that you want to move.

2. Highlight all of the words that you want to move.

3. Press the cut command key. This will remove the highlighted text.

4. Move the cursor to the place you want the previously cut text to reappear.

5. Press the paste command key. The text you cut a second ago now reappears like magic in a new position in your document.

Activity: Practice cutting and pasting text with your word processor.

Moving and Copying Text

There is a difference between moving text and copying text.

When you **move text**, you are literally taking text from one section of a document and moving it to another. The text in the original location is deleted. All remaining text will then be automatically readjusted so there will not be any unwanted space left in your document. This move and relocating function may come in handy if you decide to move a sentence or a paragraph to a new location in your document.

On the other hand, there may be times when you would like to **copy** a selected portion of text from one location and place it in another portion of your document. Your word processor will automatically copy your text from the original location to a new location. However, when you copy text, the text in the original location will not be deleted, only duplicated.

Think of moving and copying this way. If you have a favorite recipe for chocolate chip cookies and you loan the cookbook that the recipe is in to a friend, you are actually moving that recipe and cookbook from one location to another. However, if you decide to copy the recipe onto a separate piece of paper and then give it to a friend, you still have the original recipe plus a copy to give to a friend. Now, if you had typed the recipe for your chocolate chip cookies one time on your computer, you could use the copy command in your word processor to copy it over as many times as you would like.

Just remember that, whenever you decide to move or copy text, you must first select and highlight the text you wish to move or copy. Once you become more proficient with your word processor, you can not only move and copy text within your document, you can also take part of one document and move or copy it to a completely new and different document. Think of all the time you could save, not having to retype text that already exists.

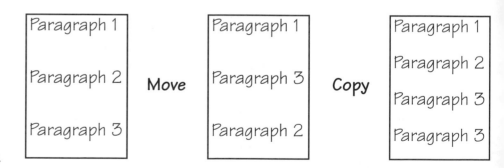

Activity: After reading how to move and copy text, practice it on your computer.

Search and Replace

The **search** and **replace** command is a function in your word processor that finds a designated word and replaces it with a new one. It is another feature of word processing.

Use the search command to locate text that you specify. Then use the replace command to change the text.

For example, you have just finished typing a ten-page report on George Washington. However, you realize after you finished that every time you typed George Washington, you forgot to capitalize his name. You made this mistake approximately 25 times. There is no need for panic. You will not have to manually search your document to find and fix every spelling mistake. This is a perfect opportunity to use your search and replace function. Here is how it works; first, you need to choose the search and replace command. Then your computer will ask you the following:

1. What word do you want to find? You type in "george washington" the way it is found in your document.

2. What word do you want to replace it with? You will type in George Washington—This is the way you want it to appear.

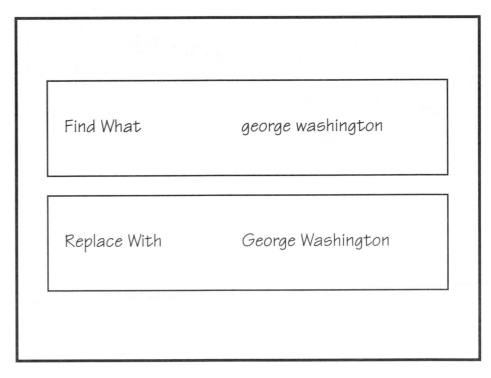

| Find What | george washington |
| Replace With | George Washington |

Using the search and replace function will save you lots of time correcting errors.

Activity: Describe another example of how the search and replace command can be used. Then practice it on your word processor.

Spell Check, Thesaurus, and Word Count

There are several functions available when using a word processor. The next three functions you will find very useful.

Spell Check

When you have finished typing a document, your word processor has the ability to check for any spelling errors that you have made. Within your word processor there is a built-in dictionary. All you have to do is activate your spell check function, and your computer will automatically begin searching for any misspelled words in your document. When a misspelled word is identified by your computer, you will be given several options of choosing the correct way to spell that word. When you choose the correct word, the misspelled word is automatically replaced with the new word you have chosen. Continue this process until the spell check reaches the end of your document.

| Not in dictionary: computr |
| Change to: computer |
| Suggest: computer
comport
compartment
compact |

Thesaurus

Not only does your word processor have a spell check, it also has a thesaurus function. Using it on a document is a great way to replace common words with synonyms, as well as increasing your vocabulary. The thesaurus function works similarly to the spell-check function. All you have to do is highlight the word you want to change, choose the thesaurus function, and your word processor will suggest several synonyms for you to choose from. Select the synonym of your choice, and the originally selected word will be replaced with your newly chosen word.

Word Count

When you are completing an assignment or report, you may be instructed to write a 500 or 1,000 word essay. You do not have to count each word manually. All you have to do is choose the word count command. Before you can blink your eyes, you will see the following:

| Words counted in document: 270 |

Activity: Practice these three features on your own word processor.

Fonts

A **font** is a special style of type that can be applied to any amount of text, ranging from one character to the entire document. Then, within each font style you have the ability to bold or italicize any piece of text you desire. There are many different font types that are available for you to use. Word processing programs come with several font styles already installed. However, if you want a font style that you do not already have on your computer, all you need to do is purchase the font software and install it onto your computer. Several common font styles are highlighted on this page.

Looking at some of the examples below, you can now see all of the endless possibilities of changing the appearance of your document. In order to change the font of your text, you need to first select the text you wish to change by highlighting it choosing the change font command, and deselecting the highlighted text once you have chosen a new font. Remember, if you change your text to a font you do not like, all you have to do is rehighlight the same text and change it back to the original font.

Times New Roman

Times New Roman Bold

Times New Roman Italicized

Avant Garde Book

Courier

Zapf Chancery

Helvetica

Roman

Script

Activity: Using your computer and word processing program, experiment with the different fonts that are available by changing your text.

Point Size

Your computer gives you the ability to change more than your font style. You also have the ability to change the size of your characters. **Point size** refers to how big or how small your characters appear on a document. A common point size used in publishing today is 12-point size. The larger or smaller the point size number, the larger or smaller the characters.

You have the ability to change the point size of any character or text in your document. You simply need to select the character(s) or text you want to change, highlight it, and and then choose the point size that you want to use. The process of changing point size is the same as changing the font type, just using a different set of commands.

Look at the examples below of different point sizes:

6 point siz

8 point size

10 point size

12 point size

14 point size

16 point size

20 point size

24 point size

30 point size

40 point size

Activity: On a separate piece of paper, write the word "computer" in five different point sizes.

Filenames and Saving Your Document to a Disk

As you write or word process a document, you should remember to periodically save your work. This simple process can save you hours of work because of an unexpected power surge or temporary loss of electricity to your computer system. There are several different places where you can save your work. One place is your c: drive or hard drive, a second place is the a: drive of your floppy disk drive, and the third place is the b: drive of your floppy disk drive. If you save it to your c: drive, then no disk is needed in this process; however, if you want to save it to your a: or b: drive, a disk is required. It is recommended that you save your work every 10–15 minutes. As you write or word process information, all your work is being written into a temporary storage area within your computer's memory. If something were to happen to that storage area, be it human or mechanical error, all the work that you have not saved would be lost. Once you save your work to a disk, it can never be erased unless you specifically use a DOS command and tell your computer to erase the information from your disk or hard drive. Remember, your disk or hard drive is a permanent storage area, just as if you were writing information into a notebook.

When you want to save your work to a disk, all you have to do is press the the "save" command. Then there will be several prompts before your work is actually saved. Your computer will ask you to name the document you wish to save. This is called making up a **filename**. A filename has to be eight characters or less and should have something to do with the topic of your document. For example, if you wrote a story about Thanksgiving, you might want to name your file "Thanks."

Remember, when you are ready to save a document, you must remember to specify which drive you want to save your document.

Your disk or hard drive is like a book. All of the filenames are like chapters. Your filenames are organized documents on a disk or hard drive, the same way chapters are organized in a book.

Activity: Practice saving your word processing files to your disk drive and hard drive.

Printing Your Document

Once your have completed writing or word processing your document, have checked your spelling, and made any desired changes in font and/or point size, you are finally ready to print your work. Remember, before printing your work, it should be saved to a disk or your hard drive. When your computer prints your document, it is taking the information from your disk or hard drive and copying it onto a piece or several pieces of paper.

Before you can print your document there are several things you must first do. (1) Make sure your printer is hooked up properly to your computer. (2) Make sure you have paper in your printer. (3) When you hook your printer to your computer, you must configure your printer to your word processing program. **Configure** means to set your hardware (printer) and software (word processing program) together so that they will work with each other. Then, when those three steps are completed, all you have to do is select the print command. You will be given several options when setting up your printer. Some of those options are shown below:

- number of pages do you want to print
- page numbers
- print from what page to what page
- draft or quality of printing

The work that you now have on paper is called your hard copy.

Activity: Print a hard copy of a story you have already word processed.

Retrieving Documents from Your Disk

Once you have printed out a hard copy of your document, you can close your word processing program and shut down your computer. As you read through your hard copy, you may realize there is something you want to add to your document. You must now retrieve your document from your disk or hard drive. Retrieving a document is the process of getting stored information from your disk or hard drive and putting it back onto your computer's screen. How are you going to do this?

• First, you must re-start your computer and open up your word processing program.

• Secondly, you must put the disk with your saved work into the disk drive of your computer. Or if your work is saved on your computer's hard drive, you can retrieve it from there.

• Finally, all you have to do is select the "open file" command and chose the file you want to open from your disk or hard drive. Your document will now appear on the screen, and you will now be ready to add to or edit your text. When satisfied with your corrections, all you have to do is save it and print another hard copy.

Activity: Practice retrieving your saved files from your disk or hard drive.

Menus

As you have learned to use your word processing program, you have probably learned that there are many options in your program from which to choose. How do you select and use these options? To access and select the options available in your program, you must use the menu bar on top of your computer's screen. A **menu** is an on-screen display which lists all the options available to you when using your word processing program. Anything that your computer allows you to highlight is usuable in your document. Some examples are printing, changing font styles, changing point sizes, checking your spelling, etc. These are only a few of the many menu items from which you can choose.

Menus are very simple to use and you do not have to be a computer whiz to figure them out. To use your menu bar, all you have to do is select the desired option with your Ctrl or Alt key along with your arrow keys, or to make it easier, just use your mouse.

Menus you use on a computer can be related to menus that you might find in a restaurant. For instance, if you would like to order French toast, you would have to look under the category "breakfast." If you want to order clam chowder, you would have to look under the category "soup." The same is true about your word processing program. If you want to save your document you would have to choose the word "file" from your menu. A listing will appear from which you can choose the save command. If you were to select the word "tools" from your menu, a listing would appear, which would allow you to select such commands as spell check, thesaurus, word count, etc.

Menu

File	Edit	View	Insert	Format	Tools	Help
open save print exit					spell check thesaurus word count	

Activity: Browse through the menu of your word processing program.

Icons

When reading your menu, there is an easier way to choose the commands you wish to use. You have the option of using the icons on top of your menu bar. An **icon** is a small picture representation or symbol of a computer command or function. It is activated by moving your cursor on top of the icon and then pressing enter or double clicking your mouse. This method of choosing commands is faster and more convenient than using the menu bar and pull-down menu.

Here are some examples of the icons you may find on the menu of your word processing program and a description of what command or function each one carries out.

Icon	Function	Icon	Function
	Opens up a file from your disk		Cuts out highlighted text when you want to move it to a new location
	Saves your work to a disk		Copies your highlighted text
	Prints your work		Pastes back into your document the text you chose to move or copy
	Allows you to preview your work before you print it	**B**	Boldfaces your text

Icons (cont.)

Icon	Function	Icon	Function
I	Italicizes your text		Opens up your thesaurus
U	Underlines your text	*ABC* ✓	Opens up the computer's dictionary so you can spell check a word or your entire document
	Left justifies your text		
	Centers your text		Activates the calculator so you can make quick calculation
	Right justifies your text		Sends current document as e-mail or fax
	Fully justifies your text	*?*	Help!

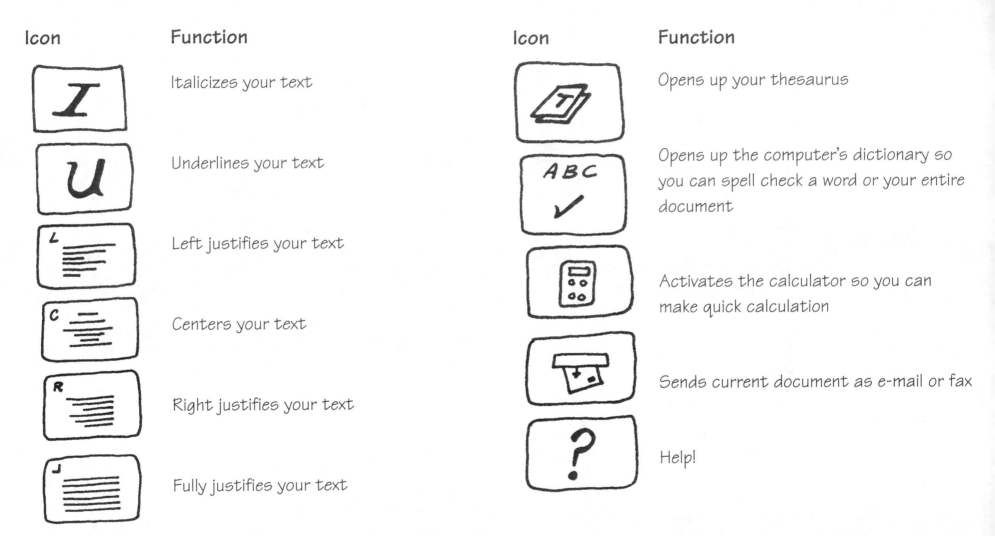

Activity: There are many other functions and commands you can use with your word processing program. On a piece of paper, draw an icon for each function.

Desktop Publishing

What Is Desktop Publishing?

Desktop publishing is an application program which allows the user to create newspapers, newsletters, brochures, and similar publications. Desktop publishing is similar to word processing except it allows the user to combine both text and graphics on the same page. However, some of the newer word processing programs also have the ability that allows you to add graphics to your text. Remember, text is letters and numbers that you type into your document; whereas graphics are the pictures, lines, shapes, circles, patterns, borders, and so on, that you use to decorate or illustrate your document.

Many desktop published documents have the following elements:

- **headline**—a large font at the top of the page

DAILY NEWS

- **smaller headlines**—for each article or story written

Feature Story   Editorials

- **text**—stories or articles

  - This is a story about a little boy who . . .

- **graphics**—pictures relating to the stories and/or articles. When you insert a graphic onto your page, your text will wrap around the graphic in a neat and orderly fashion.

In effect, newspapers and magazines are examples of desktop publishing.

Activity: At your local computer store, look at the boxes containing desktop publishing programs to see all of the different things they can do.

Computer News

Word Processing

Word processing is a type of application software that allows you to create typewritten documents. It is easy to use, and there are many wonderful features that have been designed into it. Word processors have many advantages over typewriters. You have the ability to move and copy text, check your spelling, print your document, and make changes to your document without re-writing it, among many others.

Desktop Publishing

Desktop publishing is a wonderful type of application software which you can use to type newspapers, magazines, newsletters, flyers, and the like. With desktop publishing you can add graphics on the same page as your text. You can be very creative and produce very eye-appealing documents.

Activity: On a separate piece of paper, design a newsletter layout about your summer vacation. Then try to design it using your desktop publishing program.

Resizing and Cropping

What do you do if you have finished your headlines, text, and graphics and then realize that they will not fit onto the layout of your page? Well, you can change the point size of your headlines and text, but what do you do about your graphics. You have two options:

1. **Resize**—Make your graphic either bigger or smaller. Resizing does not delete or insert anything into your graphic. It only changes the size of your graphic by enlarging or shrinking it so that it will fit into the allotted space on your page.

2. **Crop**—Cut off part of your graphic so that it will fit into the space provided. Cropping will actually change the look of your graphic.

Look at these examples to understand the differences between resizing and cropping.

Resized Graphics

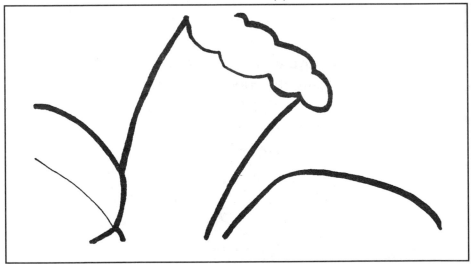

Cropped Graphics

Activity: Draw a picture on a piece of paper. Now resize it and then crop it.

Graphics

Graphics play a large part in desktop publishing. However, to use graphics, there are a few specifics you need to know and understand. Remember, graphics can and do include pictures, lines, shapes, circles, patterns, borders, and just about anything that can be used to decorate and/or illustrate your document. Where do these graphics come from? You have two choices.

1. **Clip art**—is a collection of graphics within your desktop publishing program. All you have to do is select the graphic or pre-drawn picture that you want and then put it into your document. You can also import a graphic from an additional disk or from another graphic program. **Import** means to take a graphic created in one program and copy it into another program.

2. **Create your own graphics**—Many desktop publishing programs allow you to actually create your own graphics or drawings. You do not have to be an artist to draw on your computer. Really, it is quite easy.

Activity: Try to create a picture of your favorite cartoon or comic strip character.

Pixels

A **pixel** is the smallest part of a picture that a computer screen can project. Your computer screen is divided into rows and columns of tiny squares, or cells, of which each colored dot is a pixel. A computerized picture is composed of a grid of square pixels, just like graph paper. It is the smallest unit on the screen of your computer's monitor. The more pixels your monitor's screen has, the better is the resolution or clarity, of your graphics. A super VGA monitor has 640 x 480 pixels. It has a better resolution than a monitor which may only have 273 x 400 pixels.

Pixels are part of 35 mm film and photography. Think of when you enlarge a 3" X 5" (7.5 cm x 12.5 cm) photograph. The enlargement is not as clear as the smaller photograph. In the 3" X 5" (7.5 cm x 12.5 cm) photograph, there are more pixels per square inch (cm^2), so the picture is clearer and sharper. As you enlarge a photograph to an 8" X 10" (20 cm x 25 cm) photograph, there are not as many pixels per inch (cm), so your picture will not be as sharp or as clear as the 3" X 5" (7.5 cm x 12.5 cm) photograph.

Here is an example of how pixels would look on your computer screen if they were visible to the human eye.

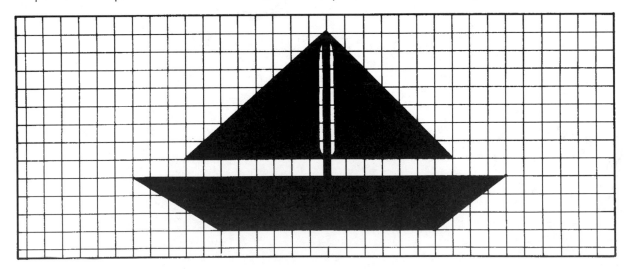

Activity: Using a piece of graph paper, draw your own picture, using each box as one pixel of color.

Drawing Tools

Whether you are using a desktop publishing program or a graphics program, you will have access and be able to use a variety of tools. Not only are there tools to make perfect circles, ovals, squares, and rectangles, but you also can choose different-sized brushes, and widths of your strokes. You also have the choice to fill in, color, or spray paint your pictures. If you make a mistake, you can easily erase all or any part of your picture. When you have finished with your picture, you have the option of printing it out. If you really enjoy dabbling in the art of computer graphics, you may want to purchase a color printer.

All of the drawing tools available are represented by icons. Remember, an icon is a picture representation of a command or function. When creating graphics, all you have to do is move your mouse to the icon of your choice and double click to pick that particular drawing tool.

Here is a sample of some of the icons and tools available for you to use within graphics programs:

Icon	Tool	Function
	Paintbrush	Makes different types of brushstrokes
	Eraser	Erases part or all of your picture
	Pencil	Lets you draw a straight line, as well as drawing freehand
	Magnifying glass	Magnifies a particular area of your picture for fine detail
	Paint can	Fills the picture or shape with color

Drawing Tools (cont.)

Icon	Tool	Function
	Spray paint	Gives the illusion of paint spraying from a can. It is great for doing airbrush work
	Grabber	Moves your picture around on the screen
	Text	Allows you to type text in different fonts within your graphics
	Gradient	Changes the texture of your paint
	Paint	You can choose the color of the paint as you draw and as you color in your drawing. All you have to do is click on the color of your choice
	Stamp pad	Some graphic programs have preset pictures that you can stamp into your picture. Select the stamp pad to view the pictures available and then choose the one you would like. It works the same way that you would use an actual stamp and stamp pad

These are only a few of the icons you will find in a graphic software program. The more sophisticated the program, the more drawing tools and options you will have available.

Activity: Using a simple graphics program, learn to use all of the available tools as you create your own drawing.

Database

#3457 Computers Don't Byte!

What Is a Database?

A **database** is a type of application software which is a collection of related records or files. Using a database's many commands, you can assess any type of information quickly and accurately and then print it in a report.

Have you ever seen a database? Sure, you have. Your phone book is a database. It organizes names, addresses, and phone numbers in a logical and organized manner. As with any database, you can locate and access information easily. Can you think of any other kinds of databases? Well, do you have any collections at home—sport cards, recipes, coins, stamps, etc.? Could you imagine if everything were thrown into one box? You would never be able to find anything! Anything that you sort and organize, even the wash, can be thought of as a database.

Think of a database as a file cabinet. In a file cabinet you have folders for each file. Within each file, you have specific records and information. In a database, you have a similar set of organized information.

There are three fundamental components of a database. They are these:

1. **Field**—the smallest amount of information that you can put into a database
2. **Record**—a collection of two or more related fields
3. **File**—a collection of related records

Let's get back to our phone book. Look at the chart below to clarify the above information.

Phone book	
Fields	Name, Street Address, City, State, Zip Code and Phone Number (6 fields)
Record	The entire information listed above (The 6 fields above = 1 record)
File	The entire phone book is one file.

Activity: List other types of databases you have or may have seen.

A Sample Database—A Phone Book

	Last Name	First Name	Street Address	City	State	Zip Code	Telephone Number
1	Bell	Frank	108 Bearch Road	Brooklyn	NY	11457	555-9876
2	Bronza	Rosanne	67 Rodeo Street	Houston	TX	10990	555-9886
3	Dolton	Maureen	5 Hallow Lane	Tampa	FL	14457	555-7364
4	Guero	Celia	4 Andrew Lane	Marysville	CA	10678	555-9784
5	Harry	Tom	64 Hanes St.	Ann Arbor	MI	12990	555-8765
6	Pero	John	74 Buswel Street	Boston	MA	16784	555-0953
7	Rusin	Julia	17 Angel Place	Rome	VA	11974	555-8573
8	Ryan	Al	6 Conway Court	Roanoke	VA	15678	555-7538
9	Smith	John	78 Spring Circle	Hollywood	FL	14497	555-8907
10	Zimman	Annmarie	8 Kinder Lane	Macon	GA	12876	555-6428

This is a sample database. As you can see, a database is a collection of data. Notice that each piece of information in each separate box is a field. Each row across makes up a record of related information. In this database there are seven fields in each record as listed in the seven field names at the top of the database. In total, there are ten records in this entire file of this database entitled "A Phone Book."

Activity: On a piece of paper, create your own database, using a collection of the books that you own.

List View and Form View

As you are working within your database, there are two options of screens from which you can work., the list view or the form view. You can work in one or the other or easily change from one view to the other. It depends on your preference.

One is the list view. When you are working in list view, you can see several records at the same time arranged in columns and rows. This, as well as the previous page, is an example of the list view of your database.

You can also work in the form view, if you prefer. When working in the form view, you can only see one record at a time. It is like turning a page in a book. This is what a form view looks like.

	Last Name	First Name	Street Address	City	State	Zip Code	Telephone Number
1	Bell	Frank	108 Bearch Road	Brooklyn	NY	11457	555-9876
2	Bronza	Rosanne	67 Rodeo Street	Houston	TX	10990	555-9886
3	Dolton	Maureen	5 Hallow Lane	Tampa	FL	14457	555-7364
4	Guero	Celia	4 Andrew Lane	Marysville	CA	10678	555-9784
5	Harry	Tom	64 Hanes St.	Ann Arbor	MI	12990	555-8765
6	Pero	John	74 Buswel Street	Boston	MA	16784	555-0953
7	Rusin	Julia	17 Angel Place	Rome	VA	11974	555-8573
8	Ryan	Al	6 Conway Court	Roanoke	VA	15678	555-7538
9	Smith	John	78 Spring Circle	Hollywood	FL	14497	555-8907
10	Zimman	Annmarie	8 Kinder Lane	Macon	GA	12876	555-6428

List View

A Phone Book

Last Name: Bell
First Name: Frank
Street Address: 108 Bearch Road
City: Brooklyn
State: NY
Zip Code: 11457
Telephone Number: 555-9876

Form View

Activity: Discuss the advantages of working in the form view, as well as the list view. Which do you prefer?

Creating and Setting Up a Database

Before you actually begin entering information into your database, you should first think about the topic of the database file. Then decide upon how you want to organize your information. Once you have done this, you can formally set up your database so that you will be able to enter information into your fields.

When you first open up your database, you will revert to the form screen. You will use this screen to define your field names, which will describe the data in each of the cells, and these cells will make up your database form.

For example:

Field Name—First Name

Cell and Cell Contents—Frank

Notice that when you are defining field names, you must add a colon after each field name, and then hit the enter key.

Continue in this manner, creating as many field names as you need for each record in your database file. When you are finished designing the form for database, you can go to the list screen, by using your menu or icons, to enter information into your database.

First Name: _____

Last Name: _____

Street Address: _____

City: _____

State: _____

Zip Code: _____

Telephone Number: _____

Activity: Open up your database and begin to create a database of all of your friends.

Entering Text into Your Database

When you enter text into your database, you must first specify the field in which you would like your data to go. Once specified, all you have to do is type in the information and press enter.

Sometimes your data will not fit into the space of the preset default field. There is no need to panic! Sometimes the specified field length (i.e., how long each field is, is just not long enough to hold each character typed. Going to your menu bar, choose the format command to increase the width of your selected field. On the other hand, if the field length is too long, you may want to shorten your field length so you will not be wasting space within your record.

For example, if you wanted to type the street address "30–15 Westward Boulevard," it would take up a space of 26 characters. Do not forget you have to count spaces as characters too. If your field length was originally set at 20, you can change it to 36 so that now you would be able to see it fully on your screen.

It is okay if you decide not to change your field length. The result will be some of your characters not fitting entirely into the field on your computer screen, but when they print, they will print complete.

| 30 – 15 Westward Bou | (field length = 20) |

| 30 – 15 Westward Boulevard | (field length increased by 20) |

Activity: Practice increasing and decreasing the field length on your database.

Sorting a Database

One of the main features of a database is the ability of putting your data in any order that you would like. **Sorting** means to arrange your records in a logical order. Have you ever sorted your laundry? When you sort your laundry, you are arranging it in a specific order. The same concept is also available in your database. You can highlight the fields you want to sort and then decide how you would like to sort your data.

Most data is sorted in ascending or descending alphabetical order. Ascending means going up so your information will be listed from A to Z. Information listed from Z to A is sorted in descending alphabetical order. A phone book is a database listed in ascending alphabetical order by the field of last names. It only takes seconds to sort a computer database. Imagine if all the last names were entered into a telephone database in random order and you had to alphabetize it with pencil and paper. It would take you a very long time!

Sometimes you may have numbers in the fields of your database, such as dates, dollar amounts, test grades, etc. You can sort numbers the same way you sort letters, in ascending or descending order, from the lowest to the highest number, or vice versa.

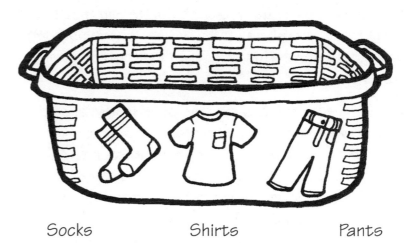

Socks   Shirts   Pants

Sorting your laundry

Last Name	Phone #
Brown	555-1122
Green	555-1234
Hall	555-5678
Jones	555-9021
Kelly	555-8356
Smith	555-3297
Winters	555-5783

Sorting your database

Activity: Describe items that you may sort at home or in school.

Querying Your Database

What is a query? A **query** is a search within a database which will retrieve certain information. When you query your database, you are asking it to display only certain information.

When you have completed setting up your database, there may be a time when you want to see or print only certain parts of your database. For example, in your telephone database, you may want to see only the records of those with last names of "B," "S," and "W." Your computer will search your database and display only those records that you requested. (The rest of your records will remain in your computer's memory).

You can even be more specific when querying your telephone database. You can ask your computer to display the records of those with last names of "P" and "B," who are also residents in New York. Obviously, the more questions you ask of your database, the shorter your list will become.

Querying is a wonderful feature of a database. The main purpose of a database is to display information in an orderly and helpful way. When you query a database, you are most definitely optimizing the use of your database by retrieving the information you need.

Which records contain addresses in California?

List all software programs that begin with "C" and "S" and are also "drill and practice."

Querying a Database

List all students with an average of 90 or above.

Which baseball cards are valued at more than $10?

Activity: Imagine that you have created a database of your entire wardrobe. One query you could make is "How many red shirts do I have?" The possibilities are endless. List other queries and then discuss their advantages.

Creating a Report

When you want to print your database, you may first want to create a report. A report will allow you to print out your database with headings and page numbers. If you have numbers and formulas in your database, a report will generate statistics. Reporting allows you to print your database with explanatory text.

In order to make a report, you must first create a report definition. A report definition tells the database what information will be in the report and where it will be positioned on your printed page.

When you create a report, you will be asked to give it a name. You should give each report a descriptive name that relates to the database so that it will be easy to identify and retrieve for future use. You can generate more than one report for each database, if you would like.

Remember, before you print your report, you have many of the same enhanced options that you have in your word processor. You have the options of changing your font and point size. You may want to use a smaller point size in your database so that it will fit onto your page. Remember to decrease your field length, if possible, so that you will not waste any space. You also have the option of changing your

page setup, thereby printing your database on your page with the longer edges of the page on top and bottom. (You also have this option in your word processing program) You can also check your spelling, as well as view your report or database, before printing.

My Phone Book

Mary	Amous	555-5589
Denise	Brown	555-1212
John	Miller	555-7632
James	Peters	555-8761

Page 1

Activity: Create a report definition for your database.

Spreadsheets

What Is a Spreadsheet?

A spreadsheet is a type of application software that allows you to arrange numerical data into a grid of cells. Spreadsheets allow you to manipulate numerical data in several different ways. Listed below are several of those ways. You can do mathematical calculations, such as adding, subtracting, multiplying, and dividing. You can also perform complex mathematical computations by entering formulas which will interact with your numerical data. You also have the ability to add text to your spreadsheet. Spreadsheets automatically compute figures faster than you could with pencil and paper or even a calculator. If you were wanting to add 100 numbers together, it would probably take you several minutes with a pencil and paper. It would take you a little less time if you were using an adding machine or a calculator. It would take less than a second if your data was loaded into a spreadsheet program.

Two other features of spreadsheet programs are the ability to make graphs and charts which will display your numerical data and calculations. These graphs and charts will make understanding and interpreting data much easier. Not only do these graphs and charts provide an easy way to understand and interpret your data, they look great in projects and presentations, especially if they are printed in 3-D or in color.

Spreadsheets are used extensively in business to keep track of money, finances, and expenses. Spreadsheets can also be used at home in a similar manner. They can an effective tools that teachers and students can use to calculate grade point averages and make graphs of analytical data. As you can see, spreadsheets are wonderful and easy to use and have many diverse applications.

Activity: Make a list on a piece of paper for all of the possible uses for a spreadsheet.

What Does a Spreadsheet Look Like?

A spreadsheet uses a grid-like worksheet, similar to that of a database. Spreadsheets are made up of columns and rows. Columns go down and rows go across. A cell is where a column and row interact. The entire worksheet is called a grid.

Each column going across has a letter at the top. The first column is lettered "A," the second column is "B," and continues through the alphabet until there are no more columns. Each row down is numbered on the left side of your grid, starting with "1," then "2," and continues in numerical order until there are no more rows.

Look at the example below:

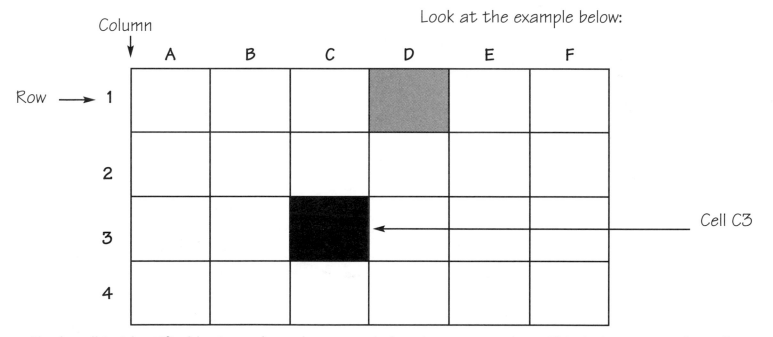

Each cell is identified by its column letter and then its row number. This is known as the cell address. The cell shaded above is identified as C3. What is the cell address of the checkered cell above? Did you say D1? If you did, you are correct.

Activity: Use the example above to identify and name all of the cell addresses in the above spreadsheet.

Entering Formulas and Functions into Your Spreadsheet

Data is entered into your spreadsheet the same way you enter data into a database. All you have to do is highlight a cell and then type in your data. Once your numerical data has been entered, you can use formulas or questions which will perform mathematical calculations.

To enter a formula into a spreadsheet, you can do one of two things. (1) You can choose from a given set of formulas which are built into your spreadsheet program. Formulas contain functions, which are built-in equations that generate values from your inputed data. A function can be a SUM (added numbers), an AVG (average numbers), or even as complex as a LOG (base 10 logarithm of x). (2) You can enter in your own formulas and functions.

To enter values into a spreadsheet formula, you must enter in your cell references. For example, if you want to average six amounts in row 1 of your spreadsheet, from columns A through F, you would have to use the following function and formula:

=AVG (A1:F1)

Notice that formulas contain numbers, cell references, operators, and functions. Formulas are preceded by an equal sign. If you wanted to add the same six numbers, you would use the following formula:

= SUM (A1...F1)

When you are using an operational symbol on a computer, the operator for addition and subtraction are (+) and (-) respectively. However, when you indicate multiplication, you must use an asterisk (*), and when you want to indicate division, you must use a slash (/).

Arithmetic Operations

add	+
subtract	-
multiply	*
divide	/

Activity: Identify some of the other many functions and formulas available in a spreadsheet.

A Sample Spreadsheet

Here as an example of a spreadsheet. It lists the children's names and scores of tests they have taken.

	A	B	C	D	E	F	G	H
1	Student's Name	Test1	Test2	Test3	Test4	Test5	Test6	Average
2								
3	Mary	88	89	100	99	68	97	90.16666667
4	John	79	87	88	93	100	100	91.16666667
5	Anne	90	79	89	84	83	94	86.5
6	Joe	100	99	97	88	100	98	97
7	Jessica	100	74	87	79	98	00	89.66666667
8	Paul	82	100	99	76	87	78	87
9	Matthew	71	78	100	98	99	77	87.16666667
10	Terry	87	71	76	93	77	100	84
11	Lynn	83	73	100	98	100	91	90.83333333
12	Jennifer	79	84	89	94	82	98	87.66666667
13	Christopher	100	75	83	99	89	92	89.66666667
14	Jeanine	75	100	98	100	99	100	95.33333333
15	Pete	76	98	100	87	87	93	90.16666667
16	David	100	98	75	88	78	90	88.16666667
17	Karen	85	75	100	87	96	100	90.5
18	Robert	86	89	99	100	100	83	92.83333333
19	Erin	98	100	100	84	89	94	94.16666667
20	Marie	80	100	99	100	95	96	95
21								
22							Total Class Average	90.38888889

The formula you must enter in order to average Mary's test grade is =AVG(B3:G3). In effect, you are telling your computer to average all figures in row 3 from column B through column G. You do not have to type a formula for each student. All you have to do is highlight column H from row 3 to row 20, and then use the fill down command from your menu. Your computer will automatically average each student's grade in less than one second. In order to get the class average in cell H22, the formula you have to enter is =AVG(H3:H20).

Activity: Practice creating this spreadsheet on your own computer.

Features in a Spreadsheet

One of the most capable features of your spreadsheet is the ability to change the value of one cell, and then, like magic, the formula will automatically and instantly recalculate all of your data.

In the example below, if you were to change the amount in cell B5 from $15 to $20, the figure in cell E5 would change automatically from $50 to $55. Also, your spreadsheet will automatically change the total amount in cell E9 from $174 to $179.

	A	B	C	D	E
1	Month	Clothes	Books	Entertainment	Monthly Total
2					
3					
4	January	$10	$20	$15	$45
5	February	$15	$15	$20	$50
6	March	$25	$5	$10	$40
7	April	$18	$9	$12	$39
8					
9			Total Expenses		$174 ($179)

Spreadsheets also have many formatting options. Aside from selecting font and point size, you can also format currency, time, and percent. Spreadsheets also have many of the features found in word processing and database programs, such as spell check, thesaurus, cut, move, copy, and paste.

You also have the option of sorting your data in ascending and descending order. This function relates to numbers from the least to the most and vice versa. Dates can be automatically listed in ascending and descending order, and you can also use the fill down command to automatically copy information from one cell down a column so that you are not continuously typing the same information over and over again.

When you are ready to print your spreadsheet, you have the option of printing it with or without guidelines. You can print the entire spreadsheet or any portion of it if that you wish.

Activity: Practice using all of the available features in your spreadsheet.

Creating Graphs and Charts

Most of today's spreadsheet programs allow you to display the information in your spreadsheet in the form of a graph or a chart. Spreadsheets can create bar graphs, pie graphs, line charts, etc. All you have to do is select "create a chart" from the menu and follow the on-screen directions. Below and on the next few pages you will find examples of graphs and charts created from our sample spreadsheet.

A Bar Graph

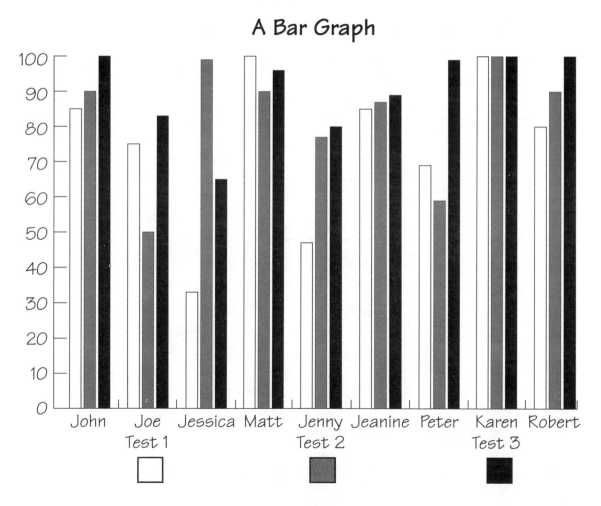

A Pie Graph

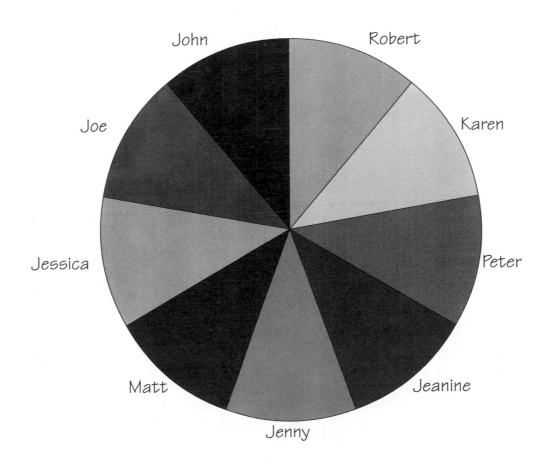

Creating Graphs and Charts (cont.)

A Line Chart

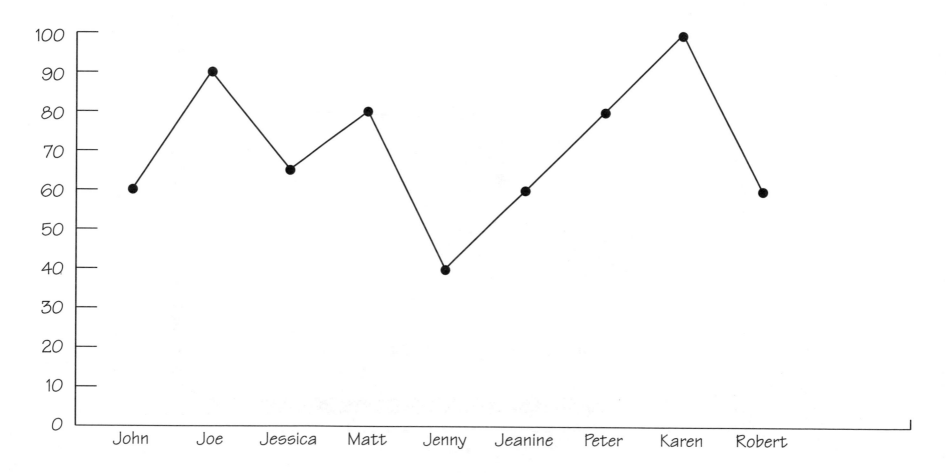

Computers at Work

Input—Processing—Output

Input is a computer term used to describe the data that is entered into a computer. **Data** are facts that a computer uses. Data can be letters, numbers, and/or graphics.

Once data is input into a computer, the computer processes that data and converts it into meaningful information. For example, if we input the number "90" into the computer, it is really meaningless data unless we process it and give it a meaning. Is it 90 dollars or 90 cents? Maybe it is 90 books or a 90 on a test score.

Similarly, if you were to input the letters "e," "a," "r," and "d," they would just be letters unless your brain processed them as a word with a meaning, such as "read" or "dear."

Data is processed in the computer's central processing unit (CPU). It is here that data is transformed or processed into meaningful information. This information is then output onto the monitor's screen so that we can see it. **Output** is information the computer gives back to us, it is the result of the processing of input. We will learn more about processing and input and output devices on the following pages.

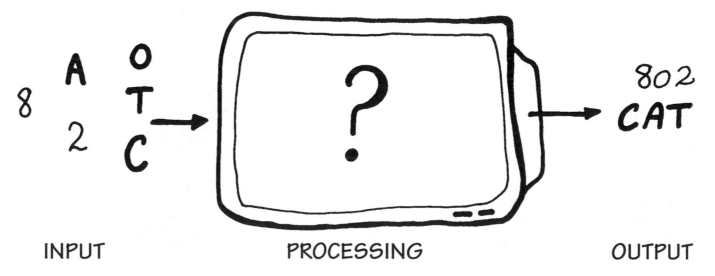

INPUT   PROCESSING   OUTPUT

Input Devices

A **peripheral device** is a piece of equipment or hardware that you can attach to your computer. An **input device** is one type of peripheral device that you can use to input data into your computer.

The following are all input devices:

1. **Keyboard**—By typing on the keys, you can input letters, numbers, and characters. You can also use the keyboard to input commands into your computer.

2. **Mouse**—A handsized device with one or more control buttons, it is connected to your computer and is used to move the cursor and other objects around on the screen.

3. **Scanner**—An optical device used to read information into your computer with the use of light, a scanner transforms pictures and photographs from a printed page into digitized images on a computer screen.

4. **Track Ball**—A track ball is similar to a mouse. It consists of a ball set upon a square or a rectangle. As you rotate the ball, the cursor moves.

Input Devices (cont.)

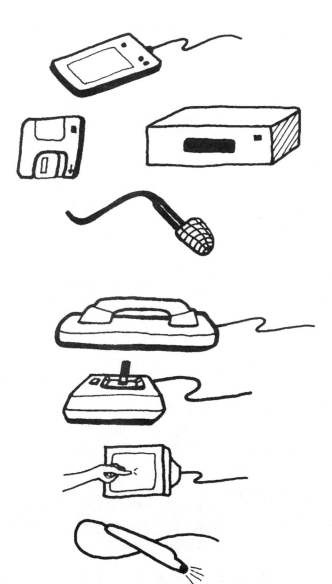

5. **Tablet**—A device upon which you can draw, it converts graphics into binary input for use on a computer.

6. **Disks and Disk Drives**—Programs from a disk are read into the computer via the disk drive.

7. **Voice Recognition System**—By enabling a computer to respond to a set of instructions spoken by your voice, it converts your voice into electronic signals through a microphone.

8. **Modem**—It converts signals from the telephone into digital pulses your computer can understand.

9. **Joystick**—It is an input device used for playing games.

10. **Touch Screen**—You press the screen with your finger to activate your choice.

11. **Light Pen**—Used to draw on-screen, on a graphics tablet, or to select menu items, you can also use it to enter data into your computer.

Processing

Processing is the computer manipulation of data so that it can be transformed into meaningful information.

The central processing unit (CPU) is the part of the computer which processes data. The CPU is made up of three parts:

1. **Control Unit**—This unit interprets data and programs instructions. It directs the step-by-step operation of your computer system. You can relate your CPU to a police officer who directs traffic in the middle of a big city street.

2. **Arithmetic Logic Unit**—This part of the CPU is where mathematical and logical (yes or no) operations are performed.

3. **Memory Unit**—This is where data and information are stored. RAM and ROM are the memory units in your computer.

When you make an ice-cream shake, your blender is simulating a computer's processing unit. Follow the diagram below.

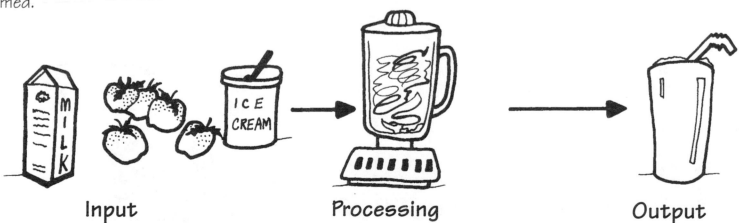

Input   Processing   Output

Activity: A washing machine is a processing unit. Can you think of any others? Make a list.

Output Devices

An **output device** is a type of peripheral or piece of computer hardware that displays output to you.

The following are examples of output devices:

1. **Monitor**—This is similar to a TV. The screen displays words, numbers, and graphics.

2. **Printer**—Many kinds of printers will print a hardcopy of your document onto a piece of paper.

3. **Modem**—Aside from being an input device, the modem also acts as an output device when it converts digital pulses from your computer into analog signals for telephone transmission.

4. **Disks and Disk Drives**—Programs from a disk are read into your computer through a disk drive. Both can be output devices when you save your data onto a disk.

5. **Speakers**—Speakers output sound from your computer.

6. **Speech and Voice Synthesizers**—Some computers can imitate human speech and can be programmed to talk.

Virus

A **virus** is part of a software program deliberately designed to sabotage your computer. Just as a human virus infects your entire body, a computer virus infects the working ability of your computer. Just like a human viral infection, damage can be done to your system even before symptoms begin to develop and surface.

Once a computer virus enters your computer system, it replicates and duplicates itself by attacking other software programs. It can also affect every disk that you use with your system. If you loan one of these undetected disks to a friend, the virus will enter his/her computer system, as well.

The consequences of a virus can range from a prank message to changing colors on your monitor to falling letters on your screen. More serious consequences can be erratic software performance to total destruction of all your data on your hard drive.

To prevent a virus from infecting your computer system here are some precautions you should take:

- Purchase and use a vaccine, a computer virus program used to detect the presence of a computer virus. Before you run shareware or public domain software, you should always check it first with a vaccine.

- Use only new, unopened copies of software on your computer. Do not use pirated or illegal copies of software.

Bugs

A **bug** is a programming error. It is not as serious as a virus, which can affect your entire computer system.

A **computer programmer** is someone who writes software programs using a specific computer language. It is a very involved job. If a programmer makes an error, even if it is only one character, it will cause a program not to work, causing it to produce incorrect results or crash all together. When a computer crashes, it abnormally terminates a program's execution and usually "freezes" your computer system. In this case, all you have to do is reboot your system, that is, restart your computer. When you **boot** your computer, you are turning your computer on and getting it ready for use. Your computer automatically loads its operating system.

Not only is a computer bug much easier to fix than a virus, it is also much easier to dectect than a virus. Therefore, with a little time and patience, a bug can be "swatted" so that it no longer "stings" your computer system.

The term bug originated when a real live insect got into the ENIAC, which was the first digital computer. The insect infected one of its circuits and caused the ENIAC to malfunction. Ever since then, the term **computer bug** has been synonymous with an error within your computer.

Multimedia

Multimedia includes text, sound, graphics, still photographs, and video. Some examples of multimedia equipment are listed below:

- Video Cameras
- VCR's
- Record, cassette, or CD players
- Electronic Keyboards (musical)
- TV monitors
- Video Disk Players

A computer can be connected to multimedia equipment in order to manipulate input and generate output from the various types of media equipment. Special sofware is required.

Multimedia has uses in business, as well as in entertainment. It can be used to generate reports, as well as present demonstrations. Its possibilities are endless using creativity and imagination.

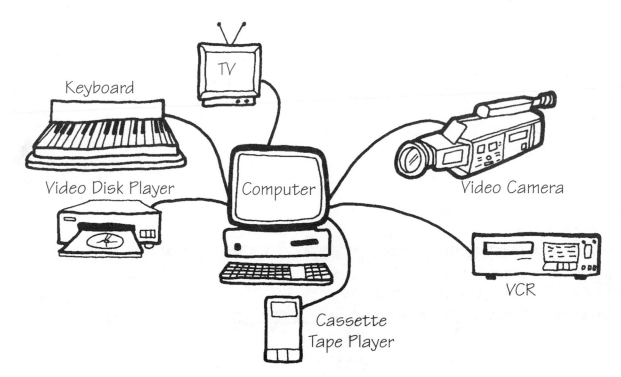

Telecommunications

Telecommunications

Telecommunications is the electronic transfer of data from one place to another.

Text, graphics, video, and voice are examples of the types of information that can be communicated from one computer to another.

A telecommunication system includes:

- A Modem
- Computers
- Telecommunication Software
- A phone line or satellite
- A telecommunications system network

The options available to you through telecommunications are diverse and numerous. Some of the more popular features of telecommunications are these:

Access to Bulletin Boards—This makes messages available to anyone . . .

E-Mail—You can electronically mail personal letters from one computer to another. You can mail a letter to a friend without paying traditional postage.

Data Bases—You can access a variety of data bases to retrieve information on a wide assortment of subjects.

Current News—You can access the news even before it is printed or shown on TV. Get information on current news topics, entertainment, sports, stock market, the weather, etc.

Shareware programs are available to the public.

The Internet

The **Internet** is an enormous network made up of thousands of interconnected smaller networks throughout the world. There are an estimated 50,000 networks on the Internet. The Internet is also known as "the information superhighway" because it provides a vast amount of information to the public throughout the world. Governments, businesses, schools, and individuals like yourself provide all kinds of information on the Internet. Currently there are more than 20 million people connected to the Internet, and the number rises each day.

How do you get connected to the Internet? First, you must have a computer and a modem. Then, you must subscribe to an on-line service. The most popular ones are Prodigy, CompuServe, and America On-line. There is a minimal fee each month for usage of an on-line service. However, the minimal fee is no comparison to the opportunities you will now have at your fingertips. Remember, you now have access to valuable information from all over the world. It is also a great way to meet and talk to people as near as in your block, in your neighborhood, your state, or in a country half way around the world. You will meet people who share similar interests with you, as well as having the opportunity to share interests and concerns on any topic you desire. You can shop and purchase anything from airline tickets to birthday presents for family members or your best friend. If you like to go to the movies, you can even check out movie reviews and look up specific time tables for local movie theaters.

So, if you have a computer and would like to travel through cyberspace and become a part of the wonderful world of the Internet, you must take a ride on the electronic information superhighway.

Taking a ride on the Internet information superhighway

Activity: Learn more about the Internet and how it can be used.

World Wide Web

The **World Wide Web**, also known as the WEB, is the star or main feature of the Internet. It is an interconnected collection of thousands of web sites. A web site can be set up by anyone, even you on your own on-line service.

There are web sites related to almost any imaginable topic; some examples are sports, culinary arts, entertainment, literature, etc. Think of the web as the largest and most enormous encyclopedia you can imagine. Using the web, you can find information about almost anything and anybody.

If you like to shop, the WEB is the place for you. Using the web you can buy anything from computer software to home furnishings. All you have to do is access the Internet.

Shopping Network, Cyberspace Malls International, and Marketplace Shops are all web shopping on-line services. Imagine being able to do all your holiday shopping without ever leaving your home. You can also comparison shop to find the best buys without all the walking from store to store. Better yet, you do not have to find a parking space or wait in long lines.

So you can see the many advantages the web offers. The freedom of movement within and throughout the web is known as "surfing the net."

Surfing the Net

Computers in Society

How Computers are Used Today

Twenty five years ago, the only computers available were very expensive and very large. They were only used in government and big businesses, mainly to keep track of finances and inventory. Over the years, computers have gotten smaller and much more affordable. Today, computers can be found almost everywhere and are used productively in a wide variety of ways. Here are some of today's uses for computers:

Banks—Computers are used in banks to keep track of customers' accounts. Money can be transferred from one bank to another electronically using computers.

Businesses—Application software programs such as word processing, data bases, and spreadsheets are used for business transactions, billing, inventory, letters, and payroll These are only a few of the the uses computers have in business.

Factories—Specialized software is used on computers to design products. Many factories use computerized robots, which assemble and package products.

Entertainment—There are many uses for computers in the field of entertainment. Computer games are very popular. The television and movie industry use computers to create cartoon, and special effects.

How Computers Are Used Today (cont.)

Advertising—Computers are used to generate many wonderful and colorful advertisements on TV, in magazines, and in all other types of media.

Medicine—Doctors, pharmacists, and technicians use computers for research, prescriptions, and x-rays. Hospitals use computers to keep track of their patients' records.

Schools—Students and teachers use computers, educational software, and computer-aided instruction. Computers are also used for record keeping of student progress and attendance.

Law Enforcement—Government law officials use computers to track down criminals by tracing license plates, comparing fingerprints and DNA evidence, and checking physical descriptions. They are also used to help find missing children.

Homes—Computers are used at home in many different and diverse ways. Aside from games, computers can also be used for anything from balancing checkbooks and financial planning to typing letters and reports with word processing programs, and for the use of educational software.

Computer Languages

A computer uses languages to communicate just as humans do. There are hundreds of different types of computer languages, just as there are hundreds of different languages people speak around the world. Each computer language has a specific style of writing, as do various languages written by people.

The most basic language of a computer is the language recognized by the computer's CPU. It is a binary code which is symbolized by 0's and 1's.

The following are some common types of computer languages:

Basic—Beginner's All Purpose Symbolic Instruction Code is the most common computer language used. Basic is simple to learn and use, and programmers use Basic to communicate with the computer when writing software programs.

Fortran—FORmula TRANslation. Fortran is a higher-level programming language used to perform complex mathematical and scientific engineering computations.

COBOL—COmmon Business Orientation Language. COBOL is a high-level language used in businesses for data application. It is used for such functions as inventory control, payroll, and billing.

Pascal—An all-purpose language designed by Blaise Pascal, Pascal is easy to learn and is used in homes, schools, and businesses.

C—A general purpose computer language, it is widely used throughout the world.

Activity: Do further research to find out about more types of computer languages.

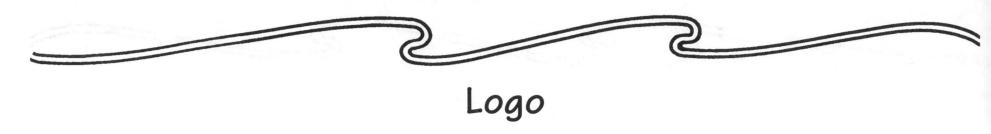

Logo

Logo is a high-level programming language designed by Seymour Papart for use by students. It gives students the opportunity to draw geometric patterns and pictures by writing simple programs which will move a small turtle around to draw. Text can also be added.

Here is a sample program written in logo. It will generate a rectangle on the screen.

TO BOX

10 FORWARD 50

20 RIGHT 90

30 FORWARD 75

40 RIGHT 90

50 FORWARD 50

60 RIGHT 90

70 FORWARD 75

In the above program, your computer will first draw a line for a length of 50 or about 1" (2.5 cm). Then the turtle on the screen will make a right turn (90°). A line will then be drawn for a length of 75, about 1.5" (3.75 cm), make another right turn, go forward 50, make another right turn, and finally go forward another length of 75 to complete the rectangle.

Activity: On a piece of paper, try following the instructions of the above logo program. Did you make a triangle? If you have a logo program, use it to create other shapes and graphics.

Networks

A network is when two or more computers are interconnected. They can communicate with one another, exchange information, as well as work independently of each other. They can also share printers and other peripheral devices.

LAN—A local area network is where two or more computers are connected within the confines of one room or building. One of the computers is designated as a file server. A **file server** is the center of the network. It contains the software and all the files for all the computers in the network. The computers that are hooked up to the file server with cables are called work stations. Some computers need a network adapter card installed in them to make it possible for the computer to be part of the network. The file server has network operating system software installed into it which allows work stations to access its files and software.

In contrast, WAN is a wide area network. WAN is a connection of computers over long distances throughout the world, through satellite and communication systems.

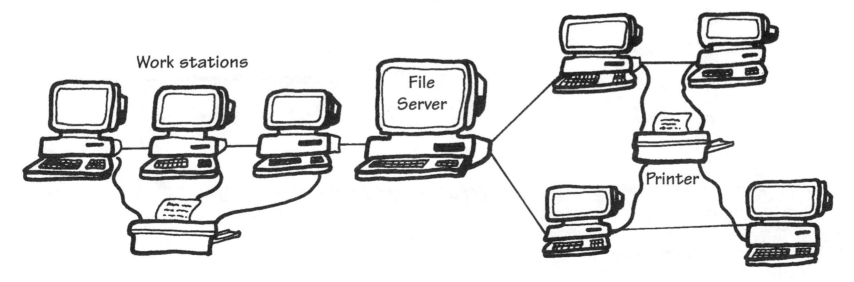

A LAN Computer Network

Computer Related Occupations

Computer Related Occupations

Computers are used in many facets of business, education, and government agencies. Many people today know how to operate computers and use them effectively.

There are certain careers related specifically to computers. They require special training and education. Here are some options available to you if you like working with computers:

Programmer—Everyone knows that a computer cannot do anything without instructions. A computer programmer writes instructions which tell the computer what to do. Programmers must know the language of computers in order to write computer software programs. Many computer programmers have degrees in computer science.

Computer Engineer—A computer engineer is someone who designs and builds computers, peripherals, chips, and circuit boards. A computer engineer must have a degree in electrical engineering. It is the responsibility of all computer engineers to put all the parts of a computer together in the right way so that the computer parts are interconnected and function properly.

Computer Technician—When computer parts are designed by computer engineers, they must be tested by computer technicians for any flaws or defects. A computer technician is specially trained to repair all the hardware parts of a computer system. Computer technicians usually have technical training from a technical school or a two-year college.

Computer Related Occupations (cont.)

Systems Analyst—A systems analyst works with a company to develop a plan to use computers in a particular business. A systems analyst must study and analyze jobs that are done and how computers can be integrated into business effectively to get these jobs done efficiently. Once the needs of an organization are identified, a system analyst will make suggestions as to the type of computers needed, what jobs they will do, where they should be placed, and what kinds of software programs will be needed. System analysts are college graduates with a concentration in business and computer engineering.

Computer Operator—Computer operators are the people who actually run the computers and print hardcopies. A high school diploma is all that is required although training in a technical school is sometimes additionally required. Many large companies often offer on-the-job training for computer operators.

Data Entry Person—A data entry person is also known as a keypunch operator. They are responsible for putting data into the computer. They do not have to know much about computers, but they do need to be good typists. College degrees are not generally needed for these jobs. However, a high school diploma is required.

Technical Writer—This is someone who writes the manuals that accompany newly purchased computers. These manuals tell you how to operate and work your computer. Technical writers are college graduates with good writing skills and knowledge about electronics and computers.

Computer Related Occupations (cont.)

Systems Manager—The systems manager is in charge of supervising the working of a computer system in an organization or business. He/she makes sure all computer activities run smoothly. It is the systems manager's job to keep abreast of all new software and hardware developments in order to maintain the most current and effective computer systems. System managers usually have a college degree in computer science.

I make sure all computers run smoothly.

Computer Teachers—Computer teachers teach people how to use computers. They can be hired by organizations to teach employees. Many schools are also hiring computer teachers who have acquired computer skills in addition to their teaching credentials. They teach students how to use computers and computer literacy. They also teach faculty members how to select software that would enhance their instruction and curriculum. Computer teachers must have a strong background and knowledge of computers.

Sales Representative—Computer salespeople sell computers to people who use computers. Not only must they know their computer products, they must also know what their customer's needs are and how to match the two. They must get along well with people and know about computers and technology.

You can buy a computer from me.

Software Librarian—Many big businesses and organizations have thousands of pieces of software containing data and files. It is the responsibility of a software librarian to file these disks in a software library. A software library must have an organized system of filing and storing disks, the same way books are stored in a library. Software librarians must be good at organizing and filing and only need a high school diploma.

Purchasing a Computer

What to Look for When Purchasing a Computer

Many people have a misconception that when shopping for a computer, they want to purchase a computer that will last forever. If this is the case, that person will never be able to find a computer to his/her liking because there is no such computer. You should know by now that computers are constantly changing, and whatever you buy today, modern technology will invent something better "tomorrow." Think of buying a computer like investing in buying a new car. Do you expect that car to last forever? Probably not. How long does the average car last? It may last ten years, or less. With advancements in modern technology, the life span of your computer will be ten years, but it will most likely become outdated well before ten years.

However, you would certainly like to purchase an updated and quality computer. So here are some things you should consider. (1) You must decide what brand you want to purchase. Will it be a Macintosh or an IBM compatible? Both have wonderful qualities. (2) It must fit the needs of what you will be using it for. For example, getting back to our analogy about buying a car, you certainly would not want to buy a subcompact car if there are a lot of people in your family. It would not suit your purpose. The same is true about a computer. Buy the computer that will match your needs.

What to Look for When Purchasing a Computer (cont.)

(3) You should try to buy a computer that has at least eight megabytes of RAM in order to run most software programs. Consider purchasing a computer that is expandable—that is, the motherboard has enough room to expand or increase your memory if you want or need to increase it in the future. And do not forget to get an adequate hard drive. Today's computer systems should have a 1,024 MB hard drive because many of the modern software programs take up lots of space on your hard drive. Remember, you want to have at least a 256 color monitor or SVGA (Super Video Graphics Adapter) Monitor. You should have at least one floppy disk drive but may also want to consider a CD-ROM drive. Now that you have a nice color monitor, what about sound? You will need 16-bit sound quality and speakers. If you are going to use a modem, you must consider the speed of your computer. You should get a computer that operates at least at 75 MHz.

So how much is all this going to cost you? Most likely around $2,000. But, like anything else, you get what you pay for. If you make wise decisions regarding the purchase of your computer, it will not run the risk of becoming obsolete the day after you buy it. Now the only other things you have to decide are what software programs you will purchase to meet your needs, where you are going to put your computer, and how will there be enough hours in the day for everyone in your household to get a turn to use it.

Computers in the Future

Only as recent as 50 years ago, computers were almost non-existent. Huge mainframe computers could be found in big businesses and government, but they were too large and much too expensive for the average person to afford and to have at home. They were in limited supply and were not available to the public.

People living many years ago laughed at the pioneers of the early calculating machines, such as Charles Babbage and Blaise Pascal. They were very reluctant to accept these newly invented calculating machines. There were those who even burned down Joseph-Marie Jacquard's home because his invention was a threat to their comfortable stability.

Throughout the years, however, technological innovations have promted the progression of computers to become more affordable. Since the invention of the computer chip and circuit boards, computers have become smaller in size and, therefore, now can be found in many businesses, as well as in schools and homes. Many people use computers in many ways as effective tools to accomplish many tasks. But even today, there are many people who are still reluctant to use computers. Fortunately, they are not in the majority.

So what will the computer of the future look like? Is it safe to assume that computers will be getting even smaller than the smallest computers today? Will they fit into your pocket and still be able to accomplish all they do now? What about computer disks? Will they become obsolete and replaced by CD-ROMs or even a newer and smaller CD-ROM which will hold even more information? Is it possible that textbooks will be on CD-ROMs, and pens and paper will be replaced by miniature computers that students will carry everywhere they go? We will have to be patient and anxiously await to see the course computers will take in the future.

Will this be the computer of the future?

Activity: What will the computer of the future look like? What will it be able to do?

Closing

Upon completion of this book, I hope you have learned many wonderful and different things about computers. You now have a greater understanding of how computers have evolved throughout the ages. You can now identify all the different parts of your computer and how each part works. The importance of proper care of your computer has been expressed. You know all the capabilities of a computer and the many various and powerful potentials for its use. Greater awareness of the many places computers can be found have also been developed.

But, most of all, you know that computers are easy to use and lots of fun to work with. I hope this book has helped you to feel more at ease with your computer. I hope that you get as much pleasure from your computer as I get from mine and that it provides you with productivity, learning, creativity, entertainment, and enjoyment.

Happy Computing!

Computer Star Award

This award is presented to:

_____

for achievement in learning that
"Computers Don't Byte."

Computer Glossary

Computer Glossary

Abacus—is the first counting and calculating machine invented by the Chinese about 4,000 years ago.

Analog Computers—are used by scientists and engineers. These kinds of computers compare and measure such scientific quantities as temperature, weight, speed, voltage, frequencies, and pressure.

Analytical Engine—was designed in 1823 by Charles Babbage.

Application Software—helps you perform a specific task on your computer.

Arithmetic Logic Unit—is the part of the CPU where mathematical and logical (yes or no) operations are performed.

Artificial Intelligence (AI)—is a computer term used when a computer seems or appears to be thinking like a human.

Babbage, Charles—is the father of computers.

Basic—Beginner's All Purpose Symbolic Instruction Code is the most common computer language.

BIT—a Binary DigIT, 0 or 1, it is the smallest unit of data that a computer can process or understand.

Bug—is a programming error.

Byte—is equal to 8 bits of data.

C—is a general purpose computer language. It is widely used throughout the world.

Cable—are used to connect peripheral devices to your computer.

Computer Glossary *(cont.)*

Cathode Ray Tube (CRT)—is inside the monitor. The screen is attached to it.

Cell—is where a column and row intersect in a spreadsheet.

Centering—is to put your text in the exact center of the page.

Central Processing Unit (CPU)—the brain of your computer. It is a chip which carries out all the functions needed to control the operations within your computer.

Characters—are letters, numbers, and symbols that are used on your keyboard.

Chip—is a single integrated circuit made of silicon.

Circuit—a set of electronic components that perform a particular function in a electronic system. It is the path that electricity follows.

Circuit Boards—are made of plastic and contain chips, metal tracks, and electronic devices such as resistors, transistors, and capacitors.

CD-ROM—is Compact Disk Read Only Memory.

CD-ROM Drive—is found on the outside of the computer. It is where you insert your CD-ROM. It is known as the d: drive.

Click—is hitting a button on the mouse which sends an electronic signal to the computer to select something on the screen.

Clip Art—a collection of graphics within a program.

Computer Glossary (cont.)

COBOL—is the COmmon Business Orientation Language. It is a high-level language used in businesses for data application.

Communication Software—is used to send and receive data through a modem with your computer over a network.

Compatible—is a software program which will run successfully on your computer.

Computer—is an electronic machine. It is also a tool used to do work.

Computer Engineer—is someone who designs and builds computers, peripherals, chips, and circuit boards.

Computer Operator—is a person who actually runs the computers and prints hardcopies.

Computer System—is all the parts of the computer together. It is made up of the CPU, memory, peripheral devices, and the operating system.

Computer Teachers—are those who teach people computer literacy and how to use a computer.

Computer Technician—is specially trained to repair all the hardware parts of a computer system.

Control Unit—is the part of the CPU that interprets data and programs instructions.

Copy—is duplicating text from one location to another.

Copyright—is legal protection for the author for bidding unauthorized copies of software.

Crop—is cutting off part of your graphic so that it will fit into a provided space.

Computer Glossary (cont.)

Cut and Paste—used to move blocks of text or graphics from one place in your document to another.

Data—are facts you give to your computer.

Database—enables you to manipulate, store, record, and retrieve data from a collection of related files.

Data Entry Person—is a keypunch operator responsible for putting data into the computer.

Daughterboards—are circuit boards which are connected to the expansion slots on the motherboard of your computer.

Delete—is to erase text or graphics.

Desktop Publishing—is an application type of program which allows the user to combine text and graphics.

Document—is the complete and finished text.

Difference Engine—was designed by Charles Babbage in 1834.

Digital Computers—perform computations and calculations, and represent pieces of data with "digits" or "bits" of information.

Disk Density—is the amount of data that can be stored on a diskette.

Disk Drive—is the part of your computer which reads programs and data from your disk.

Disk or Diskette—is a reusable storage device that holds information.

DOS—Disk Operating System

Computer Glossary (cont.)

Dots Per Inch (DPI)—is the measurement of how sharp your print will be.

Drag—is to continue to hold down the mouse button as you move the mouse to move objects on the computer screen.

Dvorak, August—in the 1930s designed a layout for the keys on a typewriter.

Educational Software—helps you learn an educational related topic.

E-Mail—is electronic mailing of personal letters from one computer to another.

Expansion Slots—spaces found on the motherboard. Smaller daughterboards are connected into the expansion slots or the motherboard.

Field—is the smallest amount of information that you can put into a database.

Fifth Generation Computers—are in the process of being invented, and we will use these computers in the future.

File—is a collection of related records or a basic unit of storage.

Filename—is characters you choose to identify a particular file. It should relate to the file itself.

File Server—is the center of a network. It is the computer which contains all the files and software for all the computers in the network.

Fingers and Toes—were the first counting tools.

Computer Glossary (cont.)

First Generation Computers—are Mark 1, ENIAC, and EDVAC.

Floppy Disk Drive—is found on the outside of your computer. This is where you insert your floppy disks. These disk drives are known as the a: drive and the b: drive.

Floppy Disks—are 5.25" or 3.5" in diameter. The disk is enclosed in a plastic case. It is used to store and retrieve data.

Font—is the different style of lettering that characters can be.

Format—initializing a disk so that it will be usable on your computer.

Formula—is a equation which will perform a mathematical calculation in a spreadsheet.

Fortran—is short for FORmula TRANslation. It is a higher-level programming language used to perform complex mathematical and scientific engineering computations.

Full Justification—is when your text is lined up evenly on both the left and right margins.

Function—is a built-in equation that can be used to generate a value from your formula.

Function Keys—are a set of keys on the top row. F1 is usually the key you press if you need help. The use of the other function keys depends upon each individual software program that you are using.

Graphics—are computer-generated pictures.

Graphic Programs—allow you to do freehand drawings, as well as create slide shows and animations.

Computer Glossary (cont.)

Hardcopy—is a piece of paper that has your printed work on it.

Hard Drive—found inside your computer. It stores and saves everything you put into the computer, even after you turn it off. The hard drive is made of several nonflexible disks, stacked together with recording heads. It is known as the c: drive.

Hardware—is all the parts of the computer that you can see and touch.

Highlighting—is the process of making part of your text stand out to select it for editing.

Hollerith, Herman—invented a machine called the Tabulating Machine in 1890. It was used to take the government census.

International Business Machines (IBM)—is the largest computer company in the world.

Icon—a small picture representation or symbol of a computer command or function.

Import—is to take text or graphics from one program and put it into another.

Information Superhighway—is the Internet.

Initializing a Disk—formatting a disk into tracks and sectors.

Input—is data we put into the computer.

Input Device—is a peripheral device used to put information into the computer.

Insert—is to add text or graphics to your document.

Computer Glossary (cont.)

Insert Mode—allows you to type on your computer by moving already typed characters over and down to make room for newly inserted text.

Integrated Circuit (IC)—was invented in 1958; it combines all the parts a computer needs to run in one small place—a chip.

Internet—is an enormous network made up of thousands of interconnected smaller networks throughout the entire world. It is also known as the information superhighway.

Jacquard, Joseph-Marie—was a French weaver who in 1801 invented the Jacquard Loom. It was a weaving machine that was controlled by punched cards.

Justification—is the alignment of the lines of text along the left margin, the right margin, both margins, and centered.

Keyboard—is a peripheral device that lets you "talk" to the computer. You press the keys on the keyboard to tell the computer what to do.

Local Area Network (LAN)—is when two or more computers are networked within the confines of one room or building.

Laptop Computers—are computers small enough to fit on a briefcase or on your lap.

Left Justification—is text lined up flush against the left side of the page.

Liebniz, Gottfried—perfected the Leibniz calculator in Germany in 1673.

Logo—is a high level programming language designed by Seymour Papart for use by students.

Computer Glossary (cont.)

Mainframe—is a large computer used to meet the computing needs of large a organization or business.

Margin—is the number of spaces between the right and left edges of a page, as well at the top and bottom edges.

Memory Unit—is the part of the CPU where data and information are stored—RAM and ROM.

Menu—is an on-screen display listing the options available to you within a program.

Microcomputers—are the personal computers or desk-top computers we use today.

Microprocessor—is an integrated circuit that contains the arithmetic, logic, and control units necessary for the operation of a computer. Minicomputers are smaller mainframe computers which were designed to meet the needs of smaller companies.

MOdulator/DEModulator (MODEM)—changes a computer's binary coded digital signals into analog signals that can travel over telephone wires.

Monitor—is a peripheral device which produces an on-screen display and also includes all internal circuitry, such as the cathode ray tube.

Monochrome Monitor—is a display device with a black background and single color characters of either white, amber, or green.

Motherboard—is the system board of a computer.

Mouse—is an input device used for moving a cursor on the screen.

Move—is taking text or graphics from one place in your document and putting it into another place within the same document or in another document.

Computer Glossary (cont.)

Multimedia—a combination of text, sound, graphics, photographs and/or video, using various types of media equipment.

Network—is when two or more computers are interconnected. They can communicate with one another, exchange information, as well as work independently of each other.

Output Device—is a type of peripheral device that displays information to you.

Overstrike Mode—is actually typing over already typed text, thereby erasing original text.

Pascal—is an all-purpose language designed by Blaise Pascal.

Pascal, Blaise—was a Frenchman and mathematician who at the age of 19 invented the Pascaline in 1642.

Pascaline—was the first mechanical and automatic calculator.

Peripheral—is each separate part attached to a computer system, usually an input or output device.

Pixel—is the smallest part of a picture that a computer screen can project.

Point Size—is the different sizes of lettering that characters can be.

Print—is putting your work from the computer's screen onto a piece of paper.

Printer—is a device attached to your computer that prints information processed by your computer onto a piece of paper.

Computer Glossary (cont.)

Processing—is the manipulation of data by the computer so that it can be transformed into meaningful information.

Program—is a set of instructions for your computer.

Programmer—is someone who writes software programs using a specific computer language.

Public Domain Software—is donated to the public by its creator. It is not protected by copyright laws.

Punched Cards—were used before the invention of disks to record and sort data or information.

Query—is a search within a database to retrieve certain information.

QWERTY Keyboard—is the keyboard we are most familiar with. It is named after the top left letter keys on the keyboard.

Random Access Memory (RAM)—is the computer's primary workplace. It is temporary memory, because once you turn off the computer, all its contents will be erased.

Read Only Memory (ROM)—is a permanent memory chip inside a computer. Its contents cannot be altered or erased.

Record—is a collection of two or more related fields in a database.

Report—is printing out a database with a heading and/or page numbers.

Resize—is to make bigger or smaller.

Computer Glossary (cont.)

Retrieve—is getting stored information from your disk back on to your computer's screen.

Right Justification—is text lined up along the right margin.

Sales Representative—is a salesperson who sells computers.

Save—is putting your work into a permanent storage area.

Scanner—is a device which you can use to copy a picture or words from a printed page onto your computer screen.

Screen—is the display area on the monitor.

Scrolling—is the movement of your text upward and downward on your screen.

Search and Replace—is a feature that finds a designated word and replaces it with a new one.

Second Generation Computers—such as RCA, IBM, and UNIVAC were built from 1959 to 1964 and used transistors.

Shareware—is software programs which can be purchased inexpensively and shared with your friends.

Simulation Software—produces a model of a real-life situation.

Software—are programs that run on your computer.

Spell Check—is a feature which checks the spelling of your words and makes correct suggestions for you.

Computer Glossary (cont.)

Spreadsheet—is a program used to create and edit rows and columns of numerical data for budgets, financial reports, grades, etc. Spreadsheet programs accurately compute mathematical formulas.

Systems Analyst—works with a company to develop a plan to use computers in the business.

Systems Manager—is the person in charge of supervising the working of a computer system in an organization or business.

Technical Writer—is someone who writes the manuals that accompany newly purchased computers.

Telecommunications—is the electronic transfer of data from one place to another.

Text—are word, sentences, and paragraphs made up of characters.

Third Generation Computers—were built in the 1960s and 1970s, and used integrated circuits.

Transistors—replaced vacuum tubes in the late 1950s to control the amount of electricity flowing in and out of the computer.

User Friendly—is a term used to express the fact that most software programs provide step-by-step directions which make them easy to use and understand.

Utility Software—tells the computer how to run by maintaining and improving the proficiency and effectiveness of your computer.

Vaccine—is a computer program used to detect the presence of a computer virus.

Vacuum Tubes—are one of the most important technological developments in the history of computers. They were electronic devices that controlled the flow of electricity in the computer.

Computer Glossary *(cont.)*

Virtual Reality—is software which creates a life-like situation.

Virus—is part of a software program deliberately designed to sabotage your computer.

Wide Area Network (WAN)—is a connection of computers over long distances throughout the world through satellite and communication systems.

Windows—is a program many computers use to manage the files within your computer.

Word Processing—is an application software program specially designed to create letters and reports.

World Wide Web (WEB)—is the main feature of the Internet.

Wrap-around Text—is when you get to the end of a typed line and your computer automatically starts the next line.

Write Protection Notch—prevents a disk from being written to, thereby protecting all the data on a disk.

Bibliography

Armstrong, Sara. **Telecommunications in the Classroom, Second Edition.** ISTE & Computer Learning Foundation, 1995.

Bergmann, Peggy, and Marlene Keanie. **More Turtle Power-Text, Graphics, and Sound with LogoWriter.** ISTE, 1995.

Boyer, B.A., and P. Semrau. "Selecting and Evaluating Interactive Videodisc Programs in Art." **The Computing Teacher,** 21 (3): 28-30, 1993.

Carter, Bruce, and Karin Wiburg. "Thinking with Computers." **The Computing Teacher,** 22 (1): 7-10. 1994.

Dana, Ann, Marianne Handler, and Jane Peters Moore. **Hypermedia as a Student Tool: A Guide for Teachers.** Teacher Ideas Press, 1995.

Dunn, S., and R. Larson. **Design Technology: Children's Engineering.** Falmer Press, 1990.

Emerging Technologies Lifelong Learning-Proceedings of the National Educational Computing Conference 1995. NECA, 1995.

Family PC Magazine. Des Moines, IA, 1995.

Harris, Judi. **Way of the Ferret-Finding Educational Resources on the Internet.** ISTE, 1994.

Kober, Nancy. "**Teachers and Technology: The Federal Role.** NTIS, 1994.

Marshall, Gail. **Travelers Through Time and Space-Multicultural Activities for the Computer Classroom.** ISTE, 1995.

Mowe, Richard. **Evaluating Technology Integration in the Elementary School-A-Step-by-Step Guide.** ISTE, 1993.

Muir, Michael. **Kindling the Fire—Integrating HyperCard into the Classroom.** ISTE, 1995.

Rathbone, Andy. **Windows 3.1 for Dummies.** IDG Books Worldwide, Inc., 1994.

Patrick, Doyle. "K–12: Linking to the National Networks." **Computers in Libraries,** 12, May 1992: 61-62.

Pfaffenberger, PH.D. **Que's Computer User's Dictionary, Thomas, Process Writing Kit—Computers, and the Writing Process-Teacher's.** Nelson Publishers, 1992.

Microsoft Works User's Guide, Microsoft Corporation, 1988.

Salpeter, Judy. **Kids and Computers.** Sams, 1992.

Bibliography (cont.)

Schrum, Lynne M. **Directory of Educational Telecommunications Services**, Revised Edition. ISTE, 1994.

Sponder, Barry, and Robert Hilgenfeld. "Cognitive guidelines for teachers: Developing computer-assisted instruction." **The Computing Teacher**, 25 (2): 187-199, 1992.

Stevens, Margaret, Rebecca Treays. **Computers for Beginners**. Usborne Pub. Ltd., 1994.

Stockley, Corinne, and Watts, Lisa. **Usborne Guide to Computer Jargon**. EDC Publishing, 1983.

Teachers & Technology: Making the Connection. U.S. Government Printing Office, 1995.

Watson, Jim. **Teaching Thinking Skills with Databases.** ISTE, 1993.

Wetzel, Keith. **The Guide to Organizing and Evaluating Student Writing plus Writing Folders**. ISTE, 1992.

Yoder, Sharon, and Irene Smith. **Lookin' Good! The Elements of Document Design for Beginners**. ISTE, 1995.

Zientara, Marguetitse. **History of Computing**. CW Communications, MA., 1981.

ISTE Periodicals (to order call 800-336-5191)

CAELL Journal of ESL Teachers

HyperNexus

ISTE Update

Journal of Computer Science Education

Journal of Computing in Teacher Education

Journal of Research on Computing in Education (JRCE)

Learning and Leading With Technology

Logo Exchange

Microsoft Works in Education

Telecommunications in Education News (T.I.E.)